KENOJUAK ASHEVAK

Life and Legacy

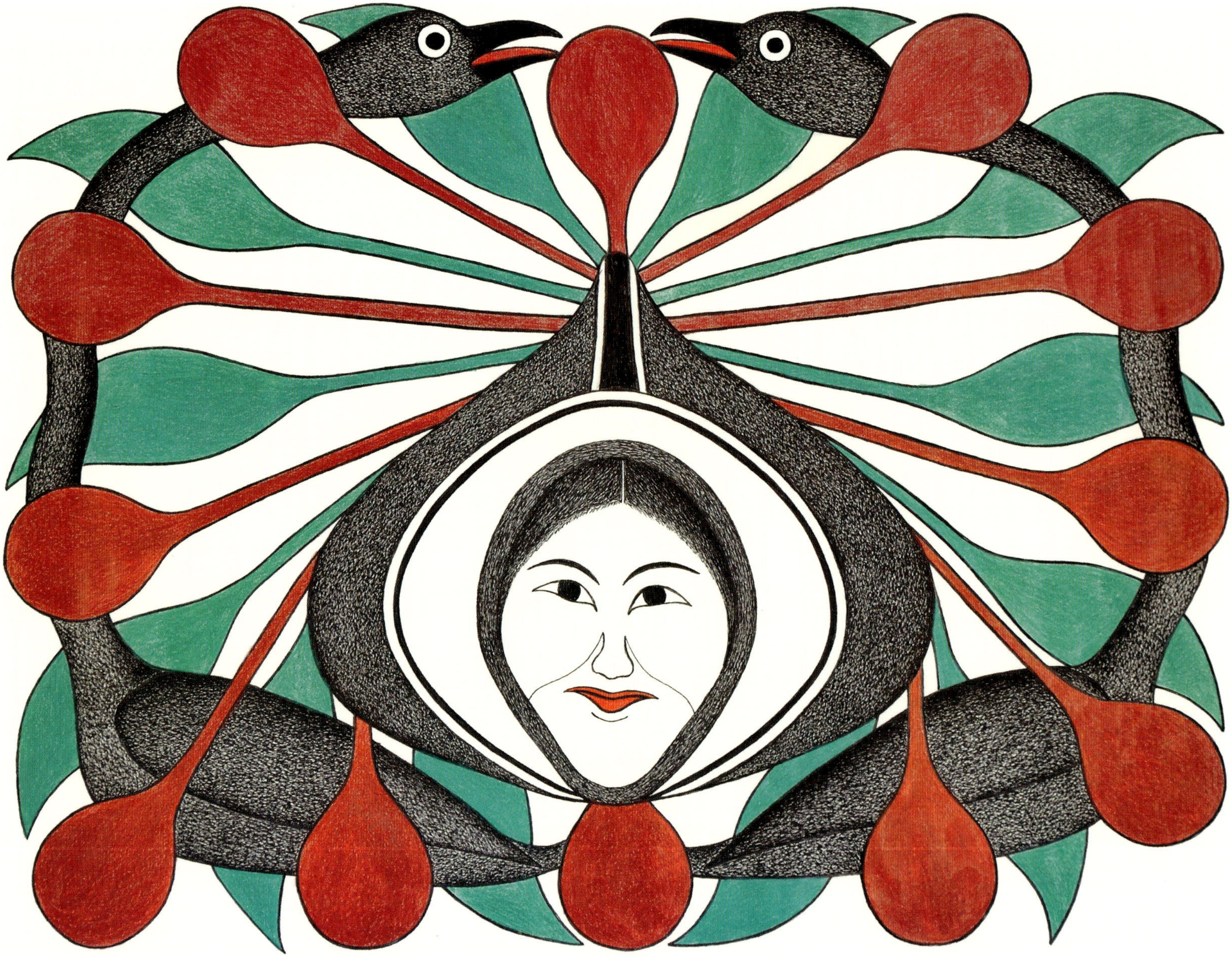

KENOJUAK ASHEVAK

Life and Legacy

Essay by Leslie Boyd

Foreword by Silaqi Ashevak

Pomegranate

PORTLAND, OREGON

Pomegranate Communications, Inc.
105 SE 18th Ave., Portland, OR 97214
800-227-1428 pomegranate.com
sales@pomegranate.com

To learn about new releases and special offers from Pomegranate, please visit pomegranate.com and sign up for our email newsletter. For all other queries, see "Contact Us" on our home page.

Published in conjunction with the exhibition *Kenojuak Ashevak: Life and Legacy*, presented by:
Kenderdine Art Gallery, Saskatoon, Saskatchewan, January–April 2020
Klondike Institute of Art and Culture, Dawson City, Yukon, June–July 2020
Kelowna Art Gallery, British Columbia, October 2020–February 2021
Art Gallery of Sudbury | Galerie d'art de Sudbury, Ontario, June–September 2021
Winnipeg Art Gallery, Manitoba, 2022
Esplanade Arts & Heritage Centre, Medicine Hat, Alberta, May–July 2022

FRONT COVER: *Untitled (Between Friends)*, 2010, ink and colored pencil
BACK COVER: *Untitled (Great Big Fish)*, 2011, ink and colored pencil
FRONTISPIECE: *Untitled (Wisdom of the Elders)*, 2009, ink and colored pencil

Library of Congress Cataloging-in-Publication Data

Names: Ashevak, Silaqi, writer of foreword. | Boyd, Leslie. Kenojuak Ashevak. | Kenojuak, 1927-2013. Works. Selections.
Title: Kenojuak Ashevak : life and legacy / essay by Leslie Boyd ; foreword by Silaqi Ashevak.
Other titles: Kenojuak Ashevak.
Description: Portland, Oregon : Pomegranate, [2020] | Includes bibliographical references and index. | In English, French and Inuktitut.
Identifiers: LCCN 2019025524 | ISBN 9780764998188 (hardcover)
Subjects: LCSH: Kenojuak, 1927-2013--Themes, motives.
Classification: LCC N6549.K465 A4 2020 | DDC 700.92--dc23
LC record available at https://lccn.loc.gov/2019025524

Item No. A288
Designed by Patrice Morris
Printed in China

35 34 33 32 31 30 29 28 27 26 11 10 9 8 7 6 5 4 3 2

CONTENTS

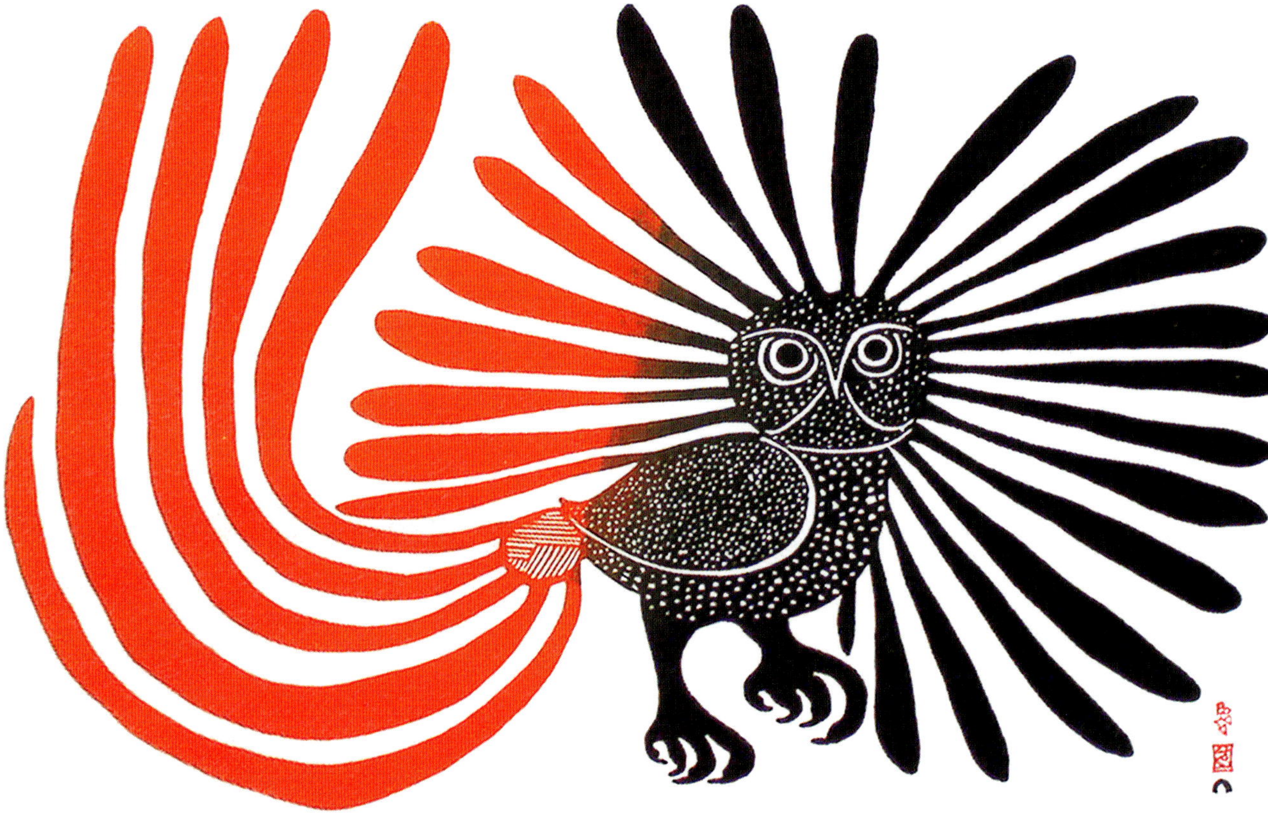

The Enchanted Owl, 1960, stonecut

FOREWORD

The first trip I took with my mother was to Kingston, Ontario, in 1991. She had been awarded an honorary doctorate from Queen's University, and she asked me to go with her as her companion and interpreter. It was an amazing experience for me—I felt like I was dreaming! I was young, only 21 years old, and I never really knew that so many people knew my mom; she had a lot of friends.

Standing up on the stage with her, I'm sure I was more nervous than she was. She was really proud. She never thought that she would get an award like that, and she was proud to be nominated. The university was amazing—I never thought I would walk into a university like that, and I kept saying, "Mom, when you travel, do you go to these kinds of places?" She told me she'd been to all kinds of big places like that.

I think my mom had a great sense of adventure, and so do I. We really enjoyed our trip to Kingston. We went to Wolfe Island and around the Thousand Islands, and toured the countryside, seeing all of the cows and sheep and horses in the fields. It was summertime, and beautiful country.

The next trip that stands out for me was when we traveled to Toronto, when my mom got her star on Canada's Walk of Fame, in 2001. I never thought that my mom would walk down the red carpet, and I would be there with her. Again, when we stood together on the stage with all those famous people, I was so nervous, and after her speech, I said, "Mom, you didn't look nervous at all!" She said, "I don't get nervous. I just think of them as a person, just like I am a person."

I traveled with my mother a lot, and I enjoyed every trip. She enjoyed traveling, too. Sometimes she got really tired, but it seemed like she was always happy traveling, and happy to get away from home for a while. Her eightieth birthday celebration at the McMichael Canadian Art Collection gallery was very special. She didn't want to cut the cake because it was so beautiful. We went to the McMichael several times, and I will always remember one lady who came up to my mother with tears in her eyes. I was amazed; I'd never seen anyone so happy to meet my mom. I said, "Mom, she was even crying!" She said, "I get that, from a lot of people." I think people cried when they met her because they love her art so much. They said that when they bought a print and put it up on their wall, it seemed to light up the whole place.

I grew up seeing her works, and to me they're all beautiful. When I really liked one of them, I used to tell her, "Don't sell it to the co-op; just keep it and put it on your wall." But she wasn't interested in keeping any of her drawings or prints—only the *Enchanted Owl*. She used to say that it was her favorite, although she never thought it would become a famous work of art. It's my *Enchanted Owl* now. I still live in the same house, and it's still there on the wall, along with some of her awards.

She was always working, here at home. In the early morning when I got up, she was already working on drawings. When I came back home after work she was still drawing. I used to tell her that she had so much patience, to sit and draw all day, and she would say, "I love it. I'm used to it and my hand doesn't want to stop. It wants to keep moving on with the pencil."

She never really talked about being famous. She used to say that, at first, when she was just starting and scared, she never thought that she would ever become a famous artist. But she was, and she said that God chose her to be a famous artist. It didn't really change her. She was always kind and friendly. When she noticed that someone needed help, she would try to help in some way.

We were very close. I was the youngest of her children, and I believe we were the closest. I miss her every day. I miss getting up in the morning and seeing her sitting here, in the living room, working on a drawing.

Silaqi Ashevak

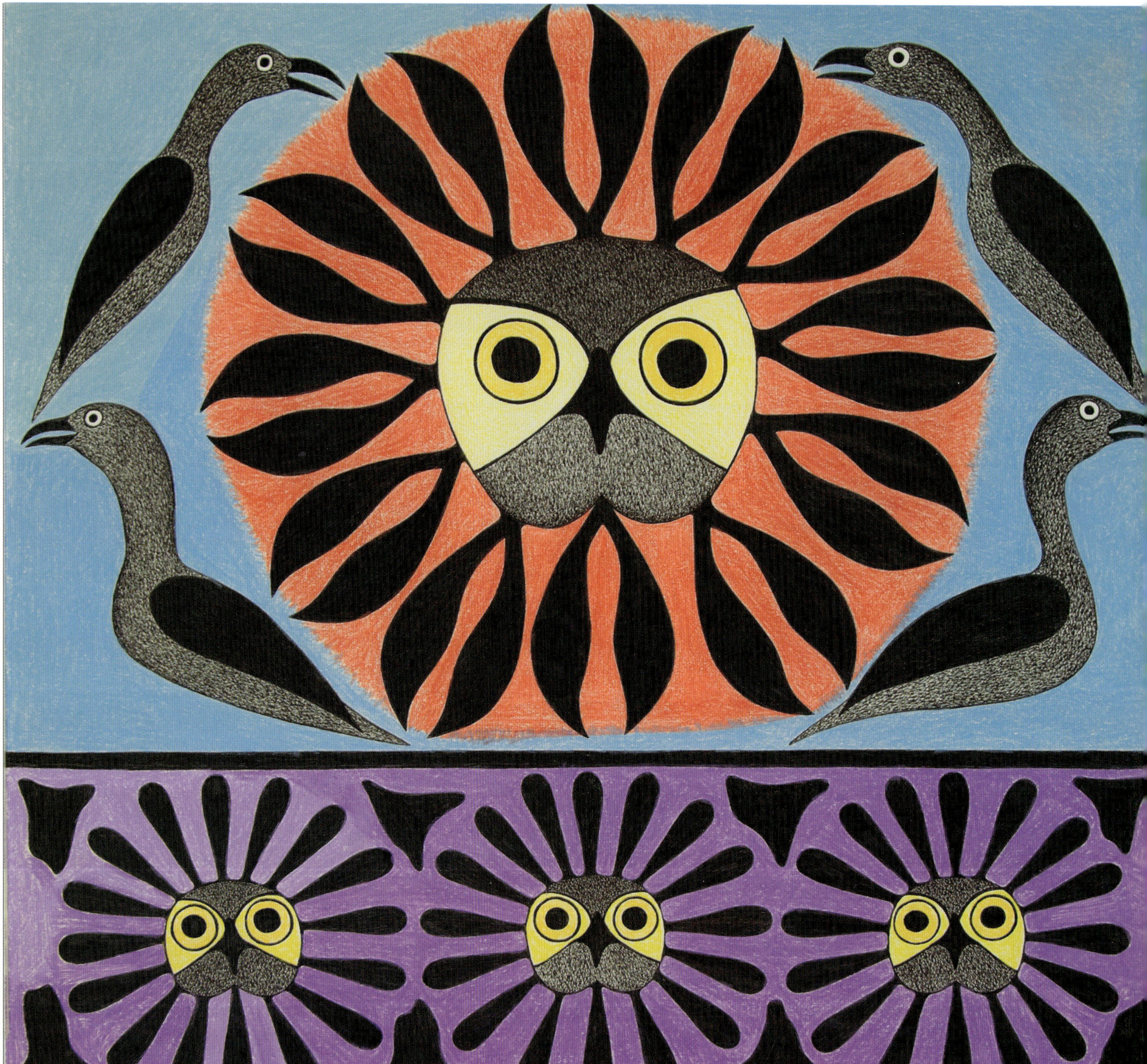

KENOJUAK ASHEVAK

Life and Legacy

Kenojuak Ashevak, the first woman in Cape Dorset to start drawing professionally, became Canada's most acclaimed Inuit artist. Her career spanned more than five decades, from the release of her first print in 1959 until her death in 2013, at age 85. During that time, her images were published in over three hundred original print editions, and she leaves an archive of over two thousand original drawings. She was born and raised on the land in the traditional Inuit way, moving from camp to camp on South Baffin Island; living in *haumuqs*, igloos, and summer tents; and relying on the animals and plants of the sea and tundra for her sustenance and survival. When she died, she had been living in a modest but modern home in Cape Dorset (known locally as Kinngait), an isolated Arctic community in the Canadian territory of Nunavut, and was lauded as one of Canada's preeminent artists and cultural icons. Her story illuminates a way of life now gone, and the profound social changes that led to her creative transformation.

EARLY YEARS

Kenojuak was born in 1927 at Ikerrasak, a traditional camp area on South Baffin Island.[1] The second child of Seelaki and Ushuakjuk, she was named after her deceased maternal grandfather. As she explained in her autobiography, published in 1985, "Inuit believe that a child who is named after someone is assured of all the love and respect previously given to the dead person. The two become spiritually related."[2] The custom is called *atikulu*, or the soul name.

Kenojuak's ancestors were from the north coast of the Ungava Peninsula, the northernmost region of the province of Quebec. The area is now known as Nunavik, and is separated from South Baffin Island, in Nunavut, by the narrow Hudson Strait. These territorial distinctions meant little to Inuit of Kenojuak's generation, however, who frequently traveled back and forth following the seasons and wildlife and the dictates of the Hudson's Bay Company. Kenojuak's first memories were of crossing the Hudson Strait in her grandfather's Peterhead boat, listening to the agitated, high-pitched cries of the *akpa* (guillemots) that nested in the high cliffs along the coast.

That journey was taking her to Pujjunaq (Mansel Island), a now uninhabited island off the coast of the Ungava Peninsula at the northern edge of Hudson Bay. The Hudson's Bay Company had established a fur trading post there in 1929, and several Inuit families were encouraged to relocate and trap for the company. Kenojuak and her family spent time there in the early 1930s, and by her account, it was an oppressive time. She recalled in her memoir that several members of the camp drowned when their small, wooden boat was driven into rocks during a storm while those on land watched, powerless to help them. Fur prices were also very low, as the rest of the country was well into the grip of the Great Depression. Disputes between hunters and traders were common, and Kenojuak's father, Ushuakjuk, was frequently at the center of those arguments. Many seemed to fear him, as he made threats against other hunters and caused tension in the

Untitled (Owl's Treasure) (detail), 2002, ink and colored pencil

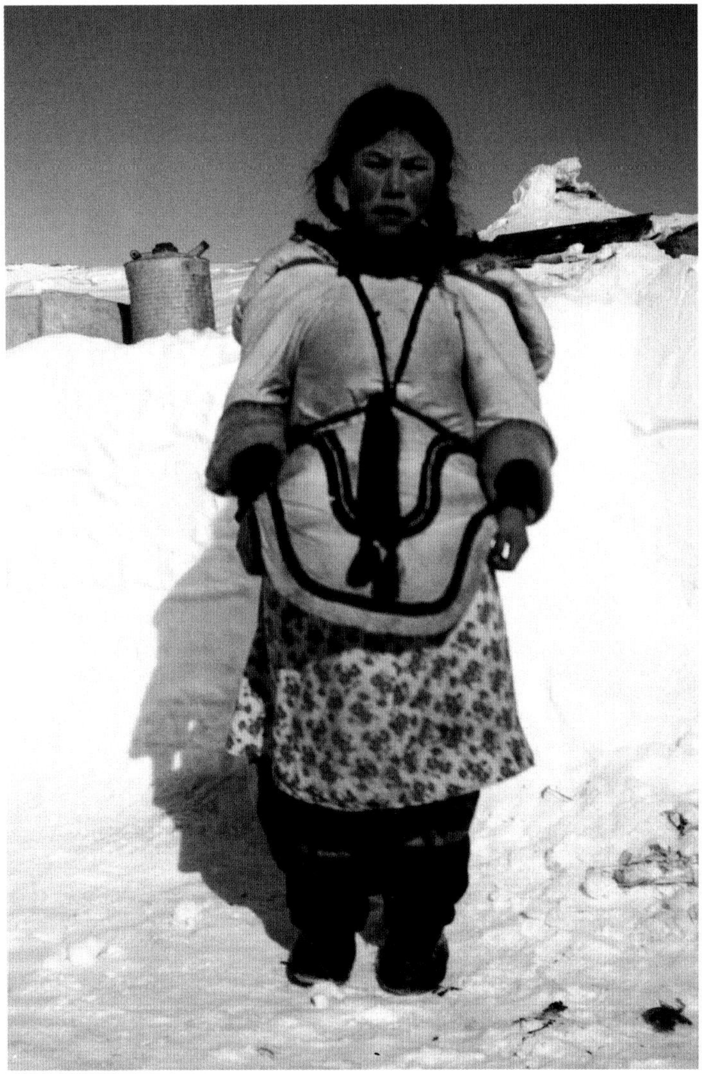

Kenojuak wearing a dress and *amauti*, 1940–1949

Photograph by Peter Pitseolak
Canadian Museum of History, 2000-679

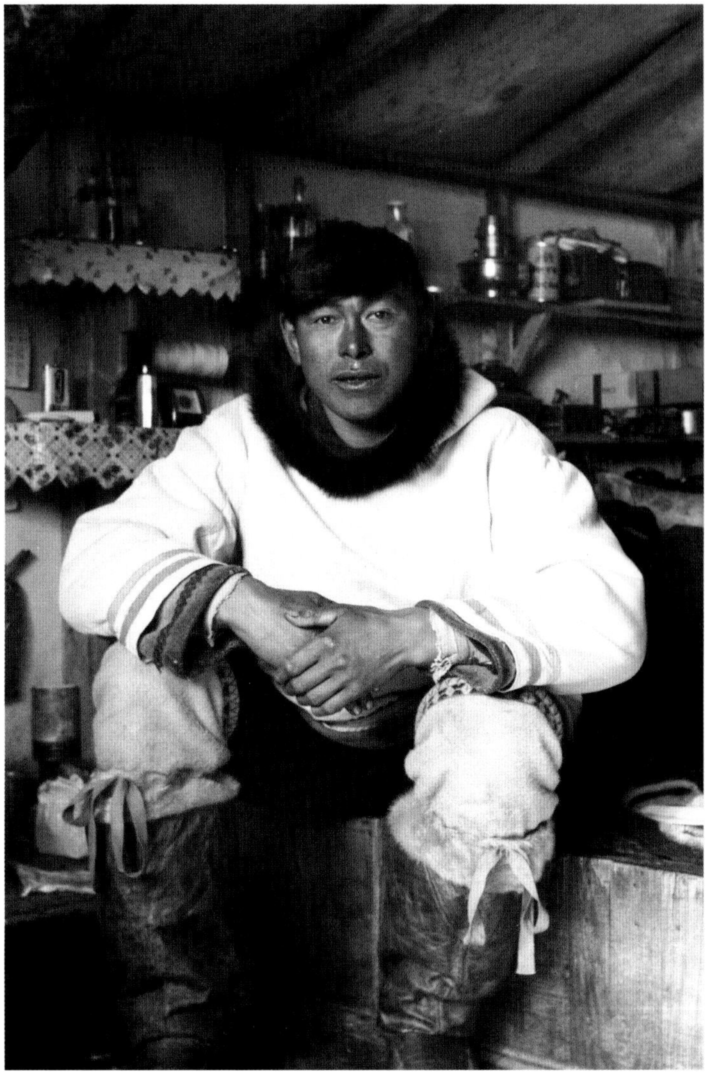

Portrait of Johnniebo, 1940–1960

Photograph by Peter Pitseolak
Canadian Museum of History, 2000-1291

camp. "Seelaki expressed fear—she believed that his sense was gone," Kenojuak recalled.[3]

Ushuakjuk became increasingly unstable during their time at Pujjunaq. Eventually, three men took matters into their own hands and ambushed him as he was leaving his snowhouse. He was shot and killed and his body tossed into the sea, along with his possessions and his dogs. Later in her life, Kenojuak acknowledged that her father's death may seem incomprehensible to some, but in those days, "Inuit justice was used solely to maintain the harmony and stability of the group. Anyone who became too quarrelsome, or lacked self-control, or perhaps robbed another man's cache, became a threat to the community as a whole. When that happened, one person or more, either self-appointed or designated by the group, would dispose of the threat."[4]

Seelaki and her children left Pujjunaq that summer and never returned. They traveled to Ivujivik, where they waited for the annual arrival of the Hudson's Bay Company supply ship *Nascopie*, which took them back to Cape Dorset and the comfort of relatives and friends. Official enquiries were made about the murder on Pujjunaq but charges were never laid.

Kenojuak spent the remaining years of her childhood in various traditional camps on South Baffin Island, frequently living with her beloved grandmother, Koweesa. She had fond memories of this time in her life: "the endless pursuit of small birds and animals in the hope of capturing one of them at last"; playing with small toys carved out of driftwood by her uncle, Niviaqsi; and learning from her grandmother how to sew with caribou sinew and make watertight seams.[5]

Her permanent home was a *haumuq*—a sturdy structure with a wooden frame and floor, covered with cotton canvas and insulated with moss. Snow blocks were piled around the exterior for added insulation. "Inside we had warmth and comfort, solely from the heat of our *qulliq*," a stone lamp that burns seal oil. In summer, they would move to a canvas tent sewn by the women, then back to the *haumuq* in fall. "We had to get all our livelihood from the sea and the land."[6]

In 1946, Kenojuak became the wife, according to Inuit custom, of a man named Johnniebo. Their marriage was arranged between the families when Johnniebo's brother, Towkie, and his wife, Elisapee, came as emissaries to discuss the prospect with Kenojuak's mother and uncles. Kenojuak pretended to be asleep during the meeting and admitted to being afraid but also remembered meeting Johnniebo in Cape Dorset—in particular "his good-natured teasing, and his tall stature," she said. "During the first few weeks of our union, I was truly a reluctant young woman in Johnniebo's company. I threw rocks at him whenever he approached me. He laughed good-naturedly, and continued his pursuit. Eventually I grew very fond of this kind, gentle man," Kenojuak recalled.[7]

Kenojuak and Johnniebo began their life together at Sukbuk, another of the frequented campsites along the South Baffin coast, but within the year, they were summoned by Peter Pitseolak to join him at his camp, Keakto, just east of Cape Dorset.[8] It was a happy time for them, and their first son, Jamasie, was born there in 1947. Keakto is a beautiful place, protected but close to the sea and only a few miles from Cape Dorset. The foxes were plenty. The year 1947 was also auspicious in another way, because the Hudson's Bay Company supply ship *Nascopie* sank off the coast of Cape Dorset—a momentous event that is still memorialized by Cape Dorset artists. Although the loss was sad, the ship lay suspended on the rocks for long enough to allow the people to salvage what they could. Peter built a wooden house at Keakto, further establishing his position as a forceful and important leader. The first known photographs of Kenojuak and Johnniebo were taken by Peter at this time.

Kenojuak and Johnniebo spent the next few years in relative security at Keakto. In 1949 they were married by an Anglican missionary who traveled to the various camps to give sermons and perform marriages and baptisms, and their second child, Mary, was born.[9] The times were reflective of the many changes beginning to affect the traditional Inuit way of life, including the broad campaign to deal with the tuberculosis epidemic sweeping the region. In 1951, Kenojuak learned that X-rays taken in 1950 showed she had contracted the disease, and she was flown to the Parc Savard hospital in Quebec City.

Kenojuak spent three years in the hospital, finally well enough to return home in 1955. In 1953 she learned that her two children, Jamasie and Mary, had died. In her autobiography, she reflected on this tragic time in her life: "Johnniebo, in his letter to me, begged me not to grieve for our two children but to concentrate on regaining my health so that I might soon return to Cape Dorset. Suffering unbearable pain over this loss, I wanted never to bear children again. Inuit in the hospital prayed for me."[10]

Kenojuak did go on to have and adopt many children, fourteen in total. Shortly after her return to Cape Dorset, she adopted Annago, in 1956. In keeping with Inuit custom and circumstances, some of her children were adopted from another family, some were adopted to another family, and some remained with Kenojuak and Johnniebo. Seven children did not survive infancy or early childhood. At the time, Inuit territories had the highest infant mortality rate in the country. It is lower now, due to significant improvements in living conditions and health services, but infant mortality is still almost three times higher among Inuit than non-Indigenous populations in Canada.[11]

BECOMING AN ARTIST

While Kenojuak was convalescing at the Parc Savard hospital, she was given sewing materials to occupy her time. She was already an accomplished sewer, and her work attracted the attention of Canadian sculptor Harold Pfeiffer, who was acting as one of the occupational therapists at the hospital.[12] He took special notice of her beautiful and perfectly made rag dolls and small-scale traditional clothing, sewn with tiny, precise stitches. In 1955, Pfeiffer accompanied Kenojuak and other Inuit back to Cape Dorset aboard the federal government's medical supply ship, the *C.D. Howe*.

Although Kenojuak had plenty of time to sew while she was recovering, she remarked in her autobiography that she had to relearn how to sew with caribou sinew when she returned from the hospital. When she started working with Indigenous materials again, she made dolls, *kamiks* (sealskin boots), sealskin tapestries,

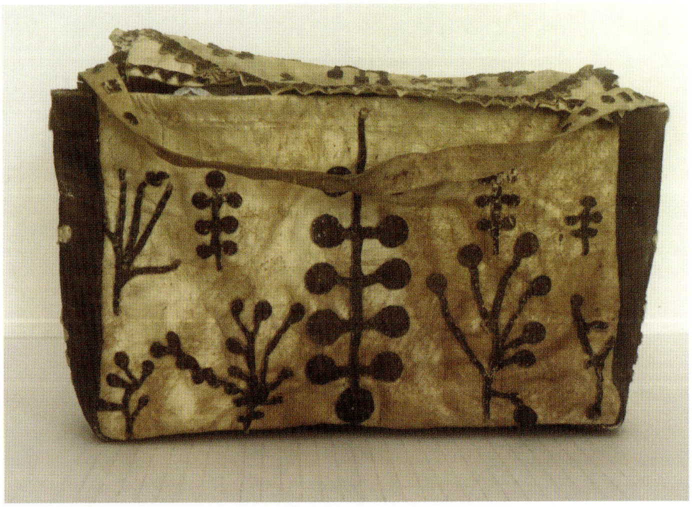

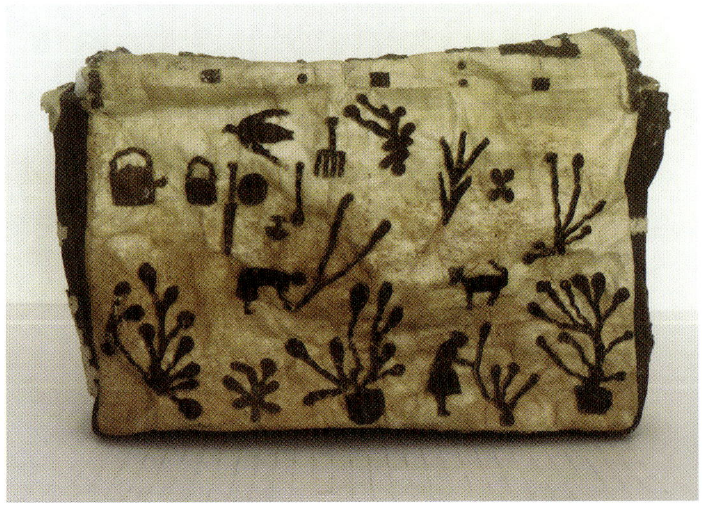

Sealskin bag, c. 1950s

and handbags with cutout designs, and it was through these creations that her innate sense of composition and design first emerged. Her talent caught the eye of Alma Houston, who, along with her husband, James Houston, established the first craft center in Cape Dorset, in 1956. Fur trapping no longer brought Inuit a reliable income, so carving and other handicrafts were being promoted by the Canadian federal government as a replacement. While James worked with the men on various projects, including the first experiments with printmaking, Alma set up a craft program with the women. "Arnakotak, the name we gave Alma Houston, meaning 'tall lady,' was encouraging Inuit women to sew and make whatever they desired," Kenojuak said. "Trying to help us gain some independence, she energetically and enthusiastically gave her time, skills, and knowledge. I began creating sealskin appliqué designs, taking them to Arnakotak for money."[13]

One of these designs was the basis for Kenojuak's first image, now one of her most famous, *Rabbit Eating Seaweed*. It was derived from a sealskin appliqué design that she created on a handbag. Impressed with Kenojuak's skill and designs, Alma suggested she make some drawings. Kenojuak was reluctant at first; at that time it was the men who made the drawings, but she did take the legal-size government bond paper from James (called Saumik, meaning left-handed) and brought back what Alma described as lovely, interconnecting pencil drawings.

Kenojuak was the first woman in Cape Dorset to start drawing, which she said was initially very difficult. "I was afraid to begin the first drawings because I had no idea in mind," she recalled.[14] "The first time Saumik gave me a piece of paper and asked me to start drawing, I asked him what kind of a drawing am I going to make. And then he just told me to draw anything that comes into my mind—it could be anything," she said.[15] "I destroyed the first drawing I did in Keakto, but I took later drawings to him when I traveled to Cape Dorset. I was pleased at the value he assigned to the work. I knew that I would continue."[16]

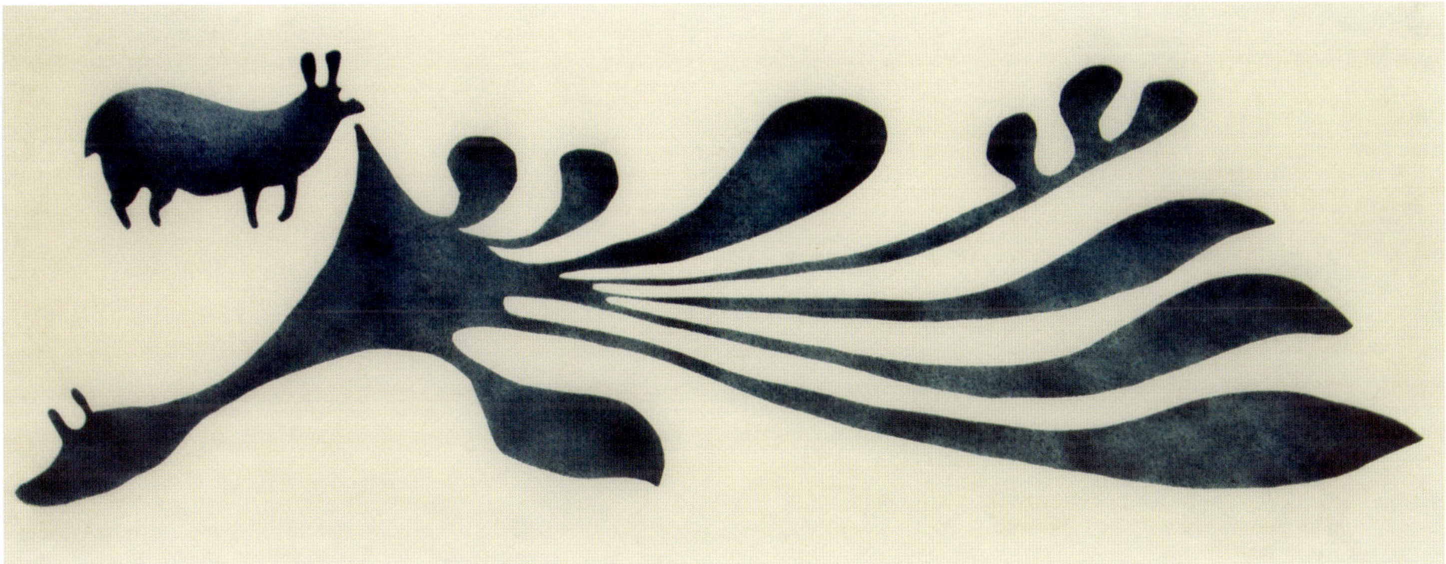

Rabbit Eating Seaweed, 1959, stencil

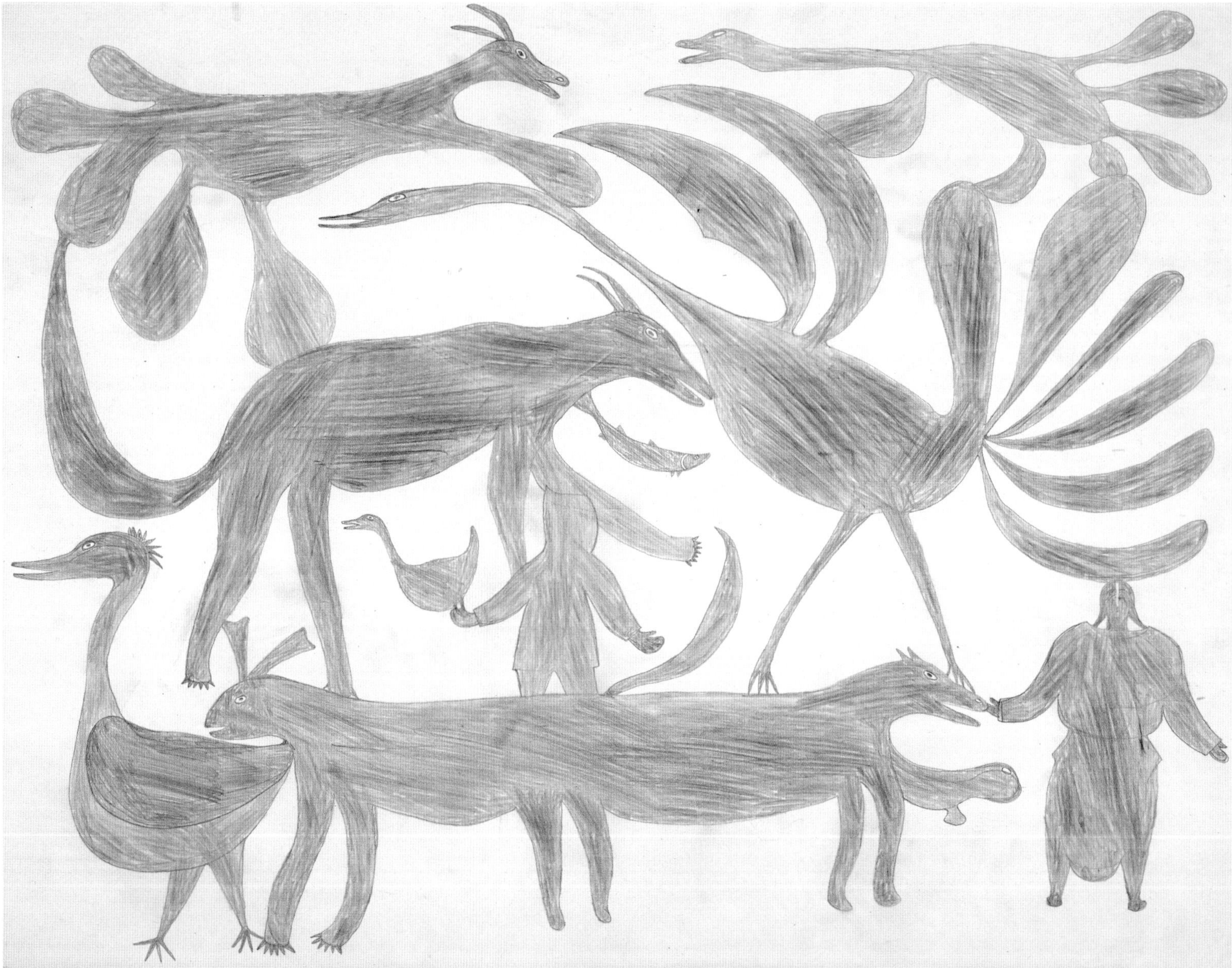

Untitled, 1959–1965, graphite

DRAWING

Kenojuak's first drawings were strongly influenced by her experience with sewing. She often used cardboard patterns, just as she had in her sewing, by placing them on the paper and tracing around them. Motifs that are repeated within a drawing were often drawn using a template, frequently as mirrored images symmetrically arranged around the central subject. Kenojuak said that she got the idea of using patterns when she saw another woman, Sheouak Petaulassie, using them, and realized that if she did that "then everything would be straight."[17]

At the same time, she also developed her own intuitive approach, a process that she described as her hand leading her mind.[18] Left-handed, she would often start at the left-hand corner of the page, slowly but assuredly building her composition to fill the page with birds and animals and people and fantastic combinations of them all. She rarely had a preconceived idea of what she wanted to draw or how the finished work would turn out, but she knew instinctively what was needed. "I'll look at it for a while and then my mind comes up with new things to further fill the space and also to further beautify the image, to enhance the image, and so then I'll add to it," she described. "As my imagination keeps working . . . I lay down more parts, until all of a sudden I look at it and say, well, it is complete; that's it."[19]

While Kenojuak's approach to composition was so fluid, her choice of palette was predetermined. As new materials became available, she moved from graphite to colored pencil and fiber-tipped pens. Before she started to draw she would lay out the colors she wanted to use and she did not adapt her choice as the drawing progressed. "I do lay the colors out in a certain way; I make sense of the colors. . . . I'll place two colors side by side that I feel would go well together . . . lined up in a way that is pleasing to my sense of color," she explained. "It's not as if something is going to come to me completely out of the blue in terms of color, although it might in terms of shape or form."[20]

Kenojuak tended to choose bright, pleasing combinations of primary colors, and used them with the same precision and clarity that she brought to her intertwining, overlapping, and flowing forms. The finished drawing was a pleasing, complex, rich image connecting all of the elements into a celebration of visual harmony.

For Kenojuak, the choice of subject was a means to an end—beautiful images. Unlike many of her contemporaries, she was not a storyteller or a narrator. Her primary interest and concern was always aesthetic. She is considered *the* bird artist of Cape Dorset—all but two Cape Dorset annual print collections include Kenojuak's birds of one kind or another, owls and ravens in particular. But even with these, her most-loved subjects, she did not usually sit down to draw them intentionally. When a member of the Canadian Eskimo Arts Council asked about the owl's importance to her, Kenojuak offered that the owl did not have any particular significance, but that every time she sat down to draw, an owl always seemed to come.[21] Although she did not depict traditional Inuit myths and legends directly in her work, she instinctively understood the interconnectedness of life and all living things that is so central to Inuit mythology and cosmology. Themes of light and darkness are represented by the sun and the moon, the owl and the raven, and, as her work matured, a serene woman's face at the center of it all.

DRAWING TO PRINT

Kenojuak is known for her prints, but she herself was not a printmaker. In the early days of the printmaking program, it was the men who were trained as printmakers and, for the most part, they editioned the work of others. The system developed for practical reasons, because at the time, most Inuit still lived in their traditional camps and came into the community to visit and trade. Those who were interested in drawing—men and women alike—were given paper and pencils to take back to their camps and then bring the finished drawings back to sell. Women tended to find—or make—more time to draw while they attended to their other responsibilities and the men hunted, sometimes for days at a time. Printers, on the other hand, were men who were prepared to stay in or near the community and work long hours in the studio. This division of labor allowed the artist the freedom to work at home and travel, and gave the printer greater freedom in decision-making about the image. Printers eventually became highly skilled and capable of making technical and aesthetic decisions. The significance of their role is recognized by the printer's signature chop, carried on every print released by the studio since 1960.

Kenojuak was acquainted with the printmaking processes, but she was not normally present as her prints were being editioned. She signed her editions as they were completed and rarely commented on them. Engravings, which were first introduced in 1962, were the exception. She made many copper plates and eventually mastered the technique of controlling the stylus, but she did not like doing it. It was hard on her wrist and hand, and she worried about cutting herself.[22] She was not alone in her feelings about engraving; many of the artists who tried it found the process tedious and difficult, and the program was short-lived.

Kenojuak's original print editions are now completely sold out. They come up at auction and continue to appreciate in value. Her 1960 stonecut *Enchanted Owl* sold in 2018 for Can$216,000—breaking the record for the highest amount paid for a print by a Canadian artist.

BECOMING FAMOUS

The world was first introduced to Kenojuak through the 1963 National Film Board production *Eskimo Artist: Kenojuak*. Her world—the Canadian Arctic—was at that time a faraway, mysterious land, little considered in the rest of the country for other than its inhospitable climate and the native "Eskimo" people, who somehow managed to survive there. This remarkable film opened the eyes of the outside world to the rich life and enchanting art of this young woman, and a lasting connection was formed. As each annual print collection from Cape Dorset was released "down south," the name Kenojuak became synonymous with the mystery, bounty, and beauty of Canada's far North.

The world fell in love with Kenojuak four years later, in November 1967, when she and Johnniebo traveled to Ottawa, where she was awarded the Medal of Service of the Order of Canada by Governor General Roland Michener. This was the inaugural investiture of Canada's new national honor, and in her attendant press, Kenojuak was described as "simply magnificent."[23] Kenojuak and Johnniebo returned to Ottawa two years later for an extended two-month stay while they worked together on a mural intended for the Canadian Pavilion at Expo '70 in Suita, Osaka, Japan. The media focus for this trip was on the artistic couple, with one headline announcing, "These artists share bed and drawing board."[24] Two years later, they were back in the south, in Halifax, for the opening of a major exhibition at the new St. Mary's University Art Gallery. This was, sadly, their last opportunity to travel and be celebrated together. Johnniebo died in 1972 when he developed appendicitis. A plane was called to medevac him to Iqaluit (then Frobisher Bay) for surgery, but it was not able to land due to weather. The circumstances were tragic, and his death was a great loss for Kenojuak.

Opportunities for Kenojuak to travel multiplied as her career flourished, taking her to Europe and across the United States and Canada. She was often cast in the role of cultural ambassador and a role model for women. Kenojuak did pave the way for other Inuit women artists, both of her generation and the next. As she matured, she spoke more candidly about herself as a working artist, supporting her family through the income she earned. She bristled at questions about when she would stop drawing: "People often treat art as though it is very different from any other profession and ask, why would you want to keep doing this? This is my job and my love. I cannot imagine life without art."[25]

Kenojuak also became a celebrity in her own land, in 1999 commemorating the creation of the Inuit homeland, Nunavut, with one of her most majestic works—*Siilavut, Nunavut (Our Environment, Our Land)*. In 2003, she was invited by Adventure Canada to join them as their guest aboard their Arctic Art cruise. At 76, she fiddled and danced her way across Hudson Bay. When the ship pulled in at Cape Dorset, one journalist wrote, "It is as though the Queen herself has arrived. . . . Relatives, well-wishers and fishermen crowd the rocky shore. Artists stop to shake Kenojuak's hand."[26] In 2009, she attended her first solo

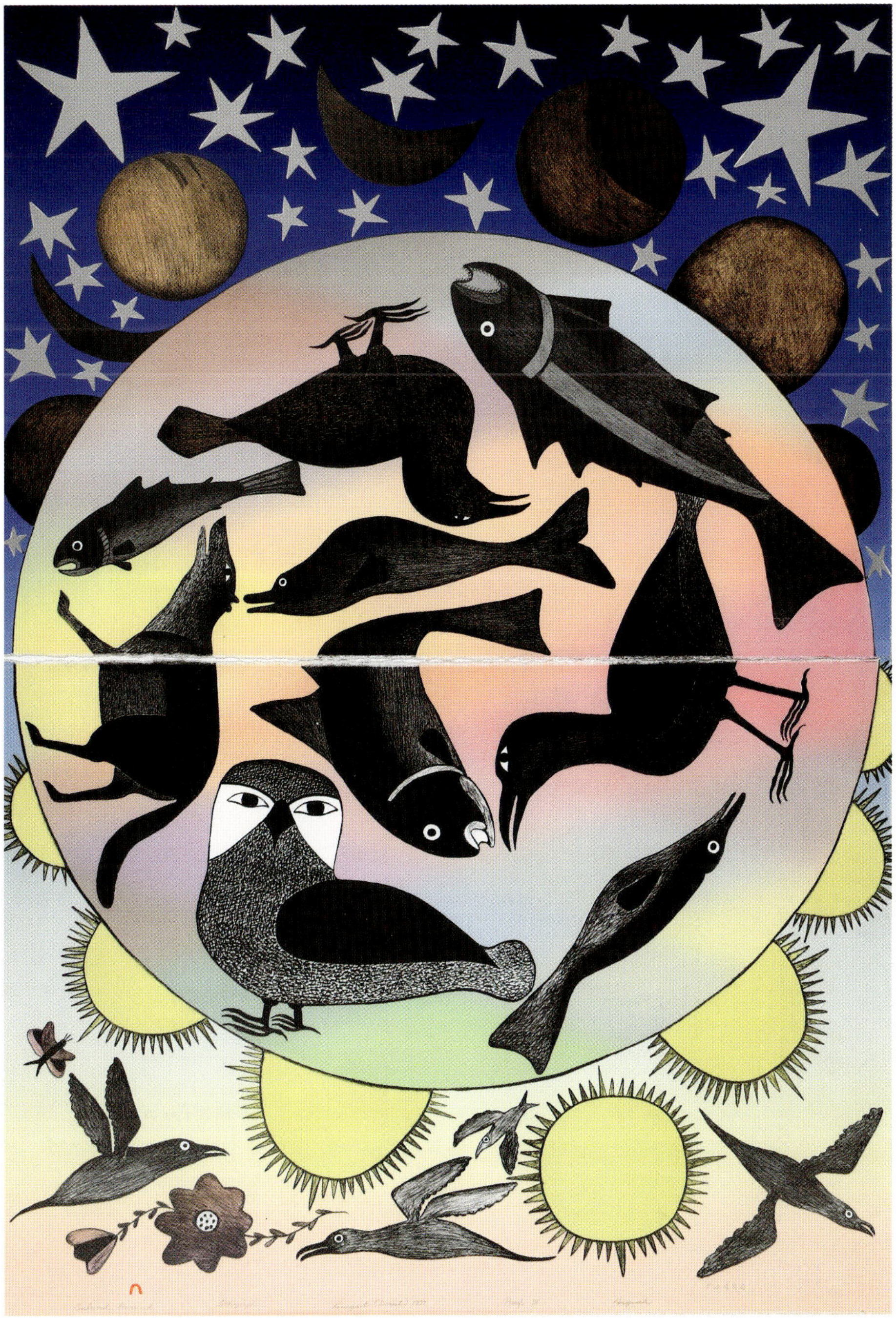

Siilavut, Nunavut (Our Environment, Our Land), 1999, lithograph

exhibition in Nunavut, at the Nunatta Sunakkutaangit Museum in Iqaluit, and in 2012, she was named to the Order of Nunavut, the territory's greatest honor.

LEGACY

The Kenojuak Cultural Centre officially opened in Cape Dorset in September 2018. It had been a long time in coming. Plans to build a cultural center in Cape Dorset date back more than twenty years, but the vagaries of politics and fundraising prevailed at the time, and the project was indefinitely postponed. But not forgotten. Cape Dorset is the most artistically famous community in Nunavut, and the reasons for building a cultural center there—to celebrate its artistic legacy—never changed and, in fact, only grew stronger as each new generation continued to produce some of the North's best artists.

The long-awaited ceremony—attended by visiting dignitaries, funders, and over six hundred members of the community—was an emotional celebration. As the sealskin rope that had been stretched across the entrance was cut using a traditional snow knife, people were welcomed inside to see the new state-of-the-art printmaking studios, studio space for artists to work, a gathering space for elders and other community groups, and the exhibition space—the first purpose-built exhibition space for works on paper in Nunavut. On the walls were thirty-one drawings and three prints by Kenojuak, for whom the cultural center is named.

The drawings in the opening exhibition are from the archives of the West Baffin Eskimo Co-operative. The co-op's collection represents the work of over two hundred Inuit from the Cape Dorset (Kinngait) area who tried their hand at drawing over the years. Some gave it up, for lack of talent or interest or both, and many continued, creating the foundation for the printmaking program and the release of the annual print collections from Cape Dorset. But many more drawings were purchased by the co-op than were ever made into print editions, eventually resulting in a trove of more than 100,000 original works. The bulk of these are on long-term loan to the McMichael Canadian Art Collection in Kleinburg, Ontario, and others are held and stored by the co-op, in Cape Dorset, and at Dorset Fine Arts, in Toronto.

The regrettable reality is that while Cape Dorset and its artists have become famous worldwide, community residents have had little or no access to their own art history. The co-op's archive of drawings and prints was moved for security reasons—namely the fear of fire, which destroyed valuable works in Pangnirtung and Baker Lake, both in Nunavut. Now, with the Kenojuak Cultural Centre open to the public, and with designated exhibition space, members of the community can see the work created by their forebears and relatives for the first time.

This exhibition—*Kenojuak Ashevak: Life and Legacy*—is the first originating in the Canadian Arctic with a subsequent national tour. Cocurated by Louisa Parr for the Kenojuak Cultural Centre and William Huffman for the West Baffin Eskimo Co-operative, the show includes never-before-displayed drawings that inspired emblematic prints in stonecut, lithography, and etching. The Cape Dorset community has also been invited to contribute personal objects, musings, and anecdotes, in addition to the works on paper, that further illustrate the seminal role that Kenojuak played in the development and appreciation of Inuit art and culture.

If Kenojuak were still alive to enjoy this achievement and tribute, she would be particularly pleased that subsequent generations now have the opportunity to appreciate and learn from the efforts of their grandparents and great-grandparents to tell their own stories in art. She was always mindful of the next generation, thinking about her children and the future, and her responsibility to provide for them as best as she could. And she was always grateful for the opportunity to become a professional artist, and "to make something beautiful." After being named Companion to the Order of Canada in 1982, she was asked what she thought about the honor: "I will not think of myself only, but will be thinking of my children as well. . . . I am not going to be thinking just about the present, but what the medal will mean in the future, and what it stands for, and that God has His hand in it. That is how I think about it."[27]

NOTES

1 The name refers to a bridge or a pathway that links an island to the mainland at low tide.

2 Patricia Ryan, "The Autobiography of Kenojuak," in *Kenojuak*, Jean Blodgett (Toronto: Firefly Books, 1985), 7.

3 Ryan, "Autobiography of Kenojuak," 8.

4 Ryan, 8.

5 Ryan, 10.

6 Ryan, 11.

7 Ryan, 12.

8 Peter Pitseolak was a camp leader and Cape Dorset's well-known documentarian and photographer. His life story, *People from Our Side,* was published in 1975 (Edmonton: Hurtig Publishers).

9 Inuit conversion to Christianity began in the early part of the twentieth century, and by the 1920s adult literacy had reached almost 100 percent.

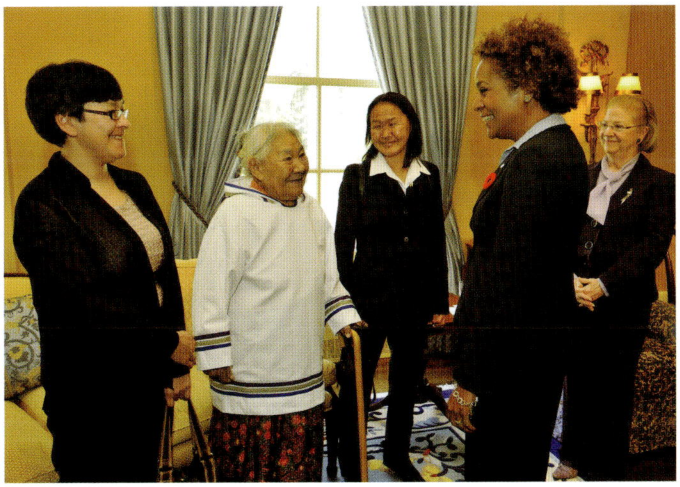

From left: Silaqi Ashevak, Kenojuak Ashevak, and Annie Pootoogook meeting with Her Excellency the Right Honourable Michaëlle Jean, 27th Governor General of Canada (2005–2010), Rideau Hall, Ottawa, 2009

Photograph by MCpl Jean-Francois Neron

10 Ryan, "Autobiography of Kenojuak," 18.

11 Inuit Tapiriit Kanatami, *Inuit Statistical Profile 2018*, 2018, 11, https://www.itk.ca/wp-content/uploads/2018/08/Inuit-Statistical-Profile.pdf.

12 Harold Pfeiffer's brother, Walter Pfeiffer, was one of the doctors attending to patients at the hospital.

13 Ryan, "Autobiography of Kenojuak," 20.

14 West Baffin Eskimo Co-operative, *Dorset 77: Cape Dorset Annual Graphics Collection 1977* (Toronto: M. F. Feheley Publishers, 1977), 48.

15 West Baffin Eskimo Co-operative, *Dorset 79: Twentieth Annual Cape Dorset Graphics Collection* (Toronto: M. F. Feheley Publishers, 1979), 37.

16 Ryan, "Autobiography of Kenojuak," 20.

17 Jean Blodgett, "The Art of Kenojuak," in *Kenojuak* (Toronto: Firefly Books, 1985), 39.

18 Blodgett, "Art of Kenojuak," 38.

19 Blodgett, 38.

20 Blodgett, 41.

21 Blodgett, 37.

22 Blodgett, 52.

23 Charles Lynch, "Our Brightest Lights," *Ottawa Citizen,* November 25, 1967.

24 "These Artists Share Bed and Drawing Board," *Star Weekly* (Toronto), June 28, 1969.

25 Marina Jimenez, "Art Is My Job and My Love," *Globe and Mail* (Toronto), October 20, 2003.

26 Jimenez, "Art Is My Job."

27 "Inuktitut Asks Kenoajuak [sic] about Her Life as an Artist and Mother," *Inuktitut Magazine*, January 1983, 13.

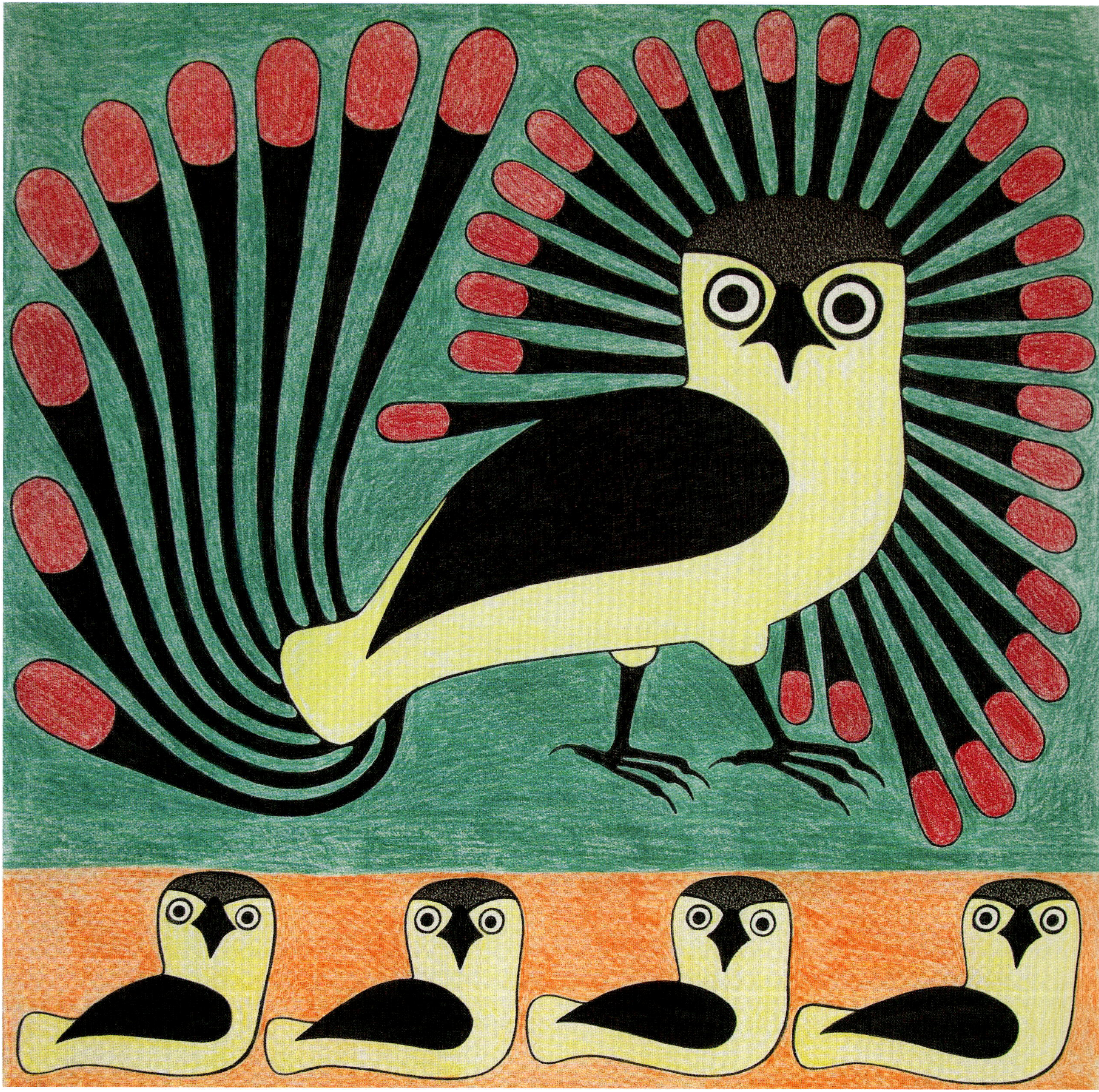

Drawings *and* Related Prints

Untitled (Tapestry of Owls) (detail), 1999, ink and colored pencil

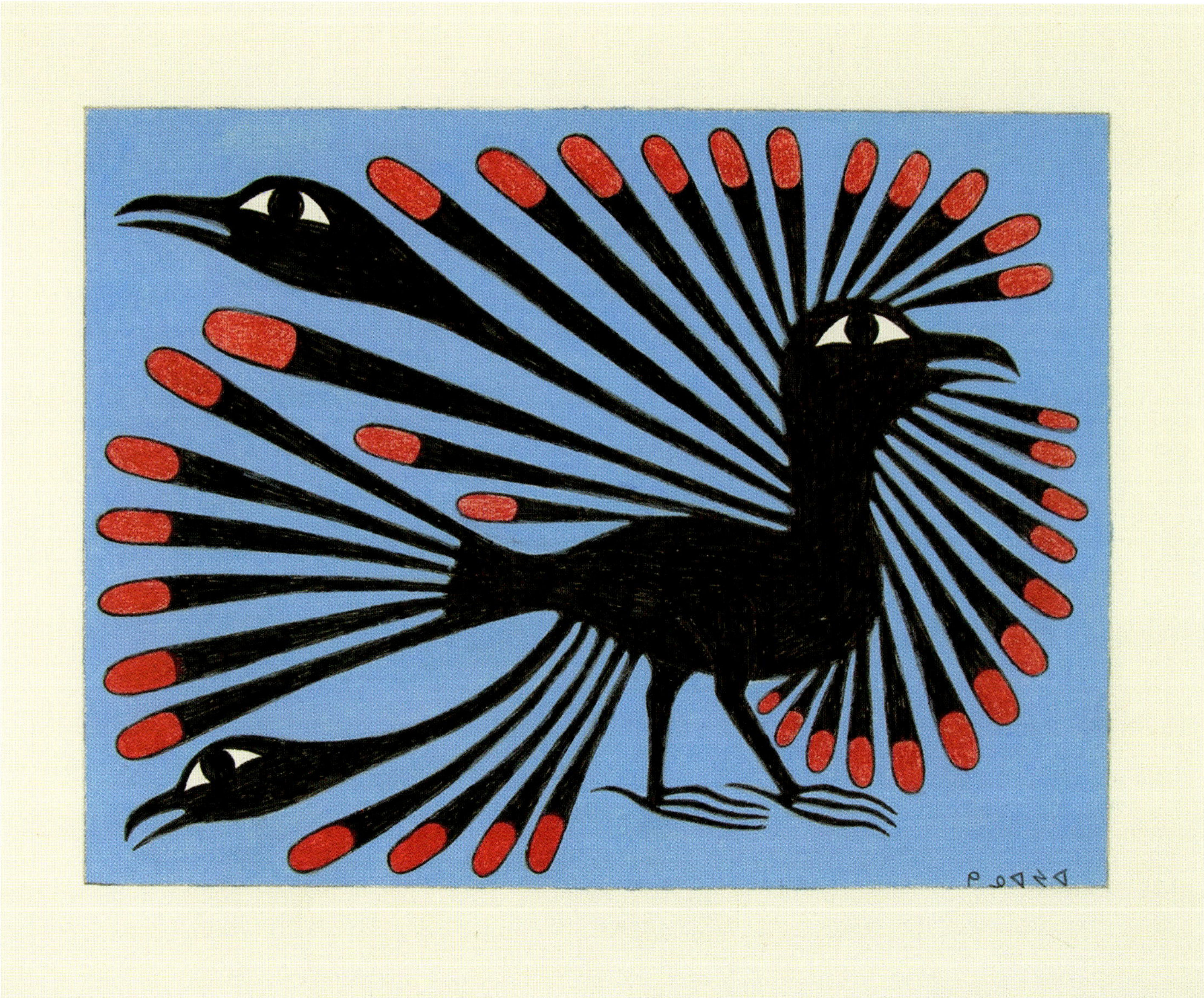

Untitled (Filigreed Raven), 1998, ink and colored pencil

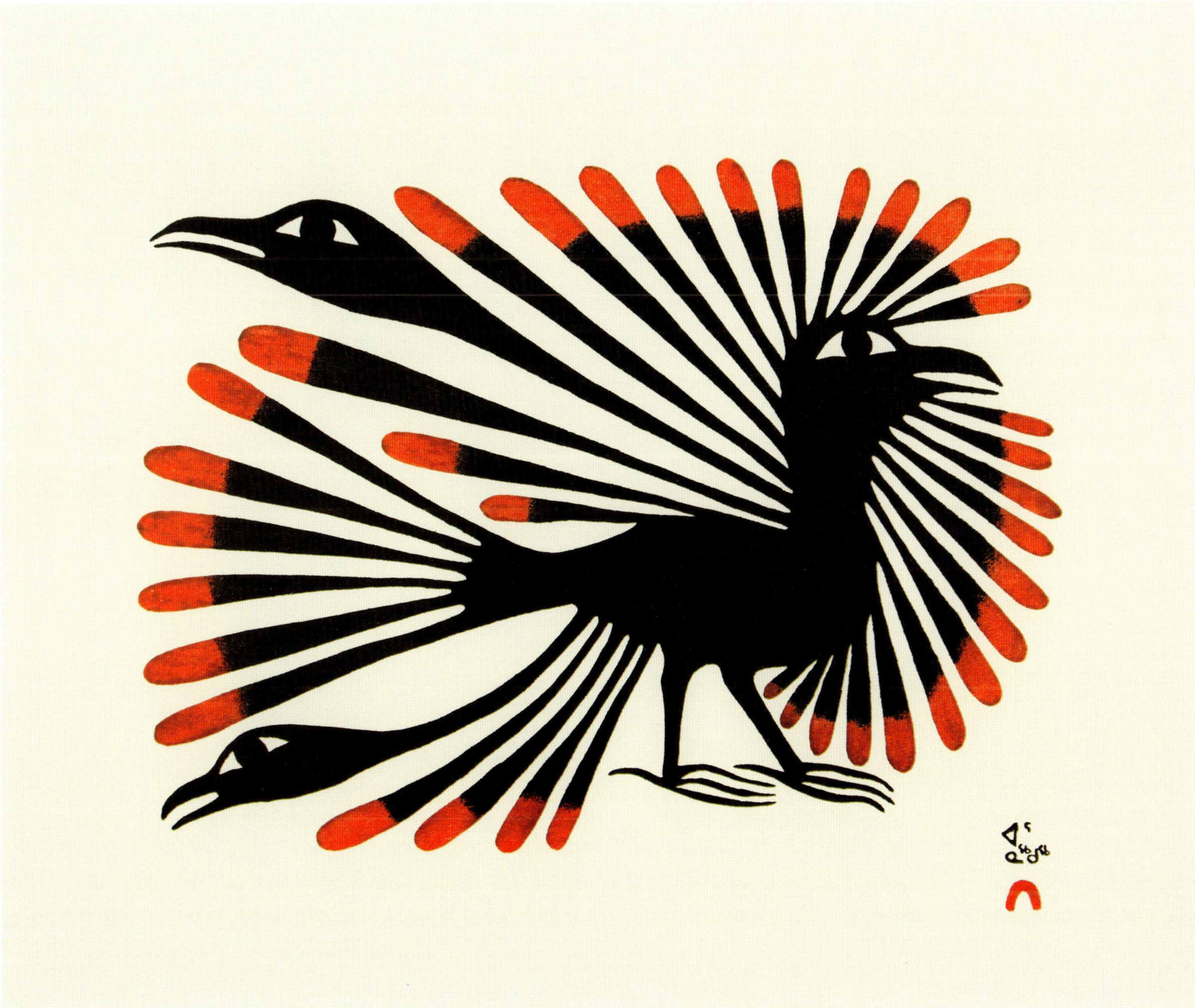

Filigreed Raven, 1998, stonecut

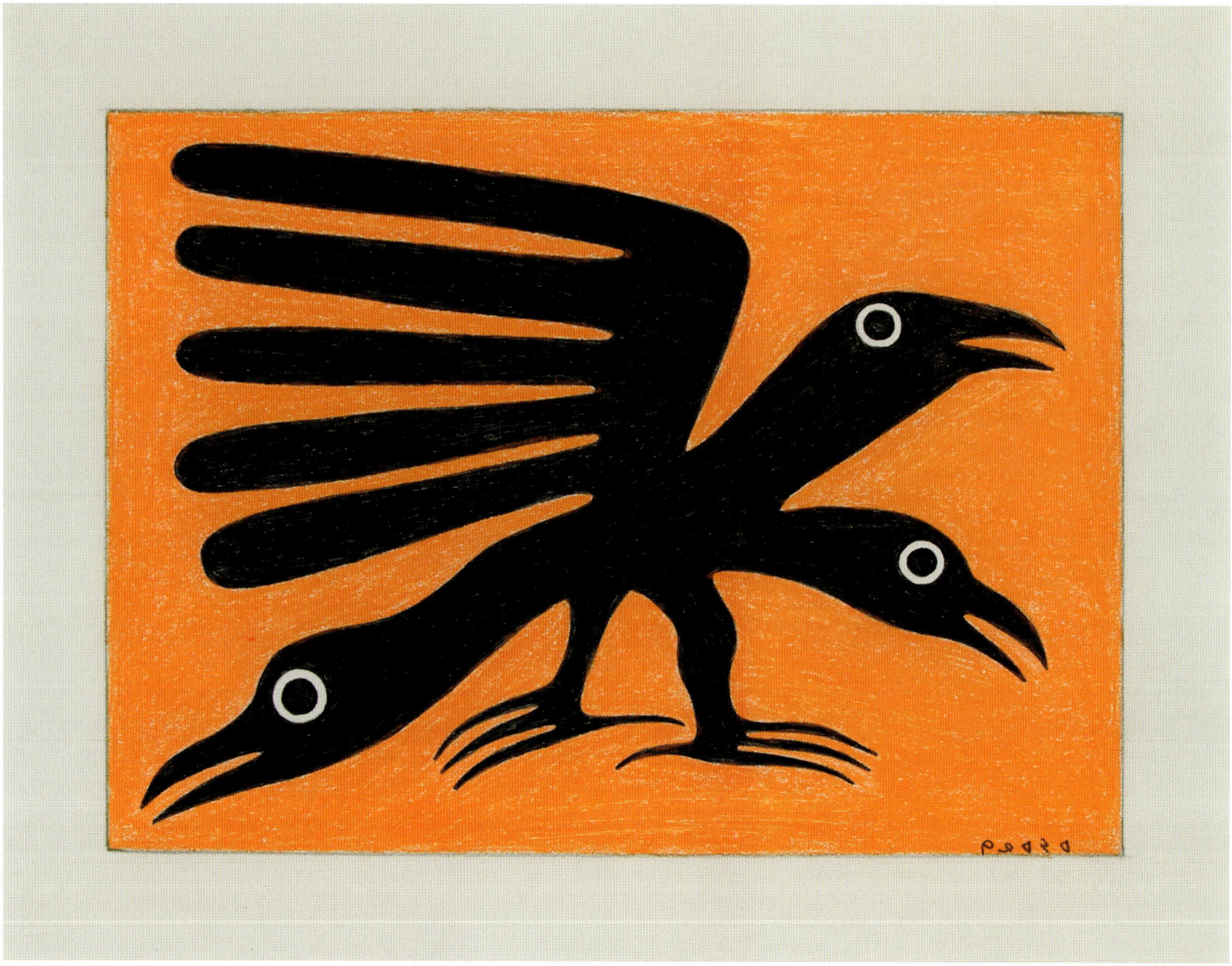

Untitled (Raven Silhouette I), 1998, ink and colored pencil

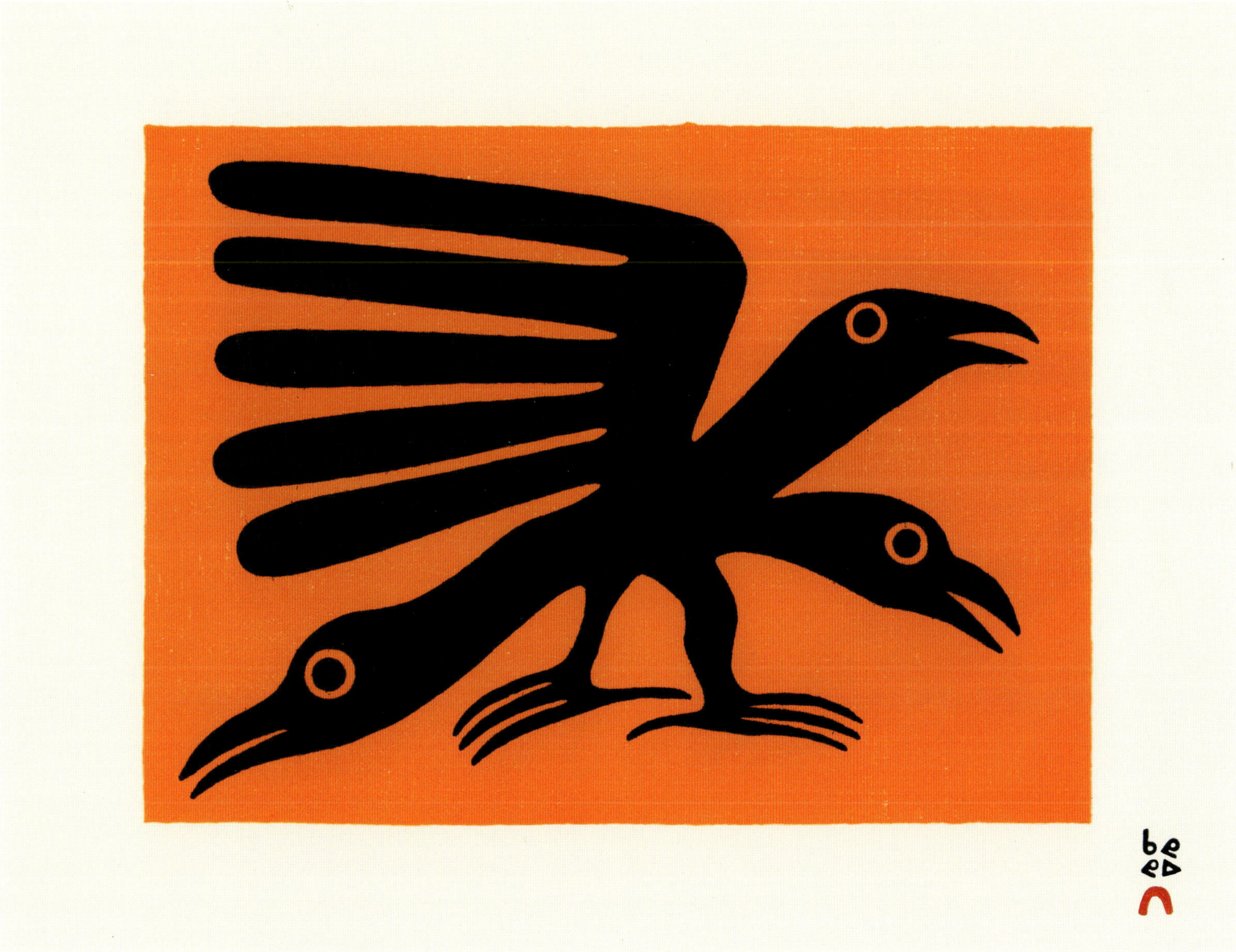

Raven Silhouette I, 1998, stonecut

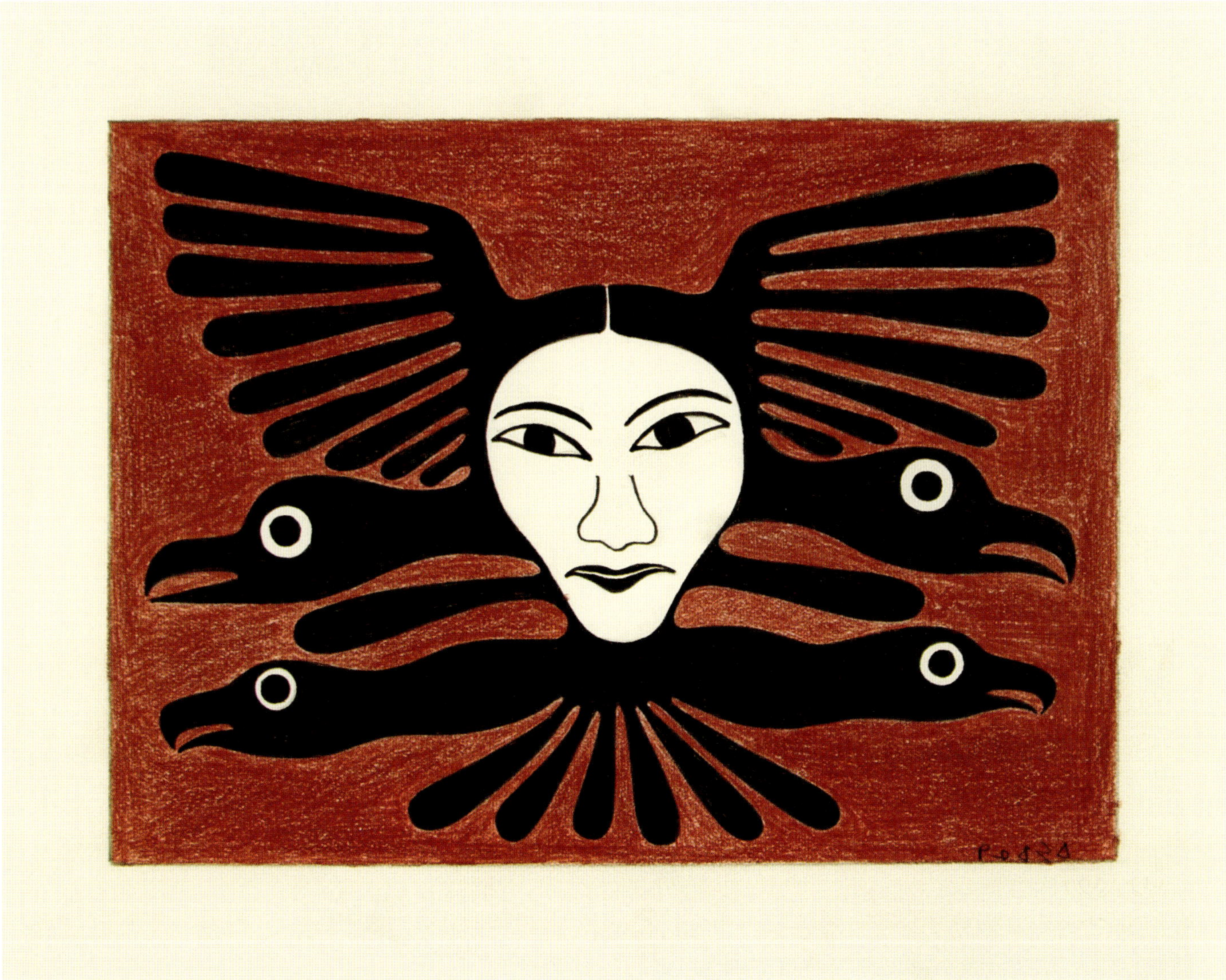

Untitled (Raven Silhouette II), 1998, ink and colored pencil

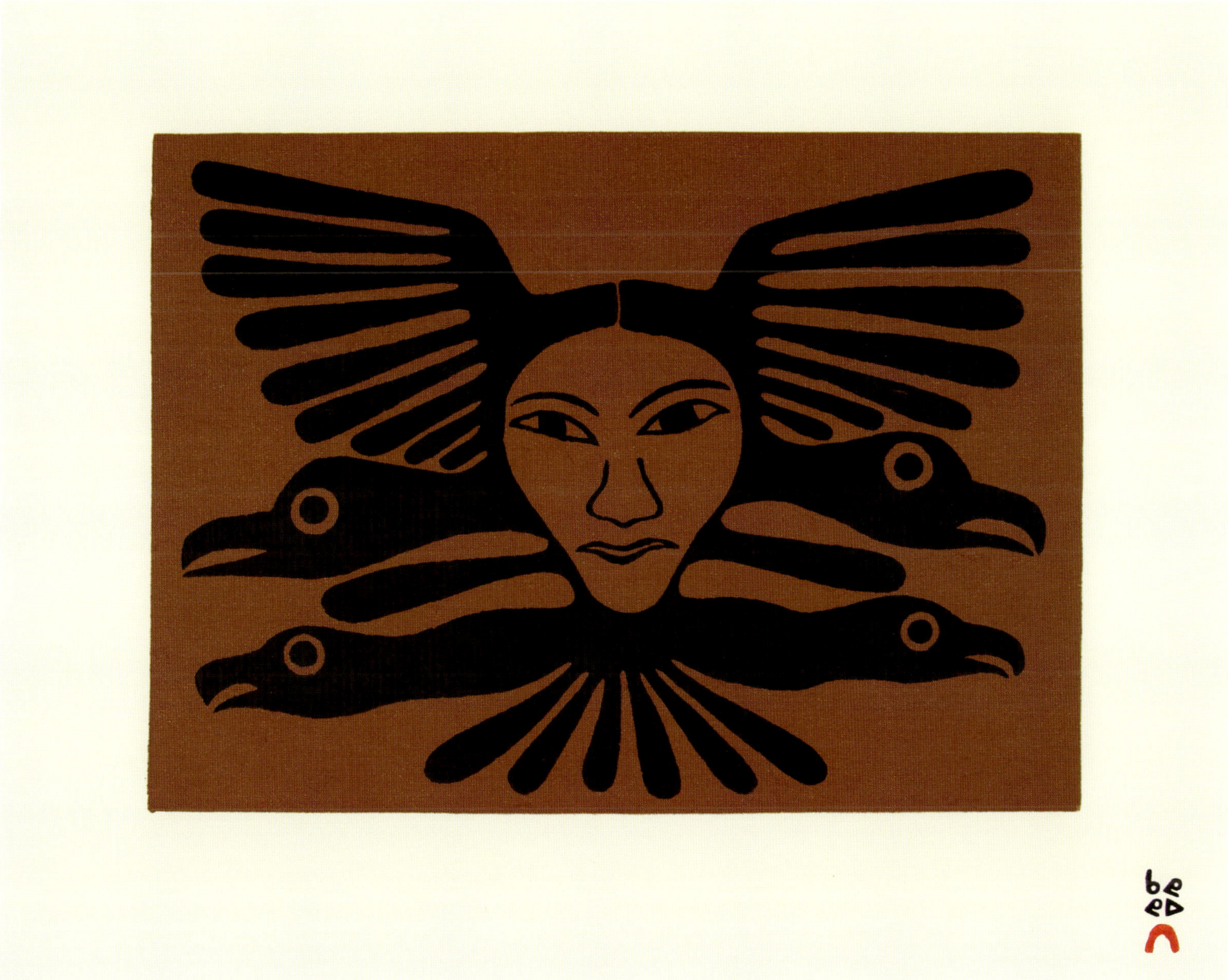

Raven Silhouette II, 1998, stonecut

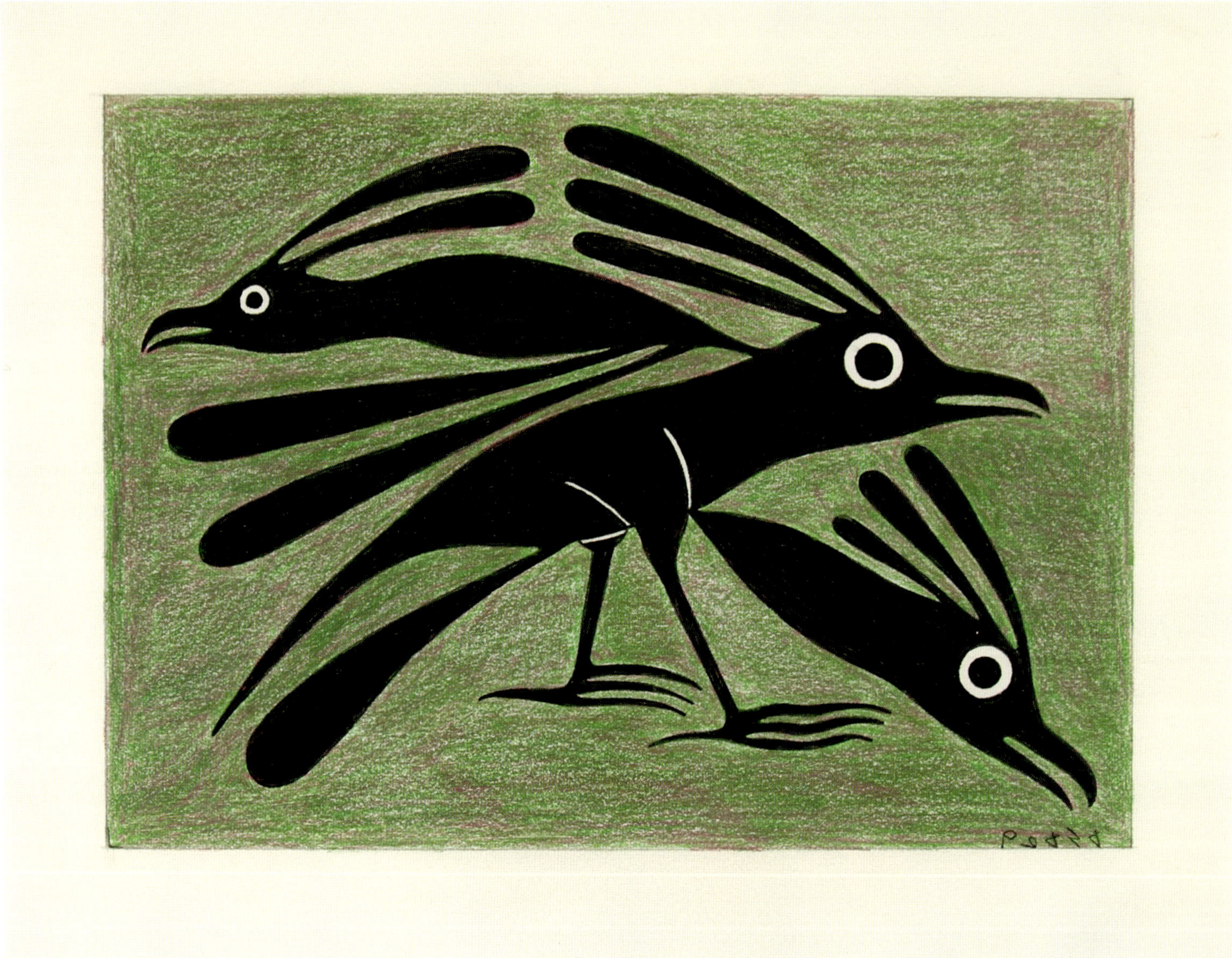

Untitled (Raven Silhouette III), 1998, ink and colored pencil

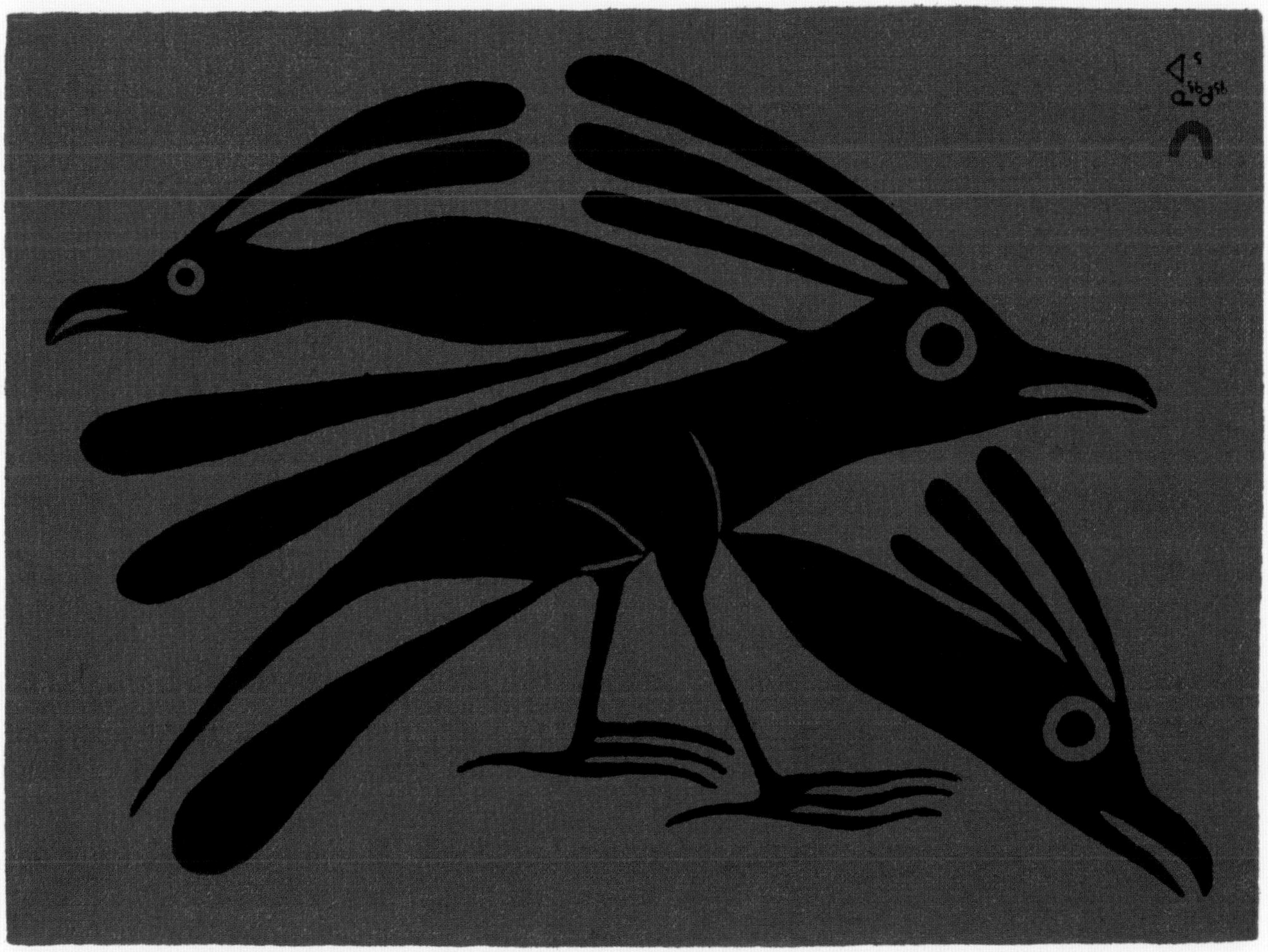

Raven Silhouette III, 1998, stonecut

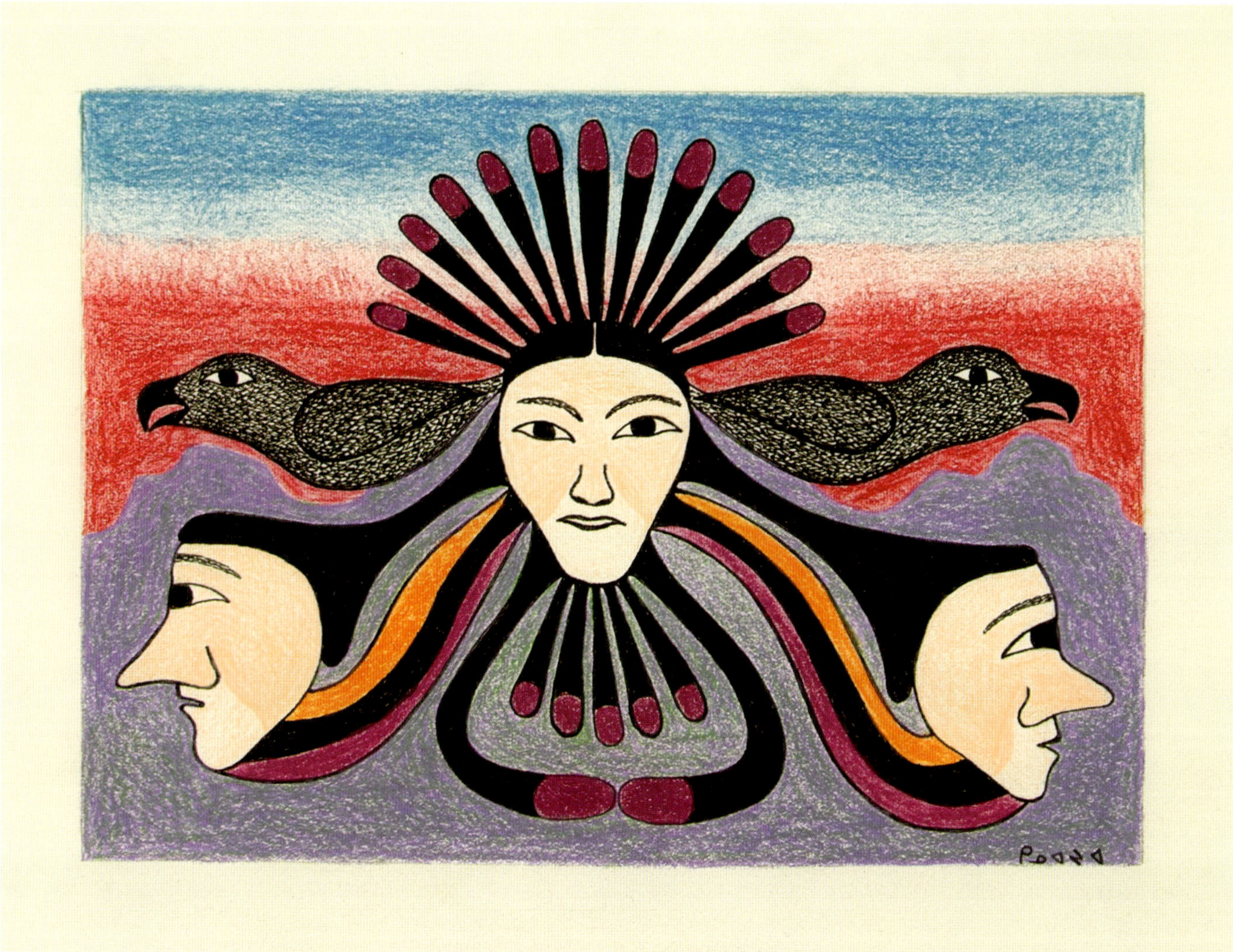

Untitled (Oracle), 1999, ink and colored pencil

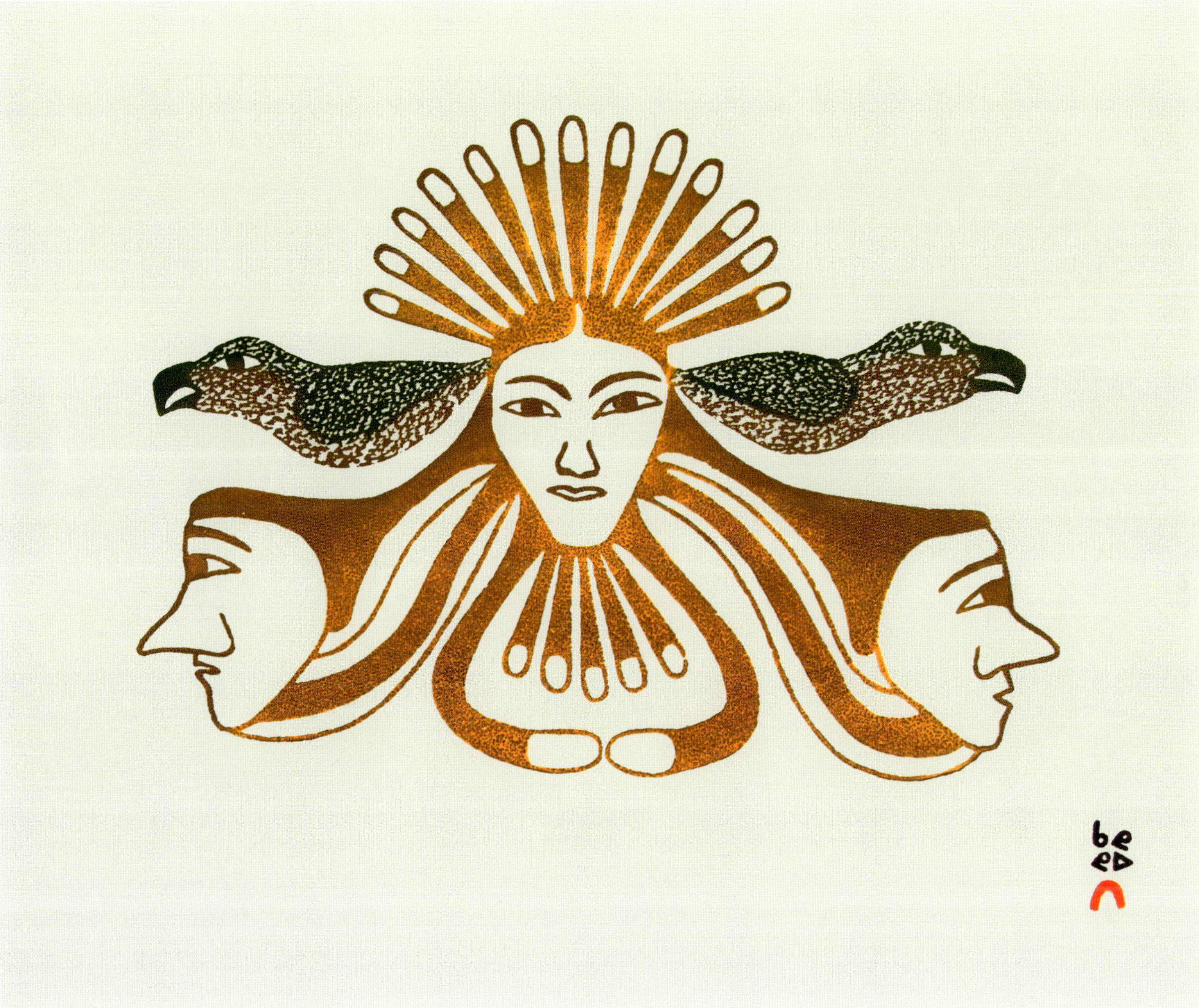

Oracle, 1999, stonecut

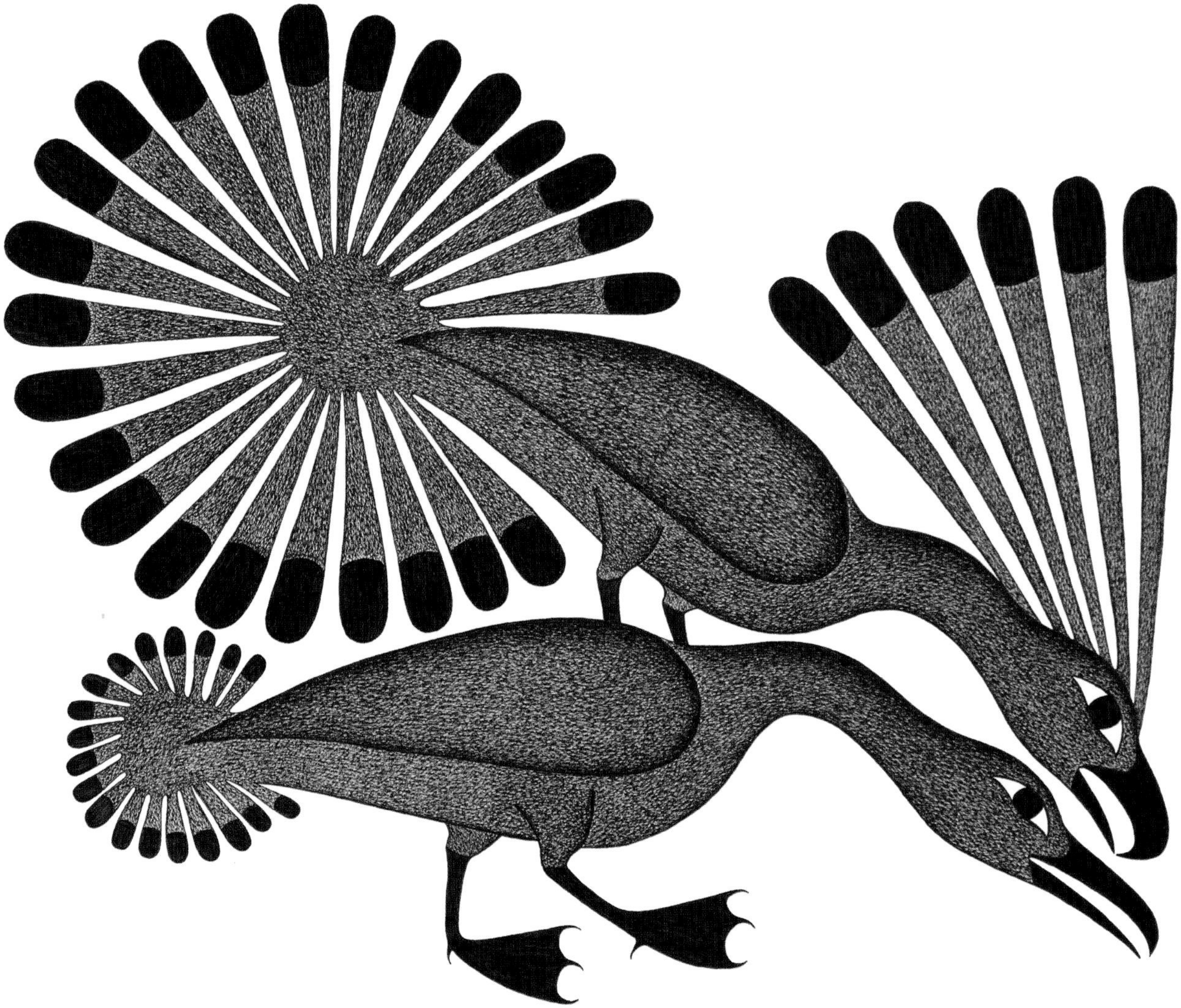

Untitled (Summer Courtship), 2000, ink

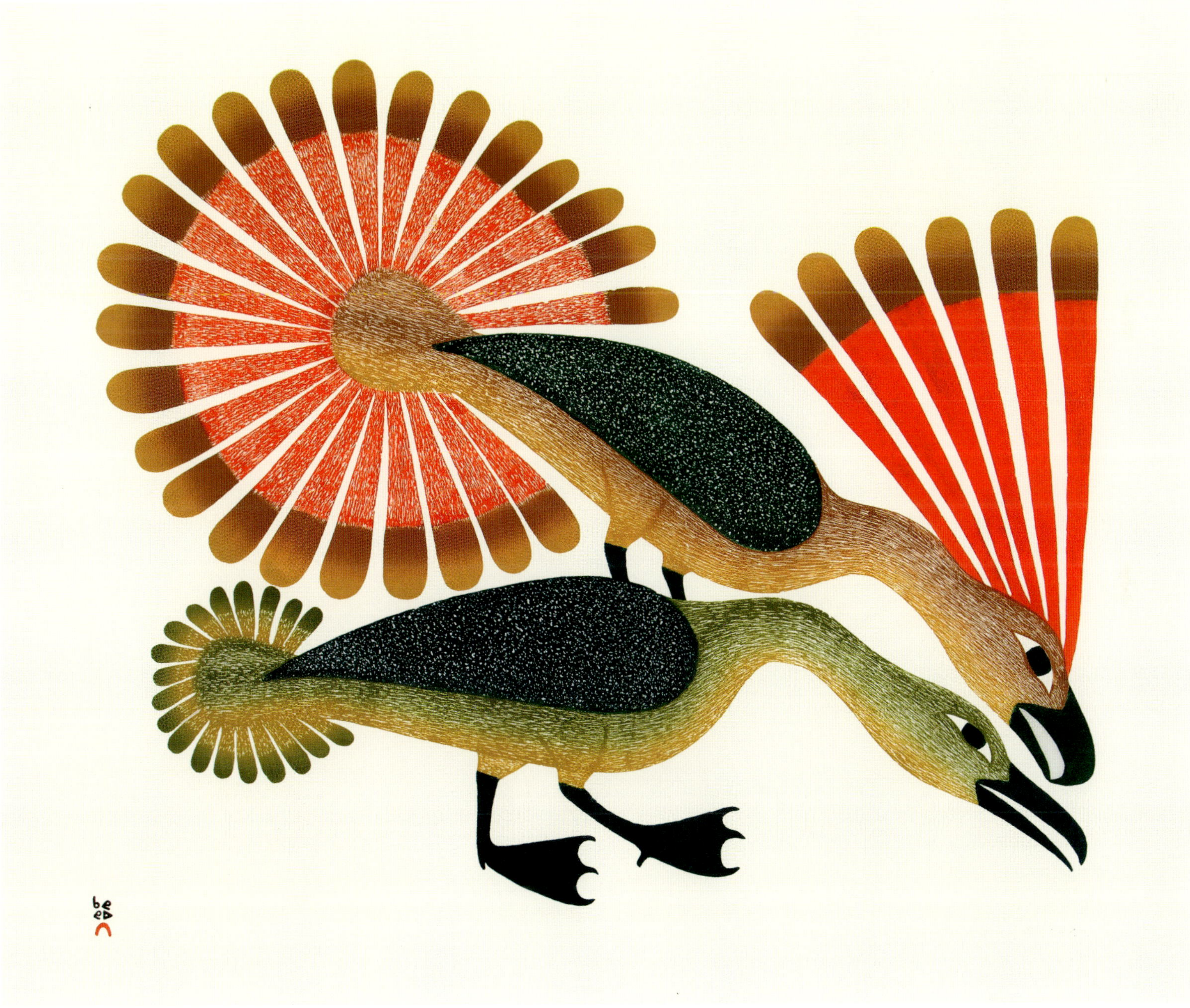

Summer Courtship, 2000, stonecut and stencil

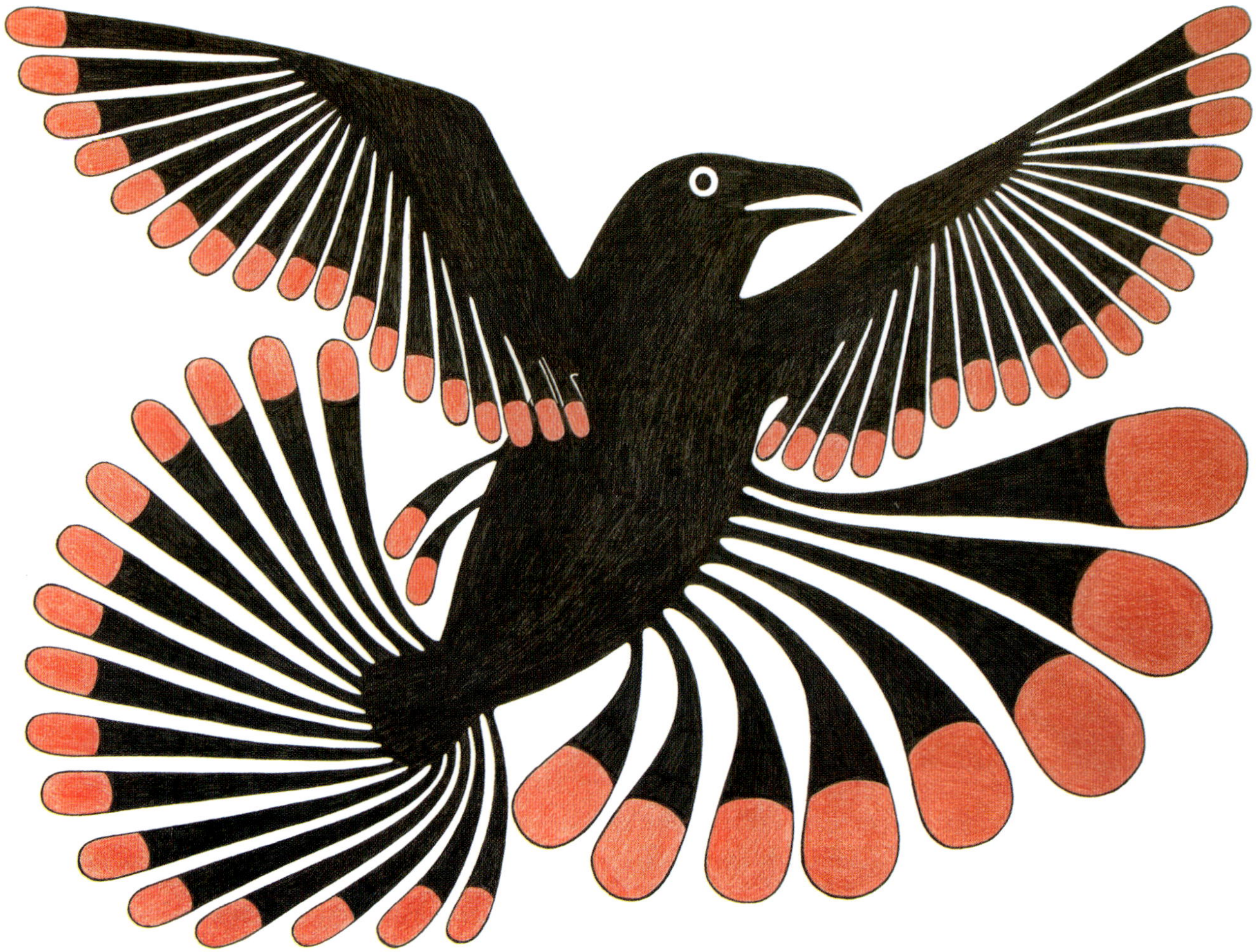

Untitled (Ravens Return), 2000, ink and colored pencil

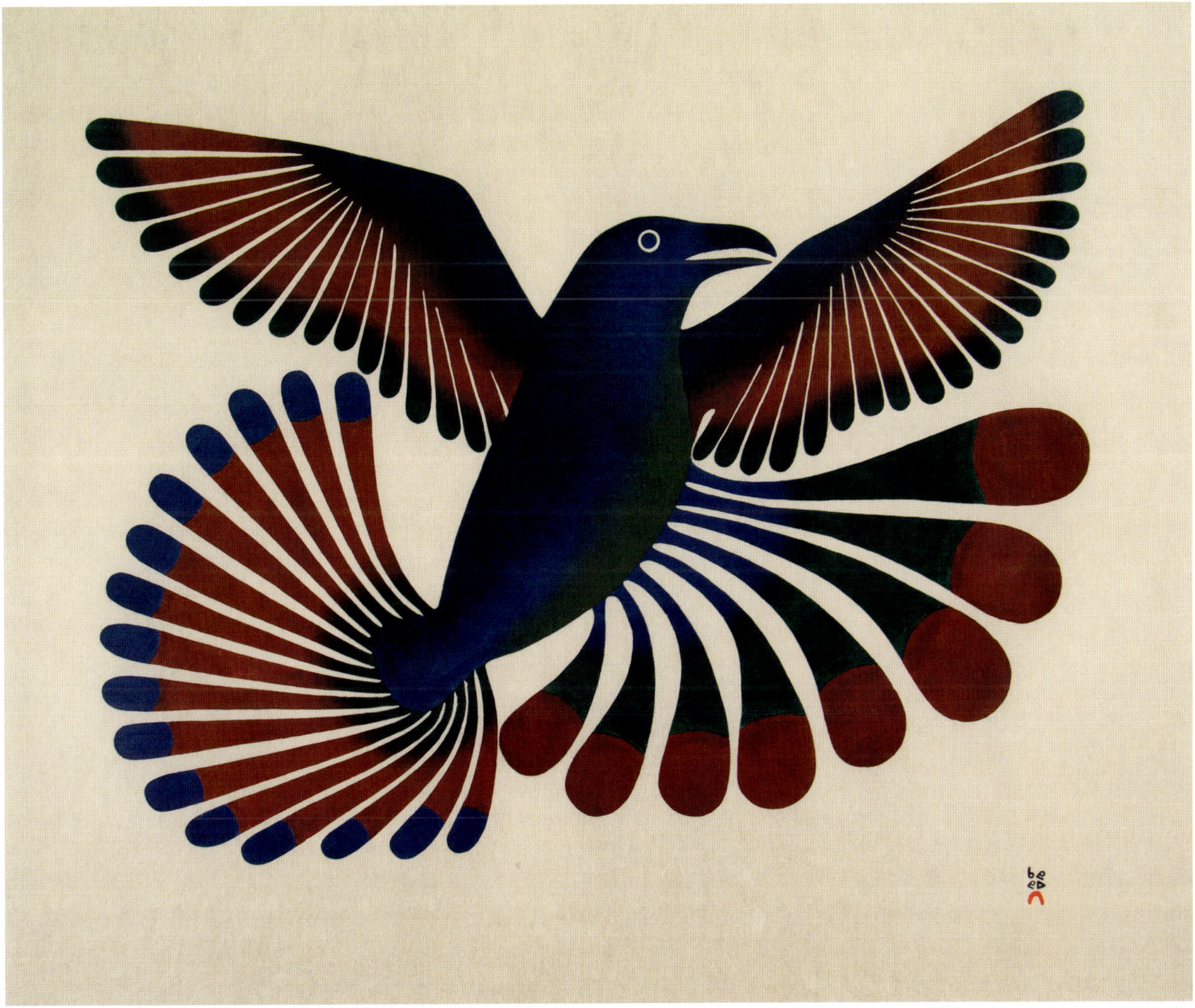

Ravens Return, 2000, stonecut and stencil

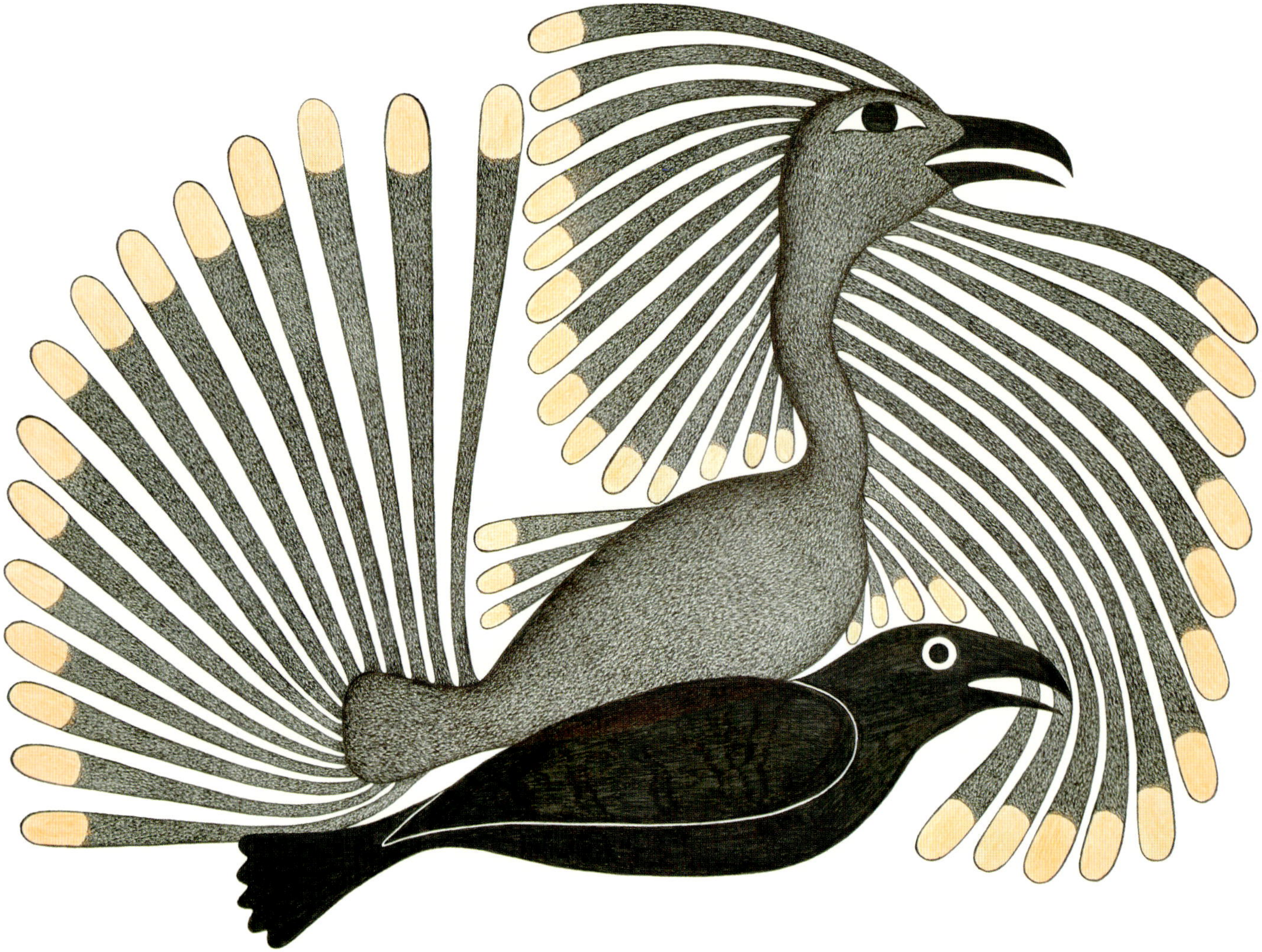

Untitled (Intruding Raven), 2001, ink and colored pencil

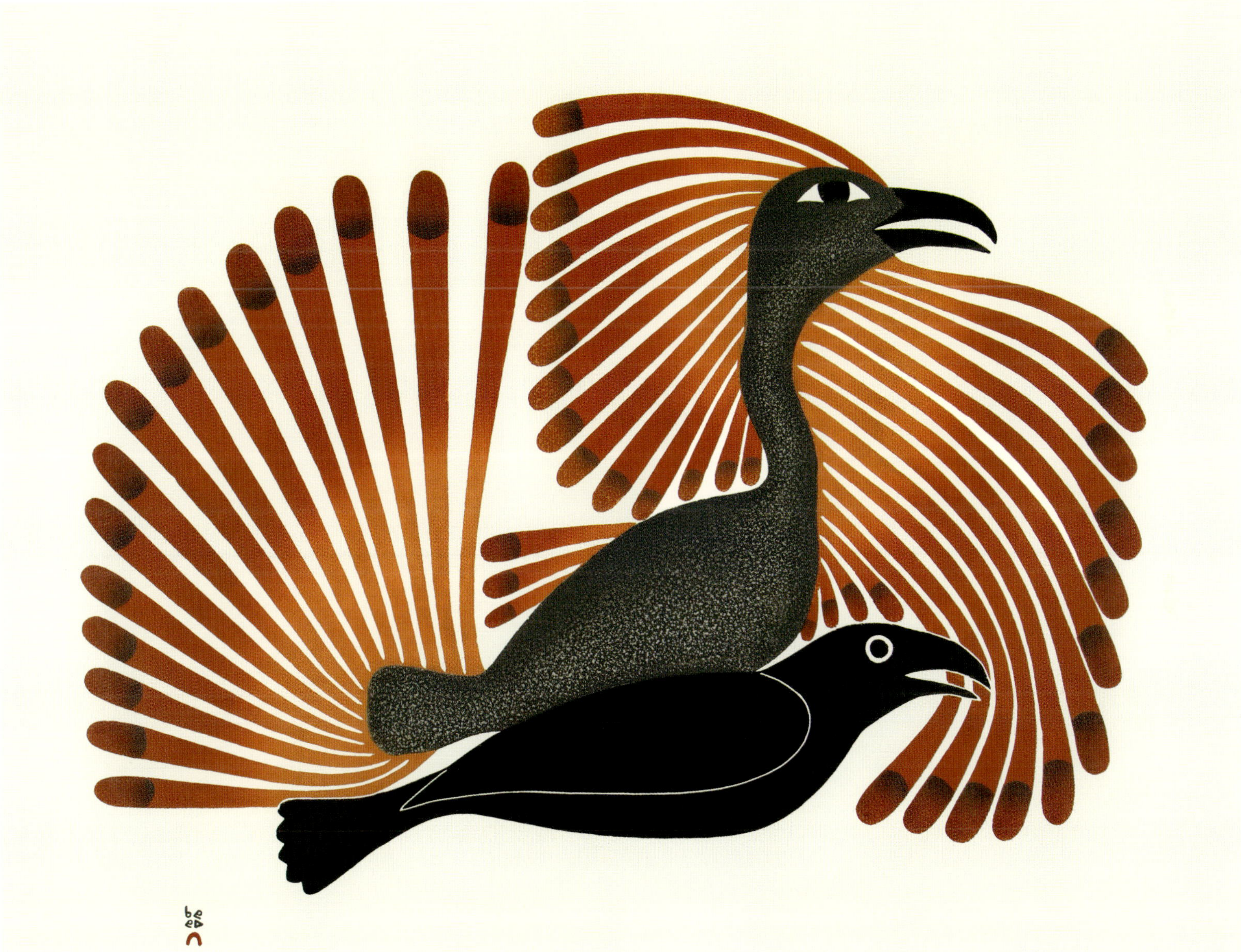

Intruding Raven, 2001, stonecut and stencil

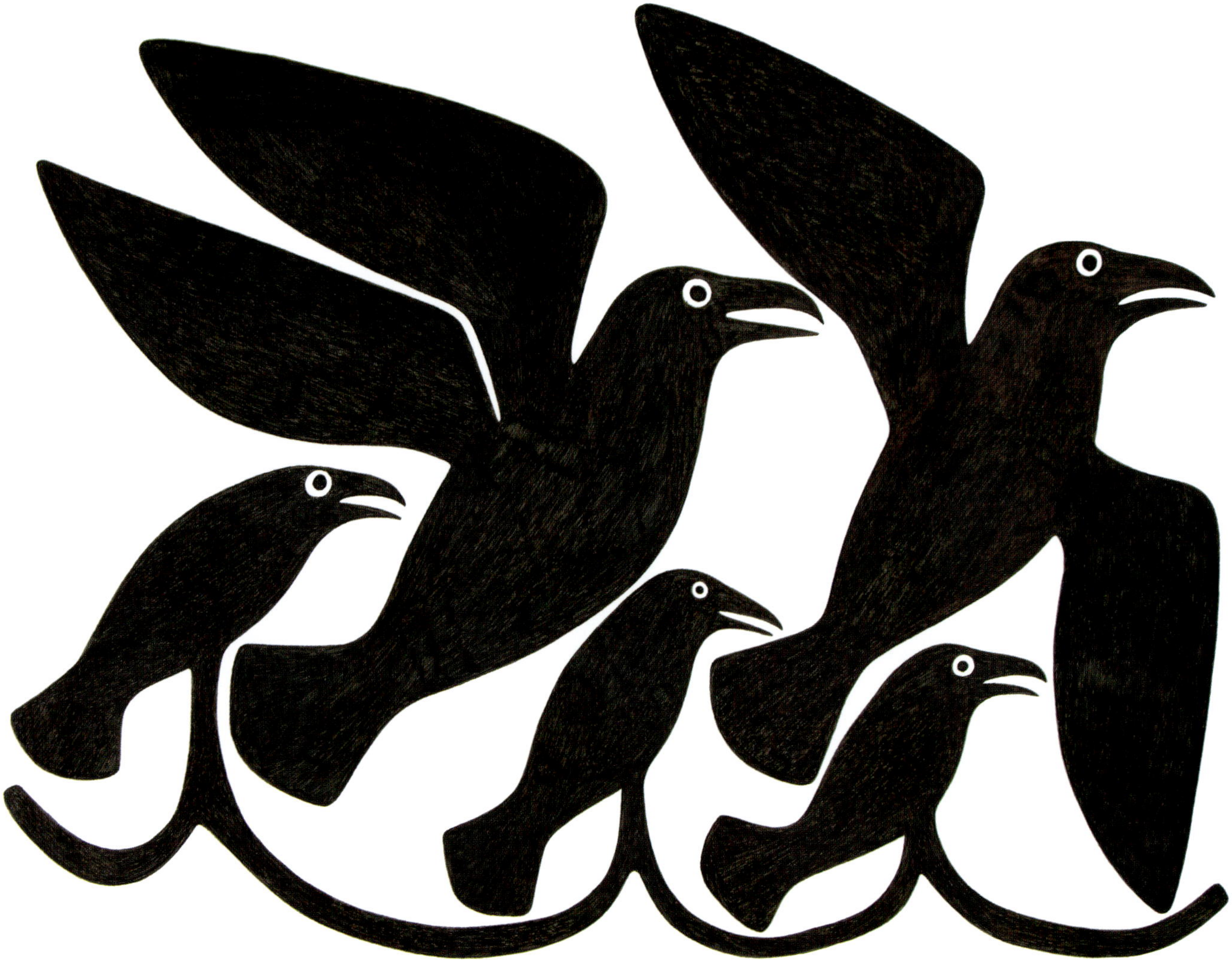

Untitled (Starlit Ravens), 2001, ink

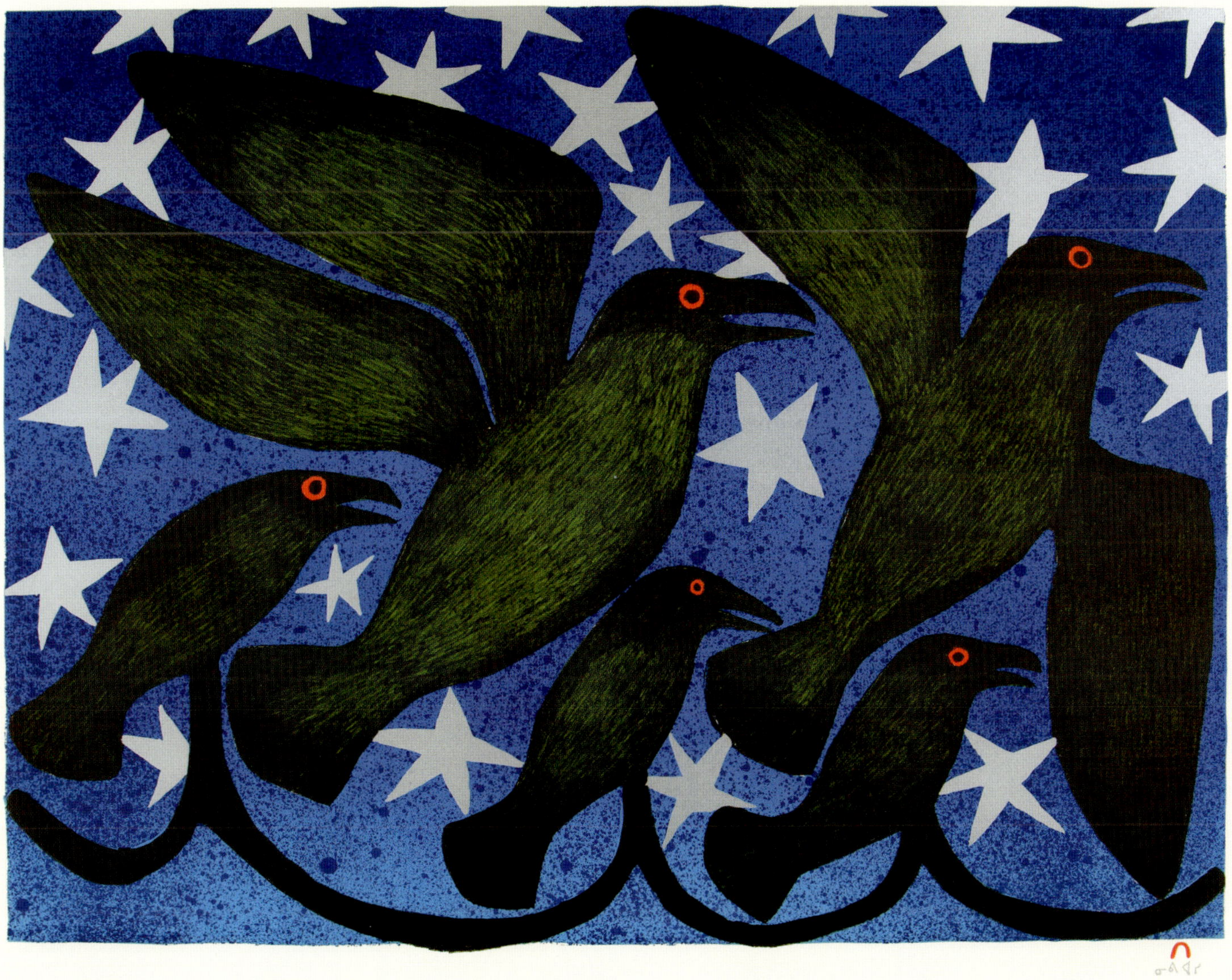

Starlit Ravens, 2001, lithograph

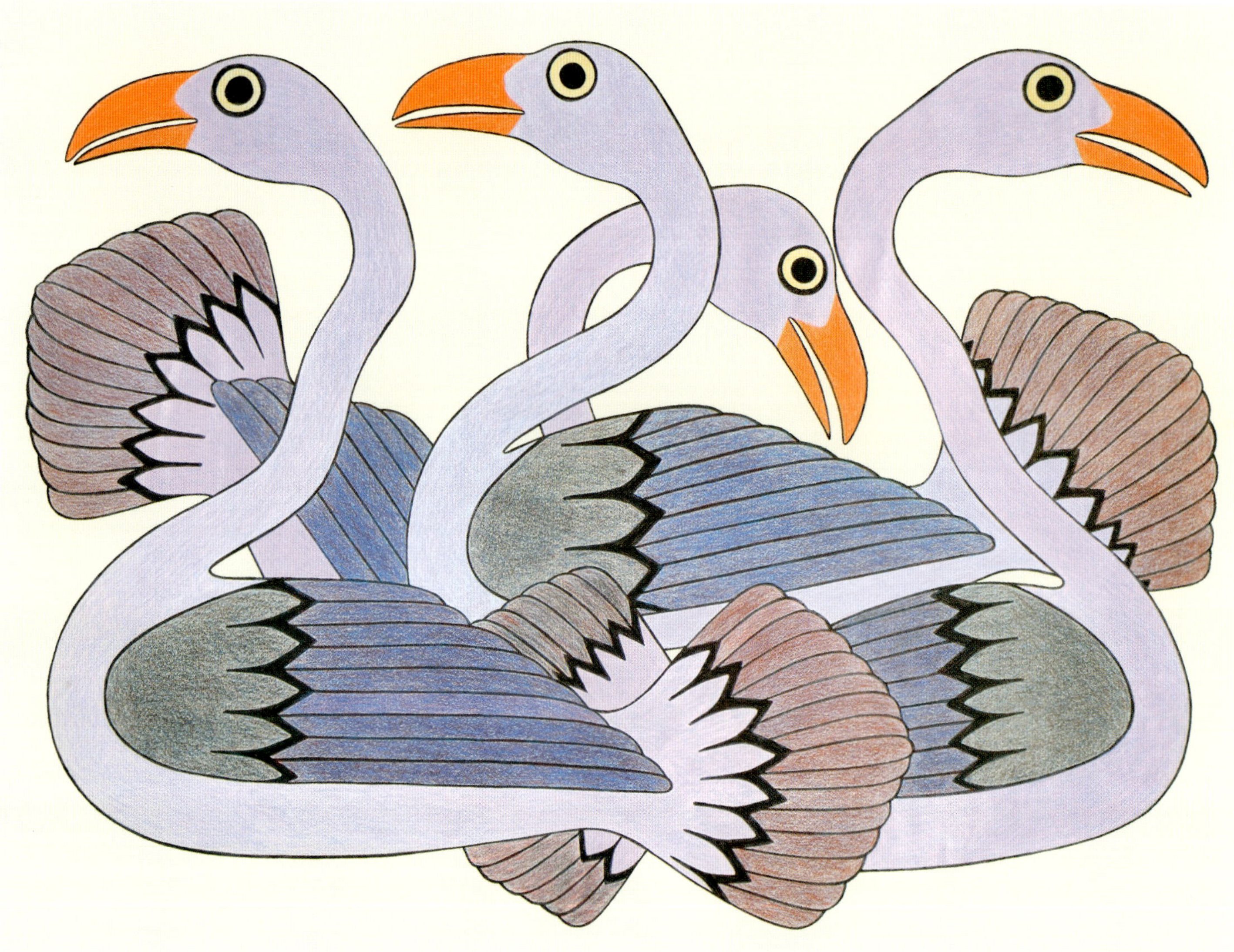

Untitled (Swans at Sunset), 2002, ink and colored pencil

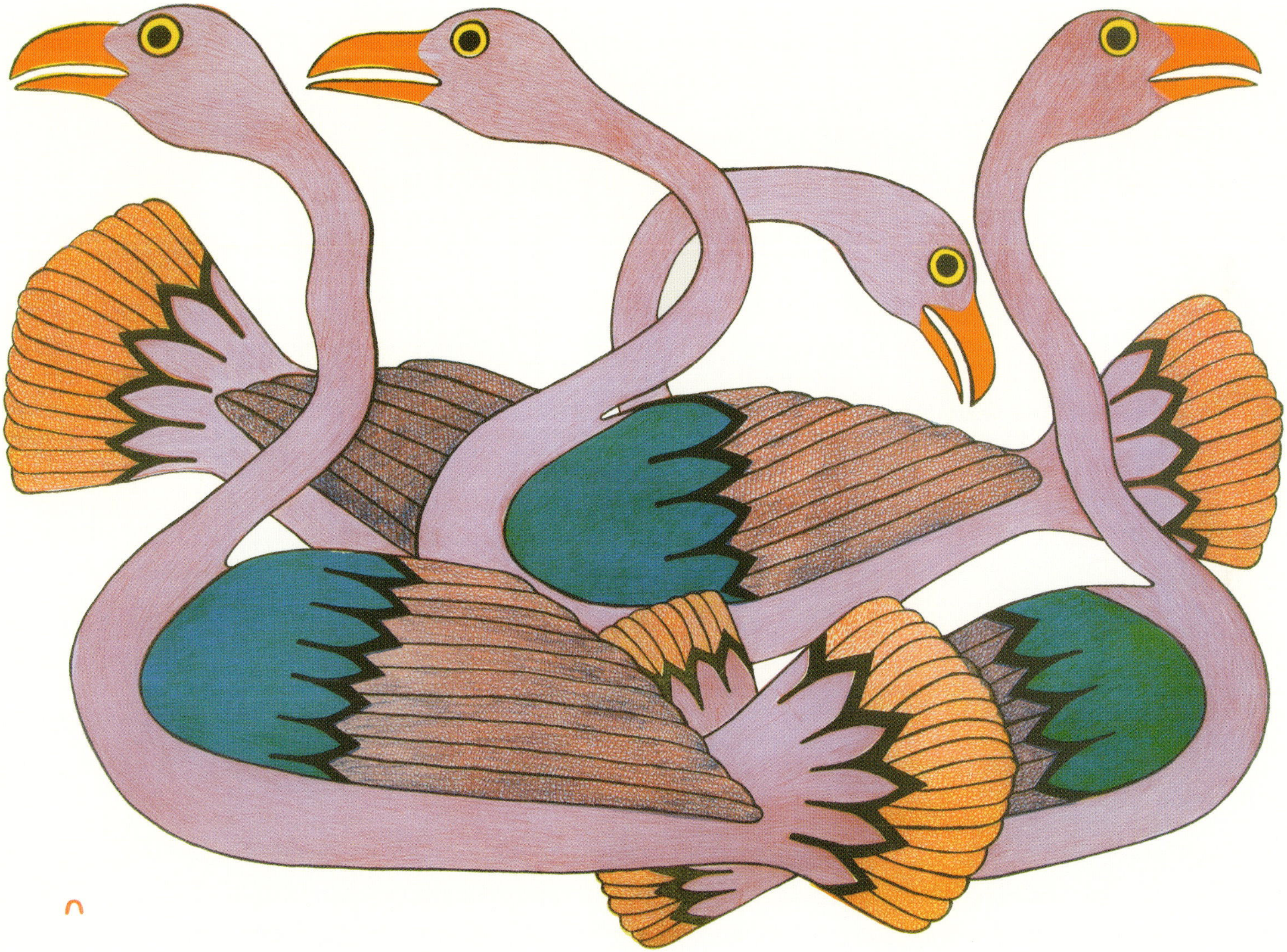

Swans at Sunset, 2002, lithograph

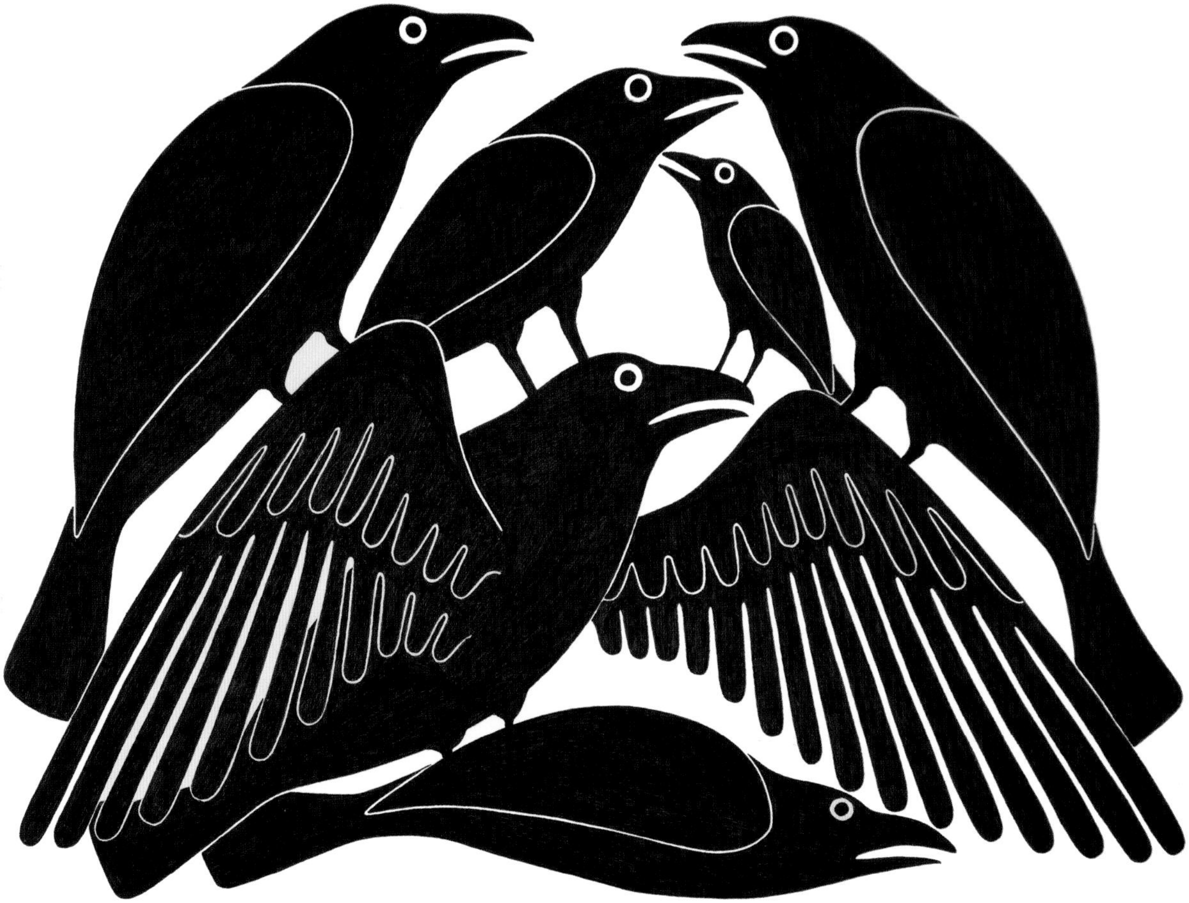

Untitled (Ravens' Chorus), 2002, ink and colored pencil

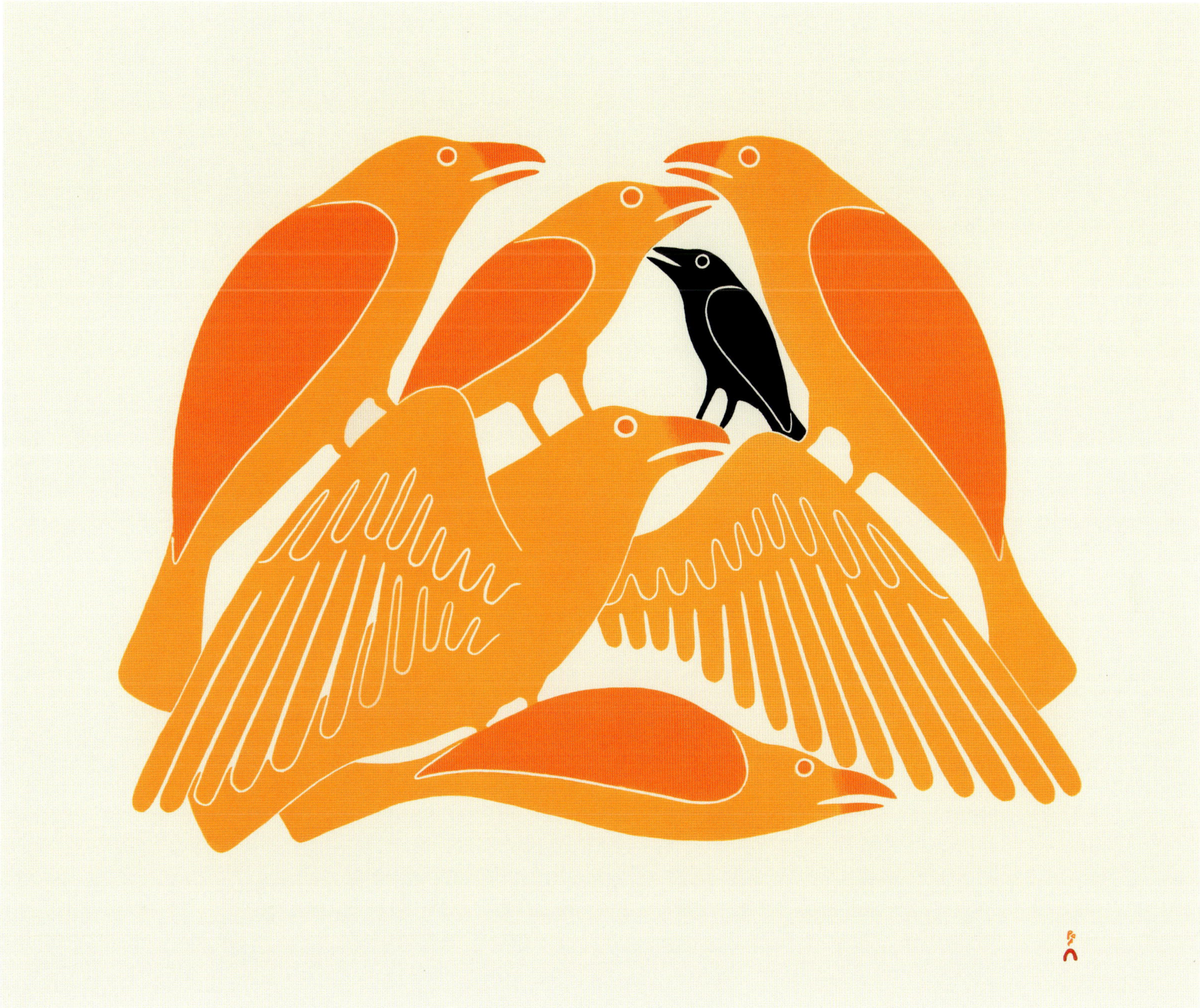

Ravens' Chorus, 2002, stonecut

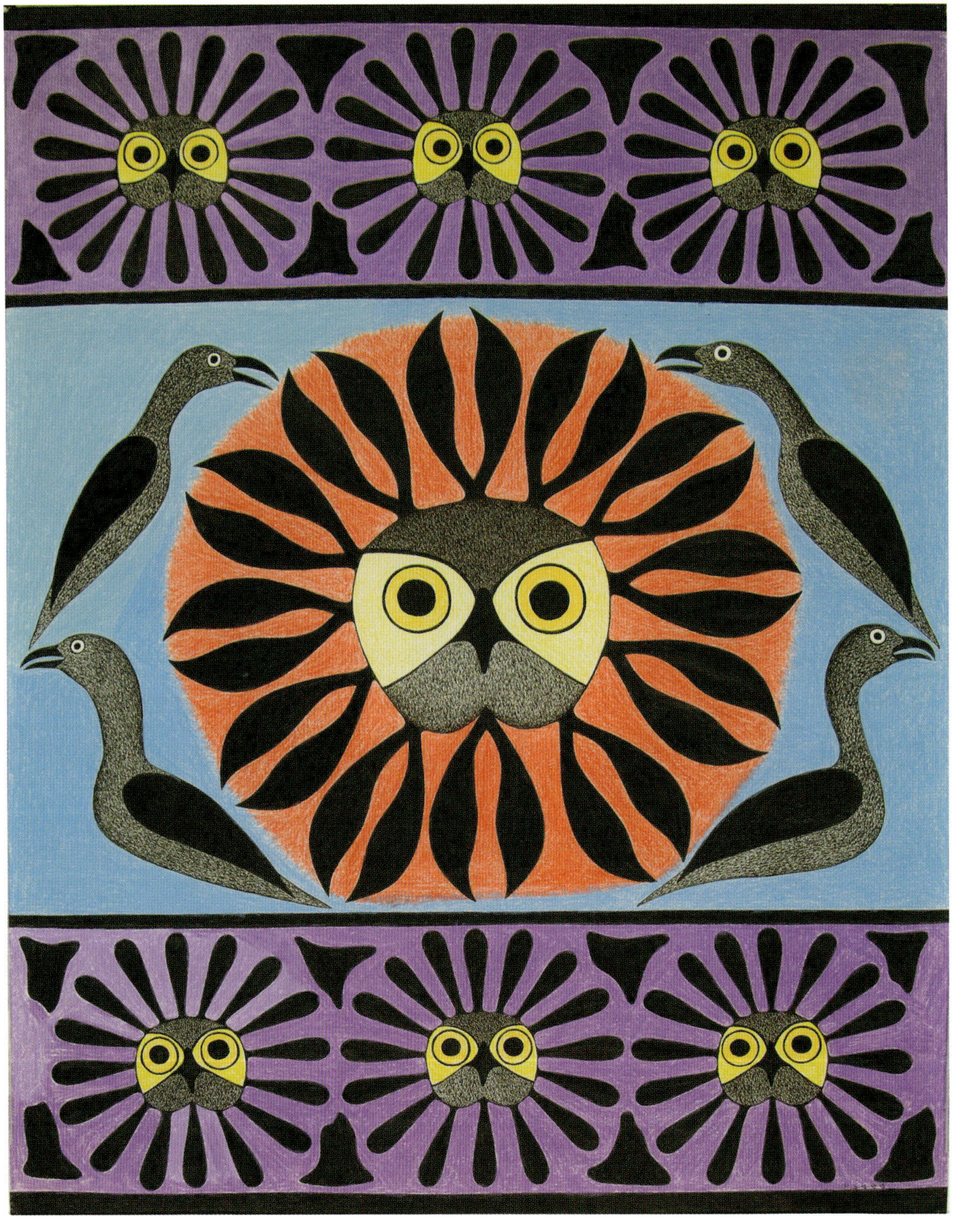

Untitled (Owl's Treasure), 2002, ink and colored pencil

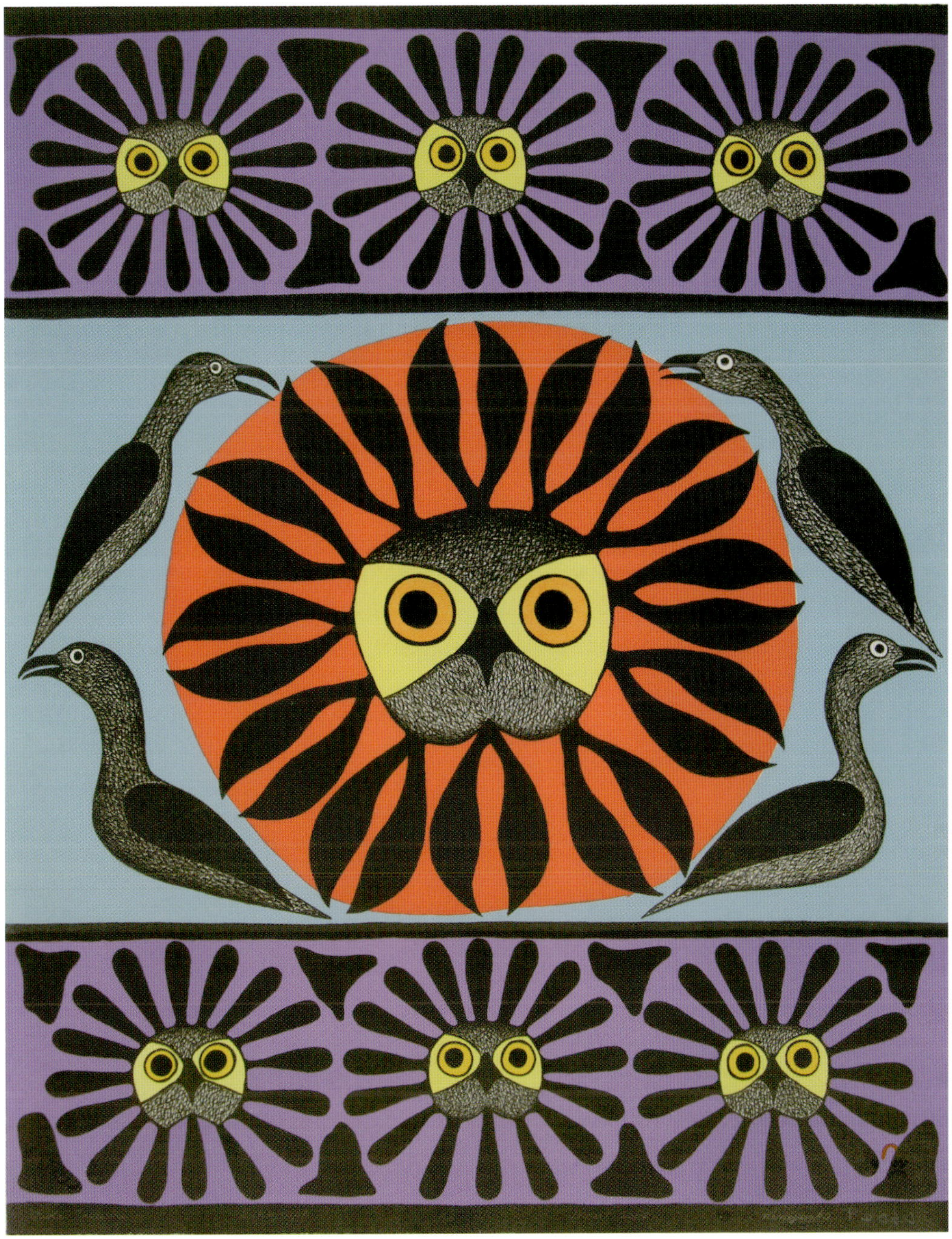

Owl's Treasure, 2002, lithograph

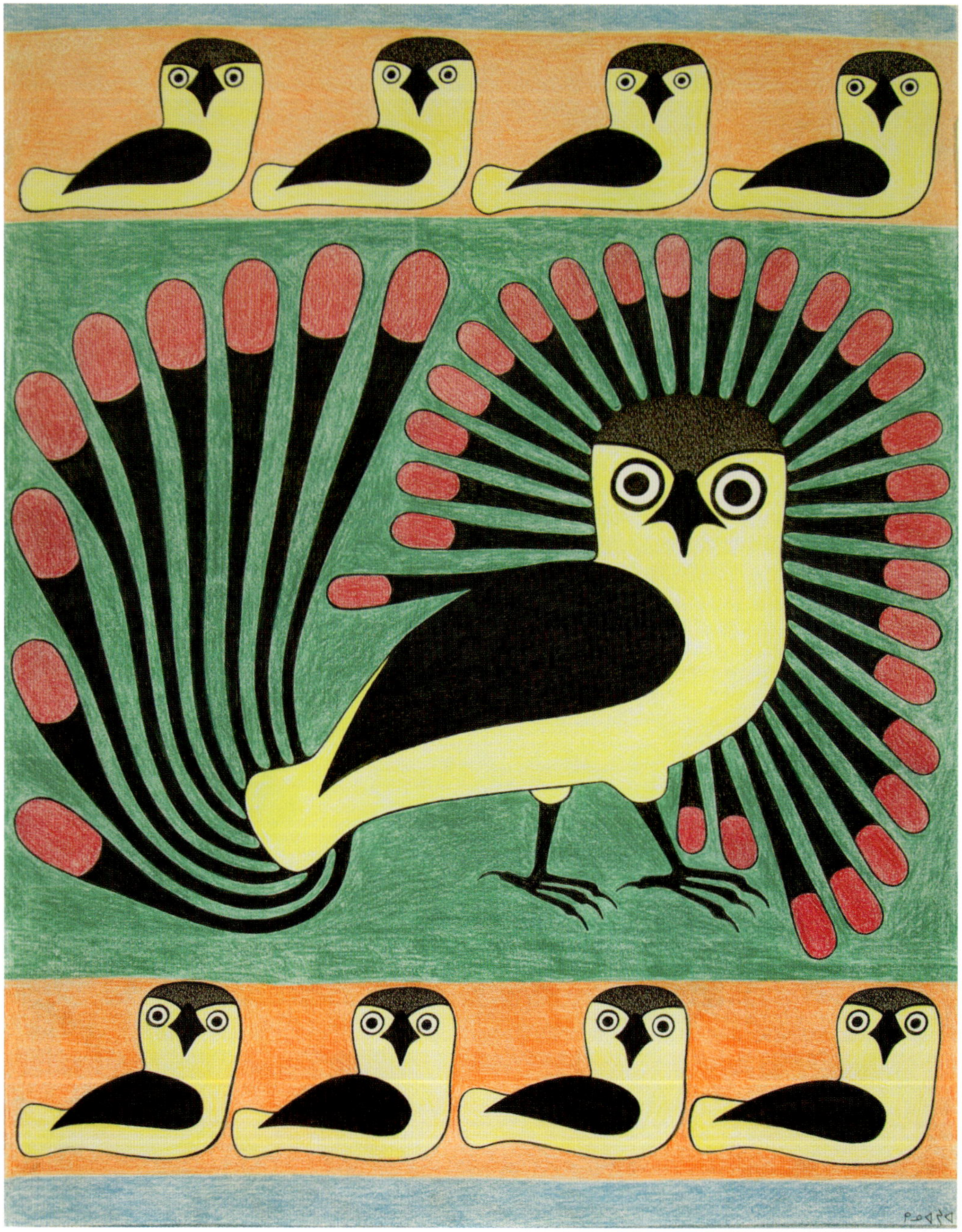

Untitled (Tapestry of Owls), 1999, ink and colored pencil

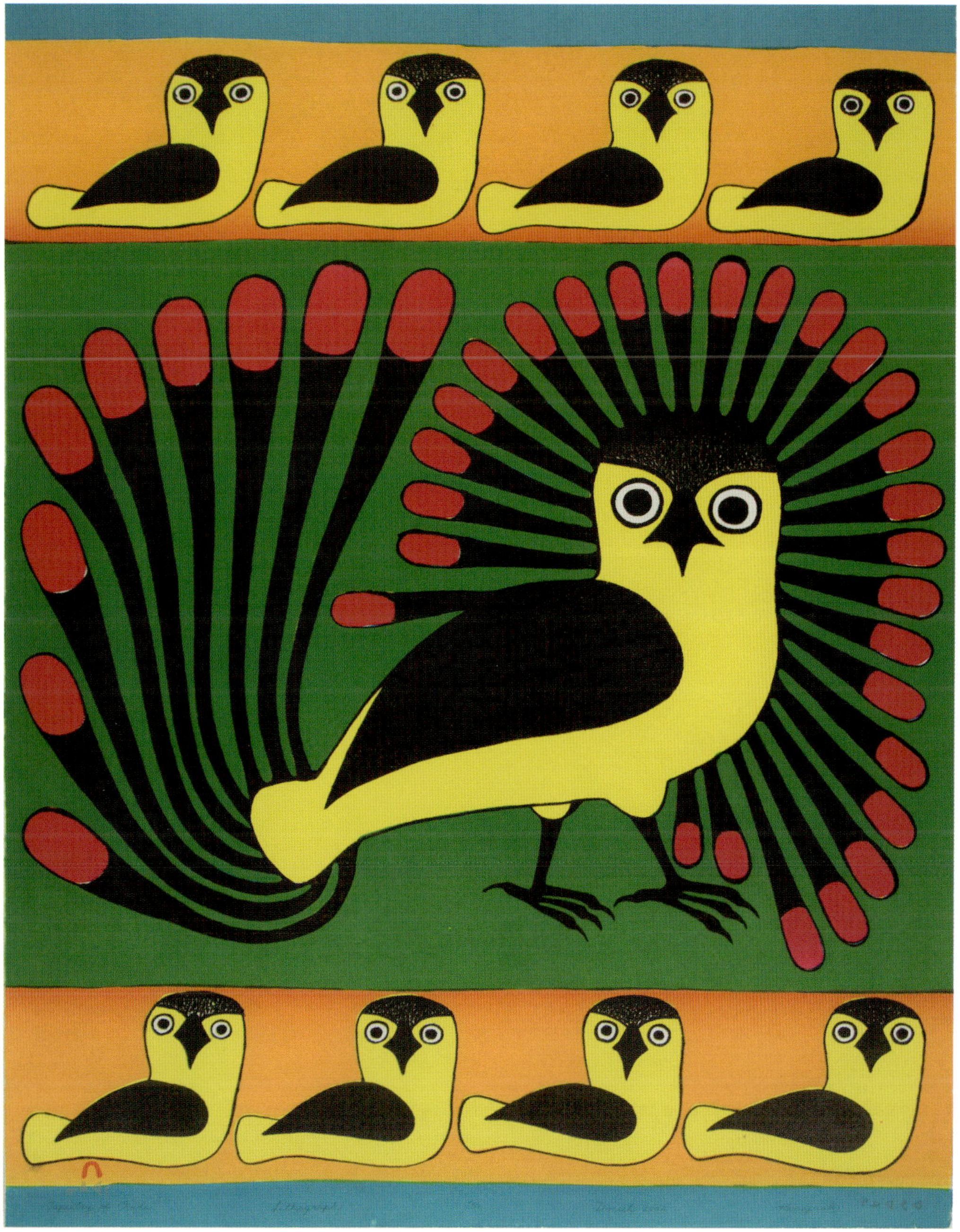

Tapestry of Owls, 2002, lithograph

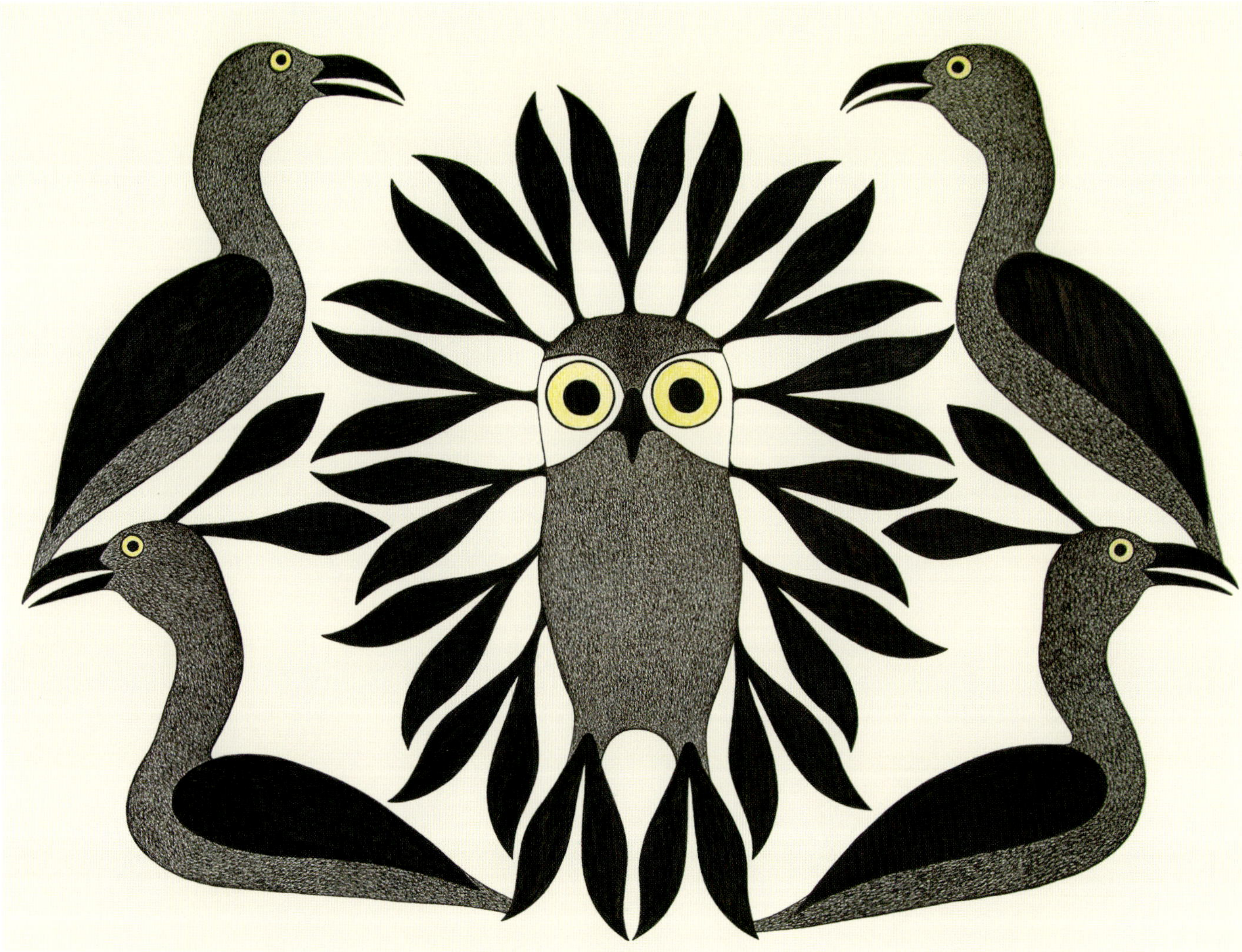

Untitled (Loons Protect the Owl), 2002, ink and colored pencil

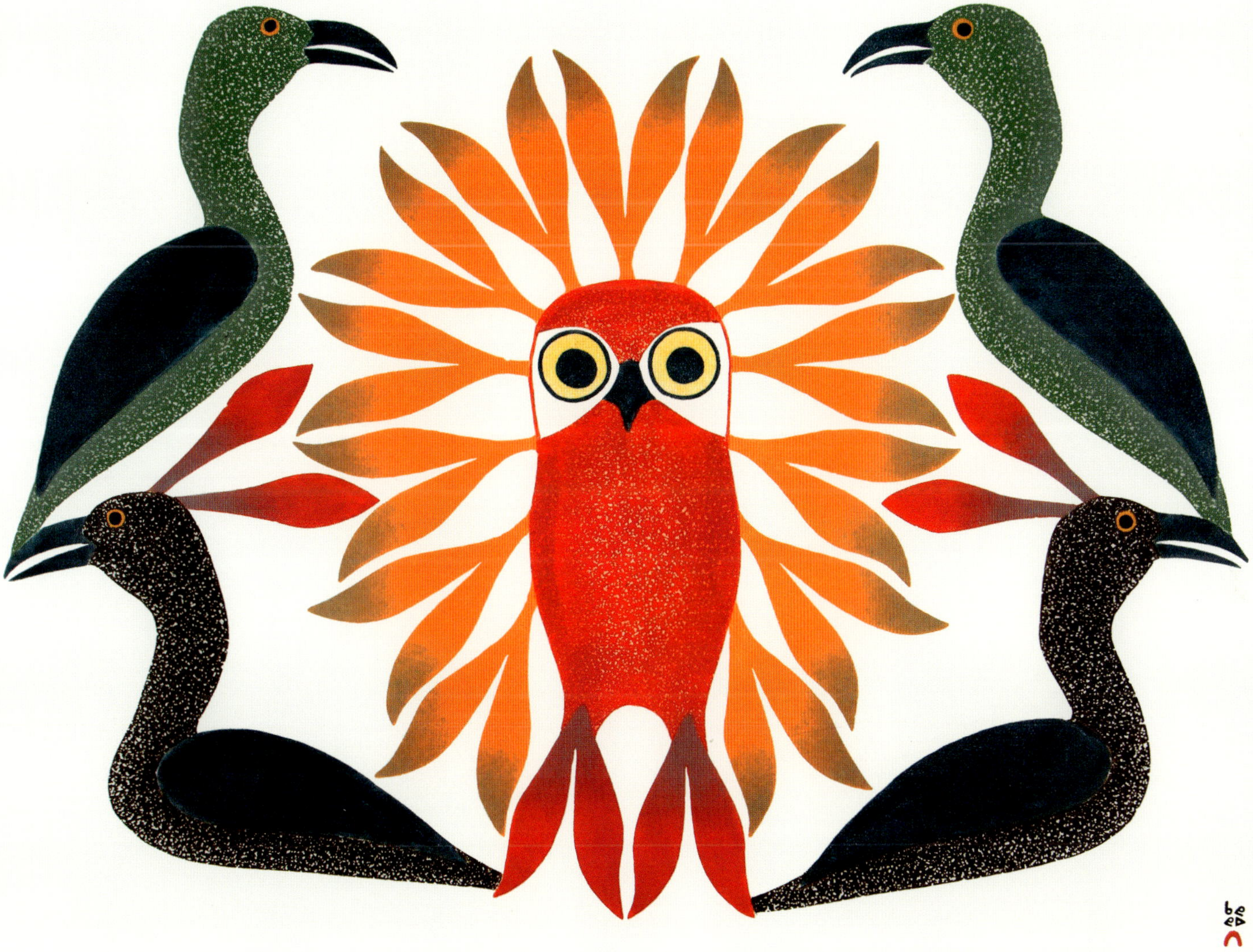

Loons Protect the Owl, 2002, stonecut and stencil

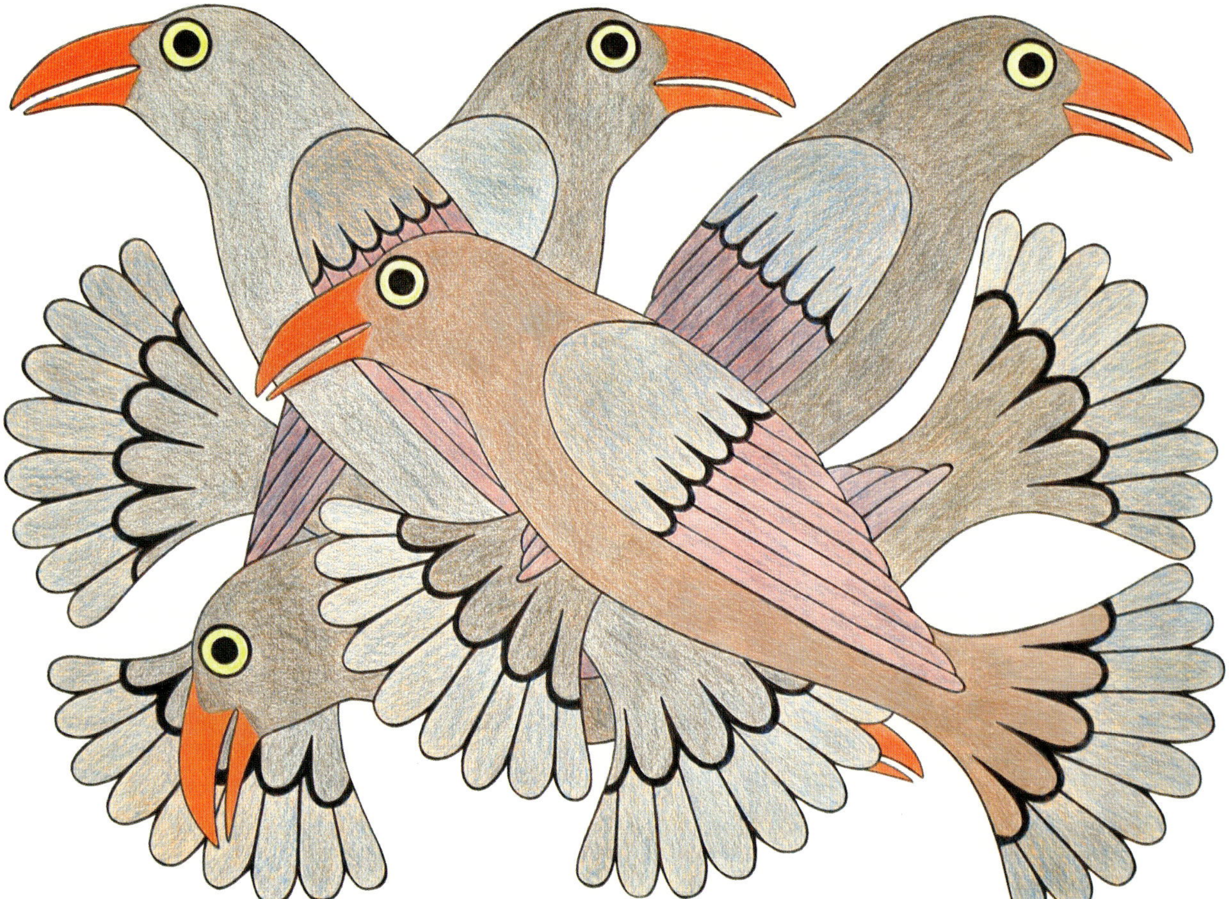

Untitled (Spectacular Ravens), 2003, ink and colored pencil

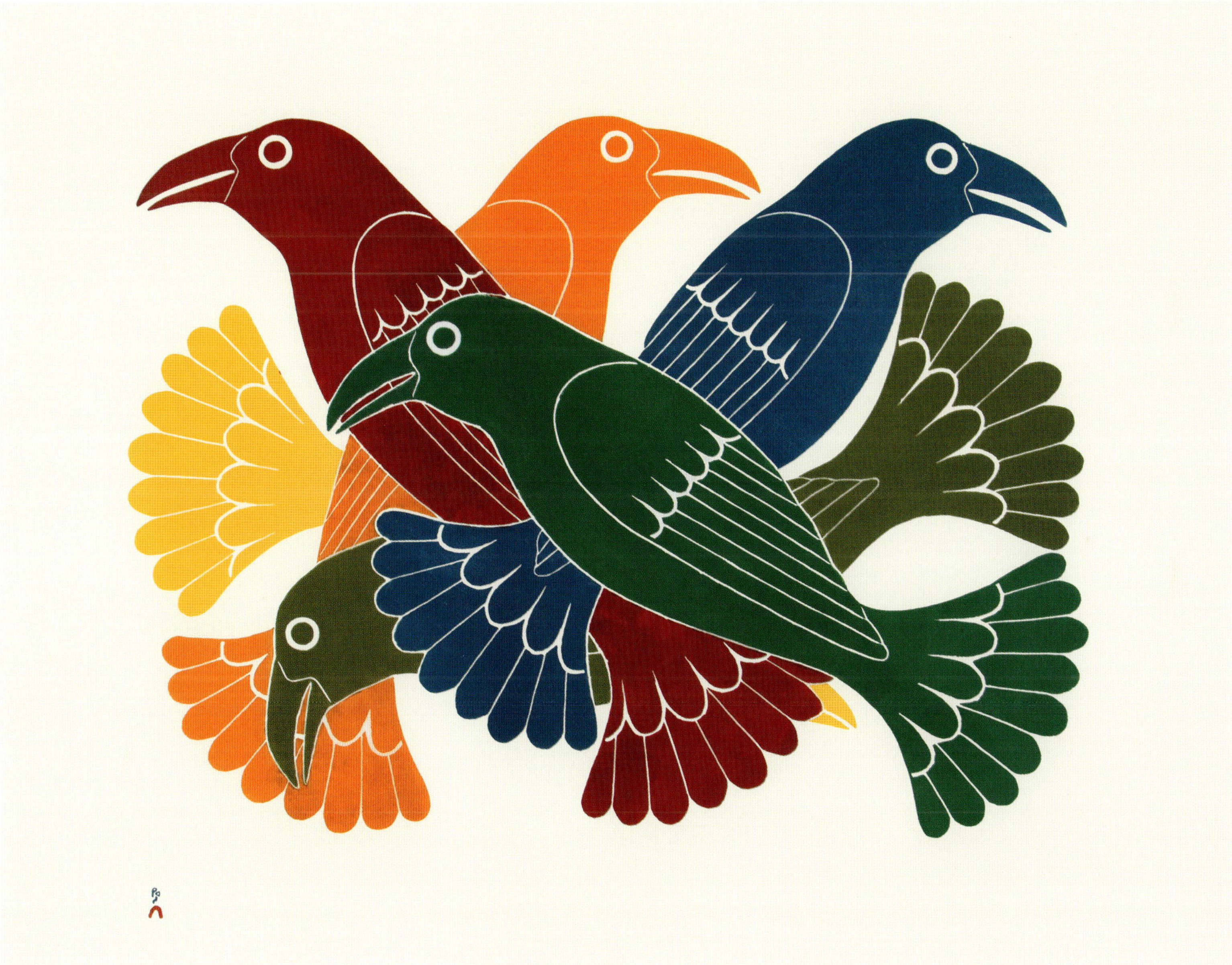

Spectacular Ravens, 2003, stonecut and stencil

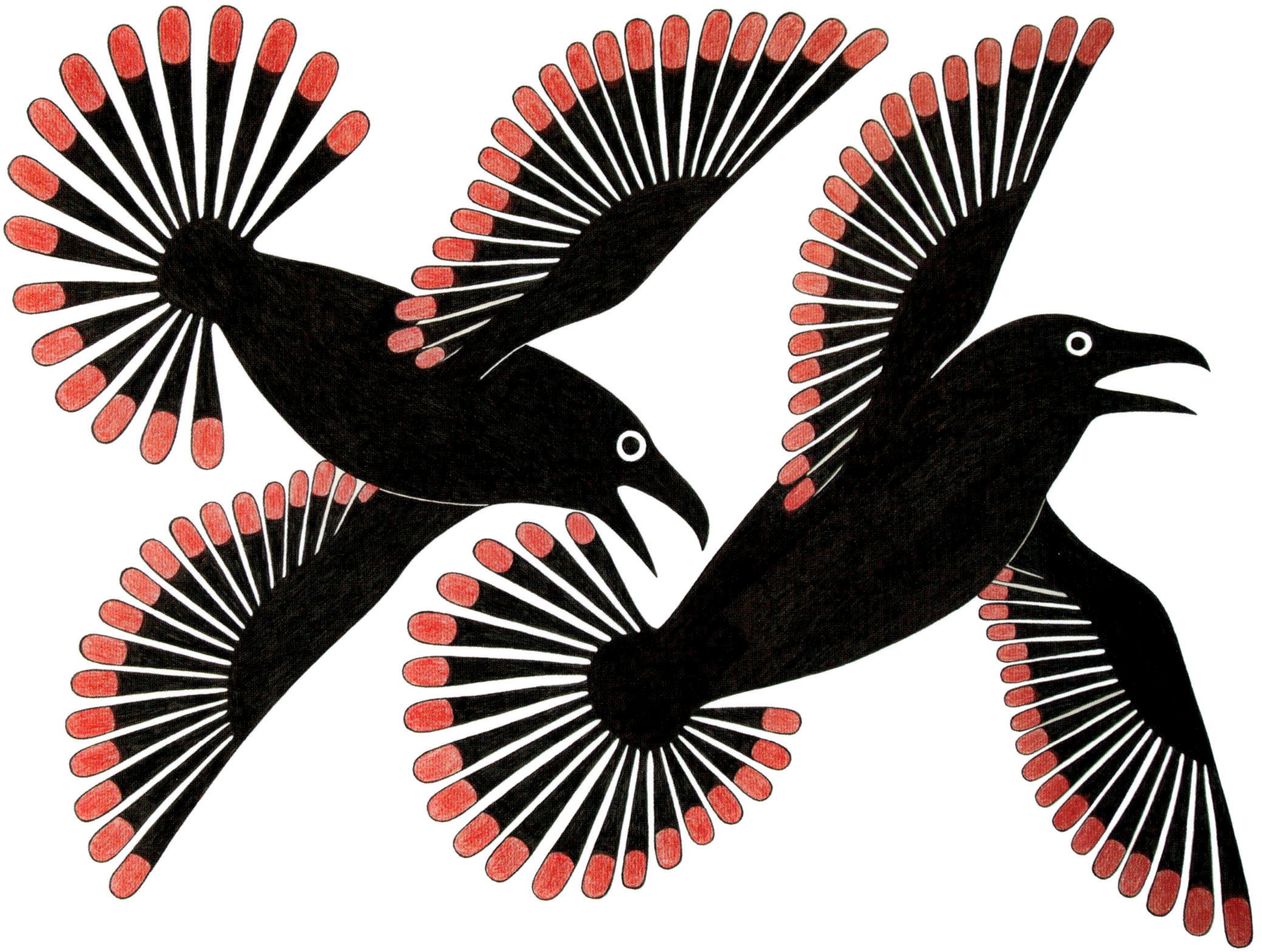

Untitled (Dancing Ravens), 2003, ink and colored pencil

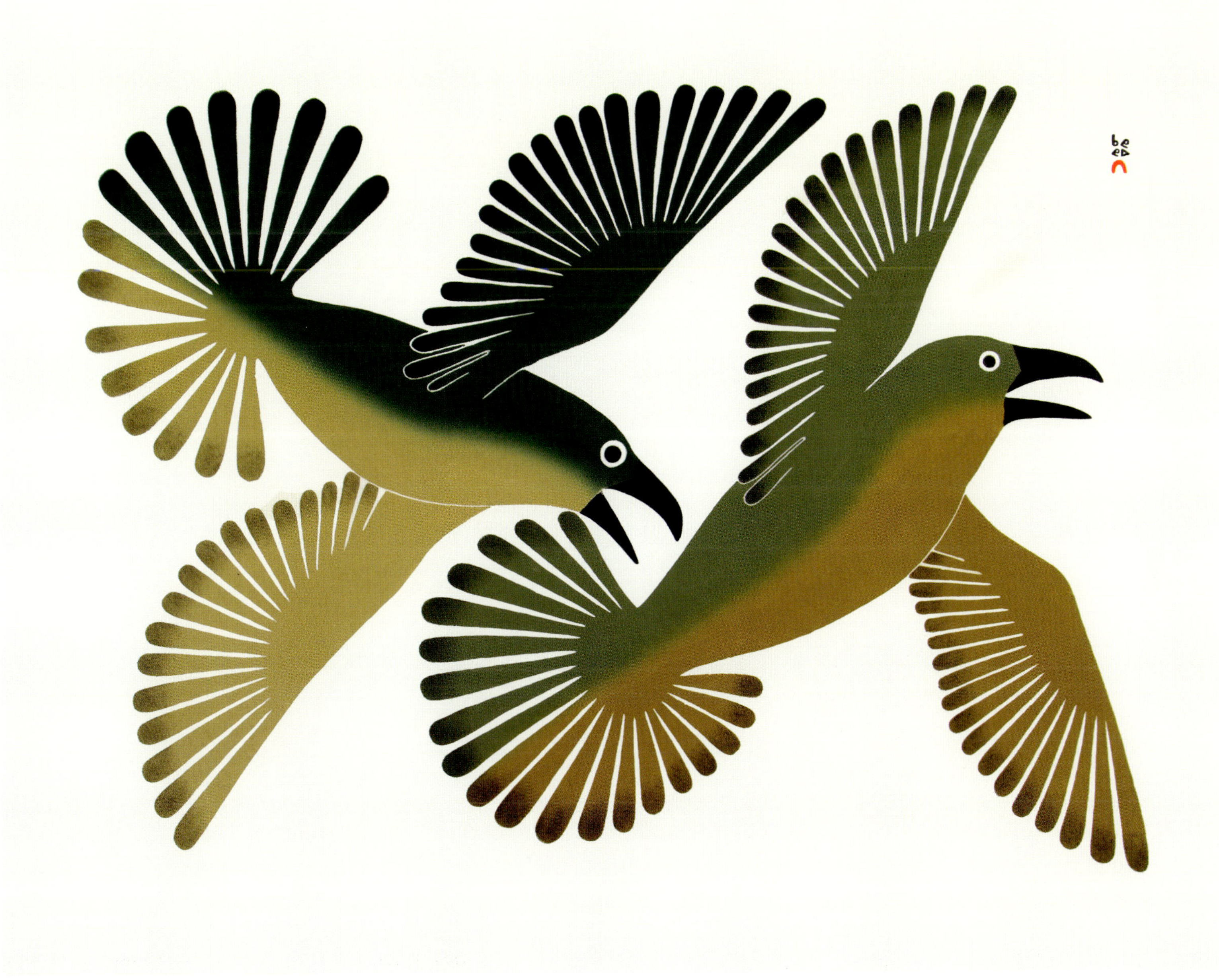

Dancing Ravens, 2003, stonecut and stencil

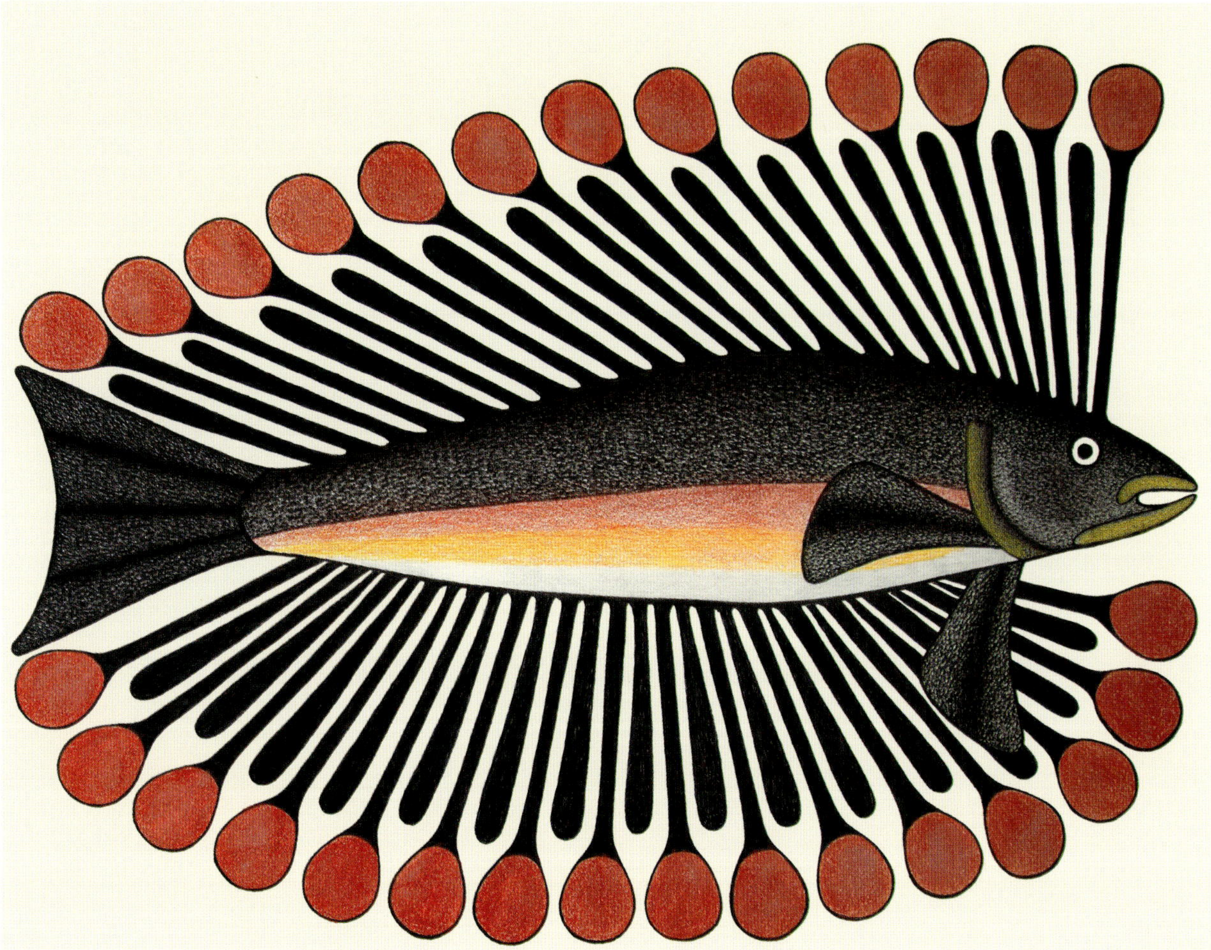

Untitled (Decorative Char), 2004, ink and colored pencil

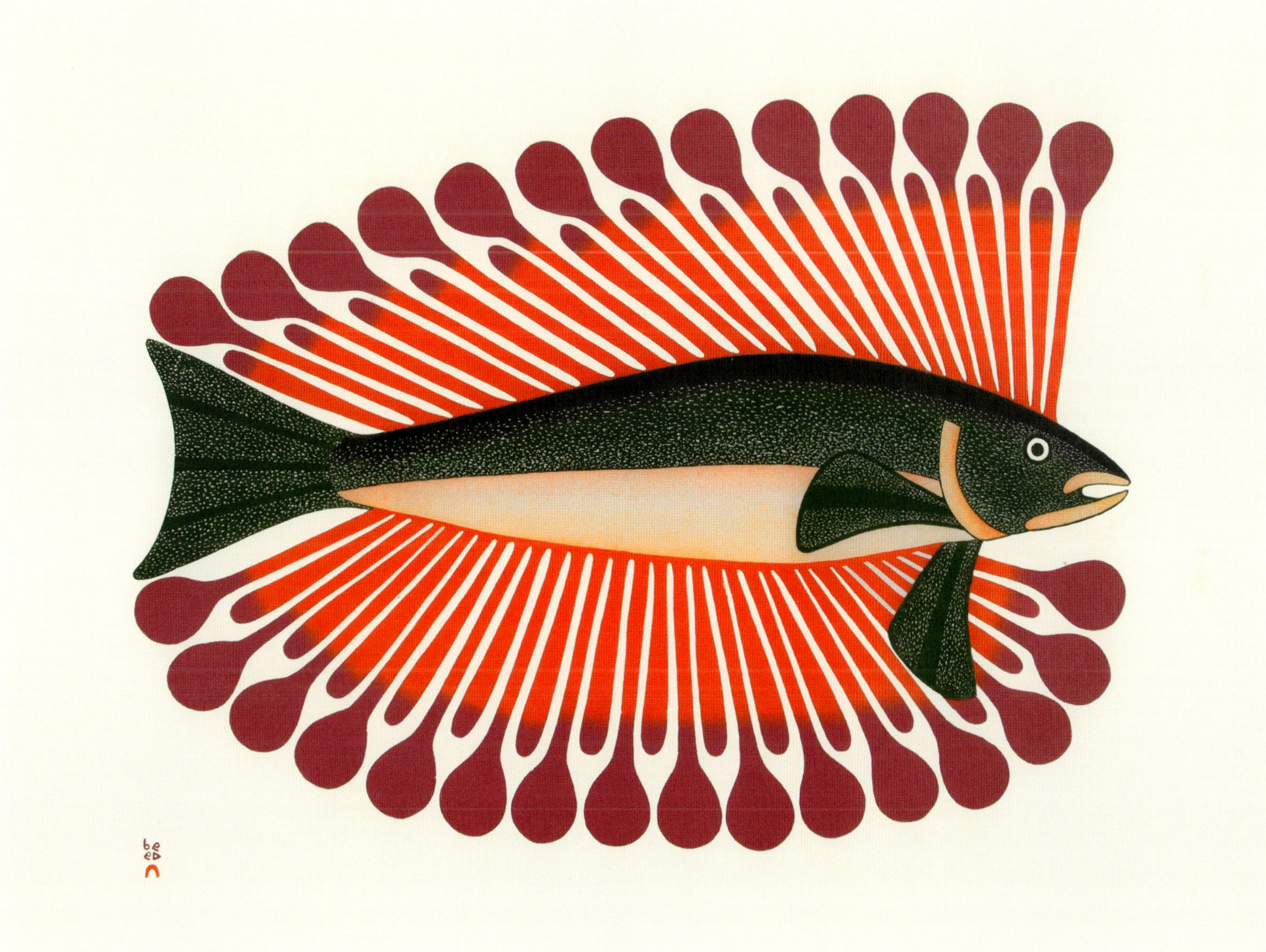

Decorative Char, 2004, stonecut and stencil

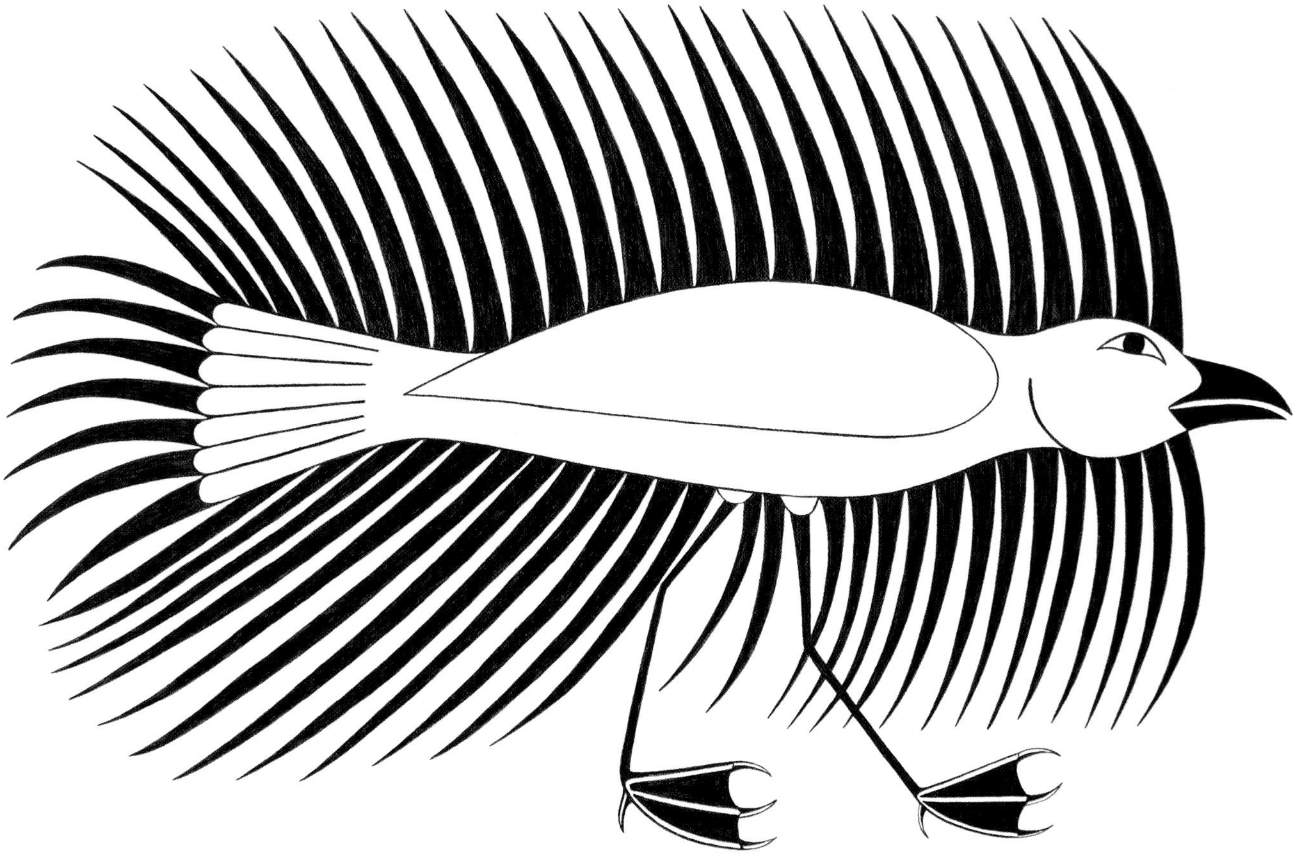

Untitled (Quivering Seagull), 2004, ink

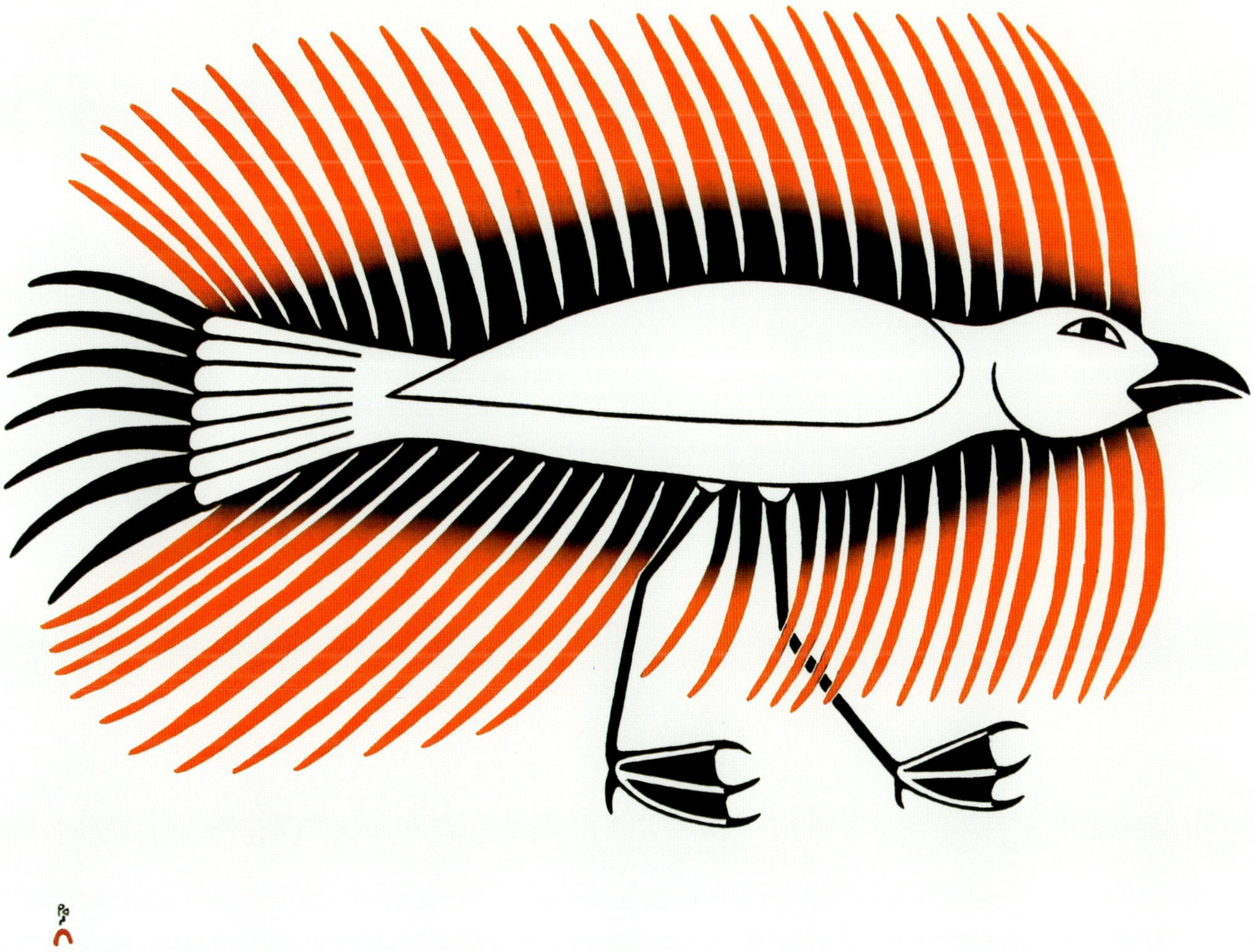

Quivering Seagull, 2004, stonecut

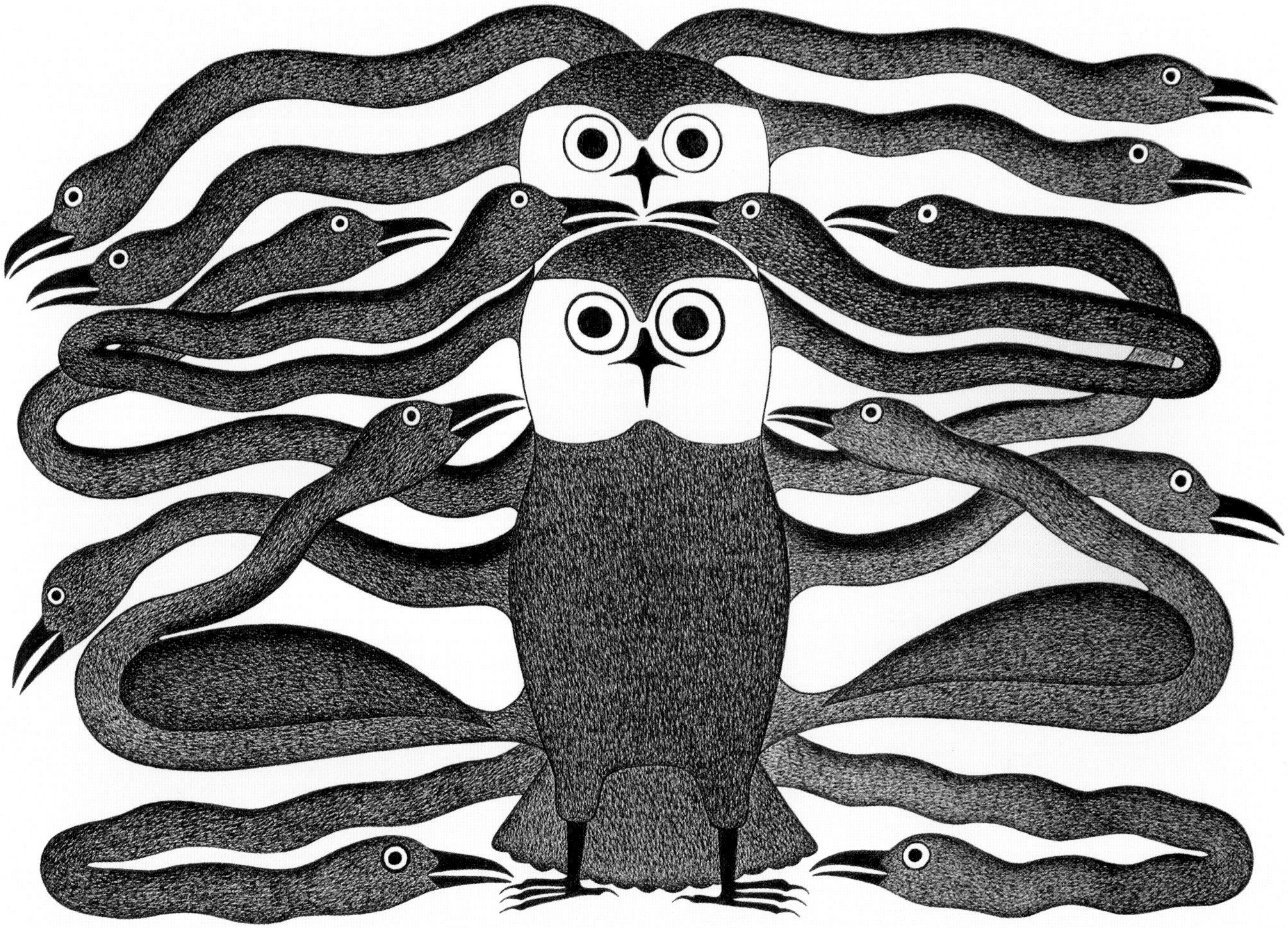

Untitled (Owls Enveloped), 2004, ink

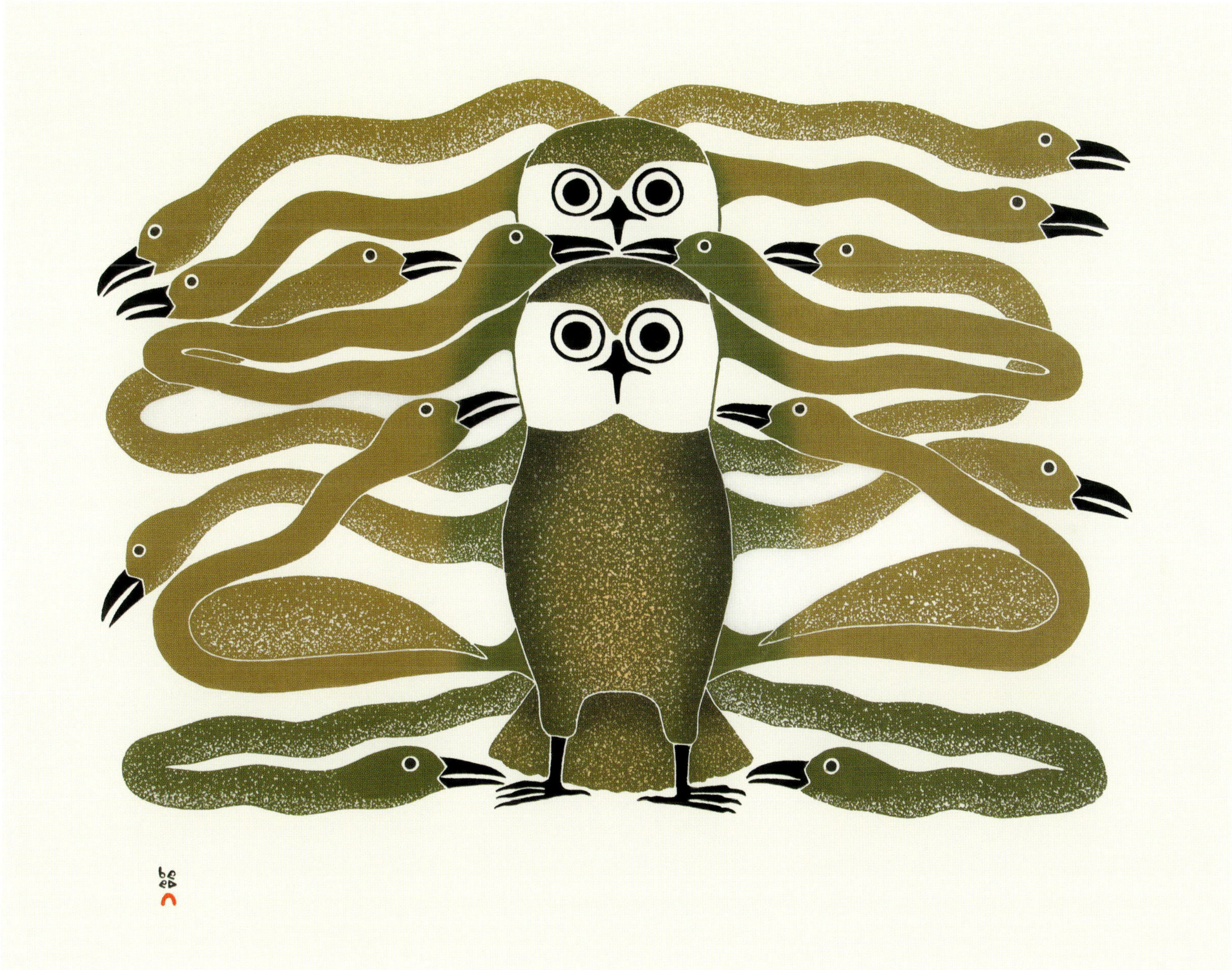

Owls Enveloped, 2004, stonecut and stencil

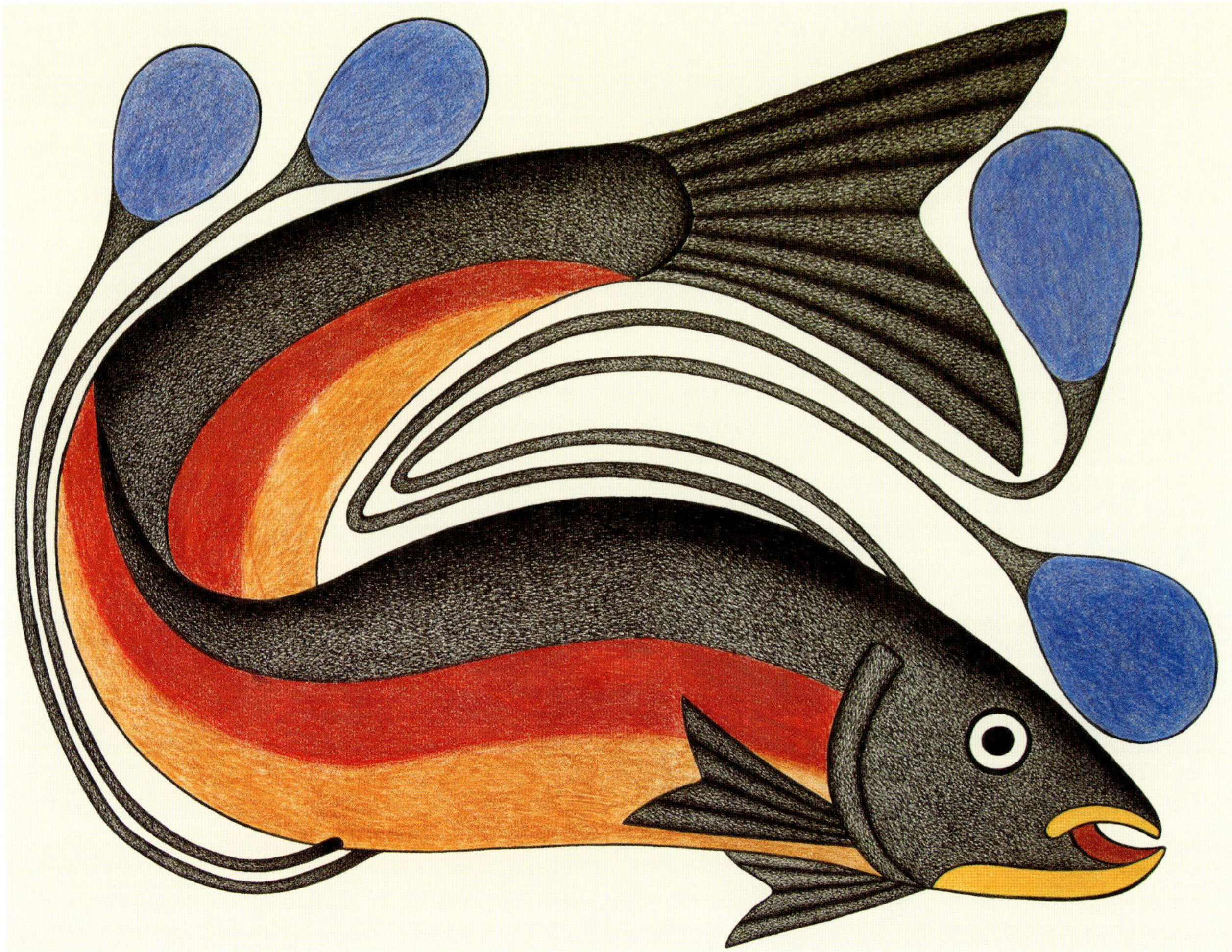

Untitled (Iqalutsiavak [Beautiful Fish]), 2005, ink and colored pencil

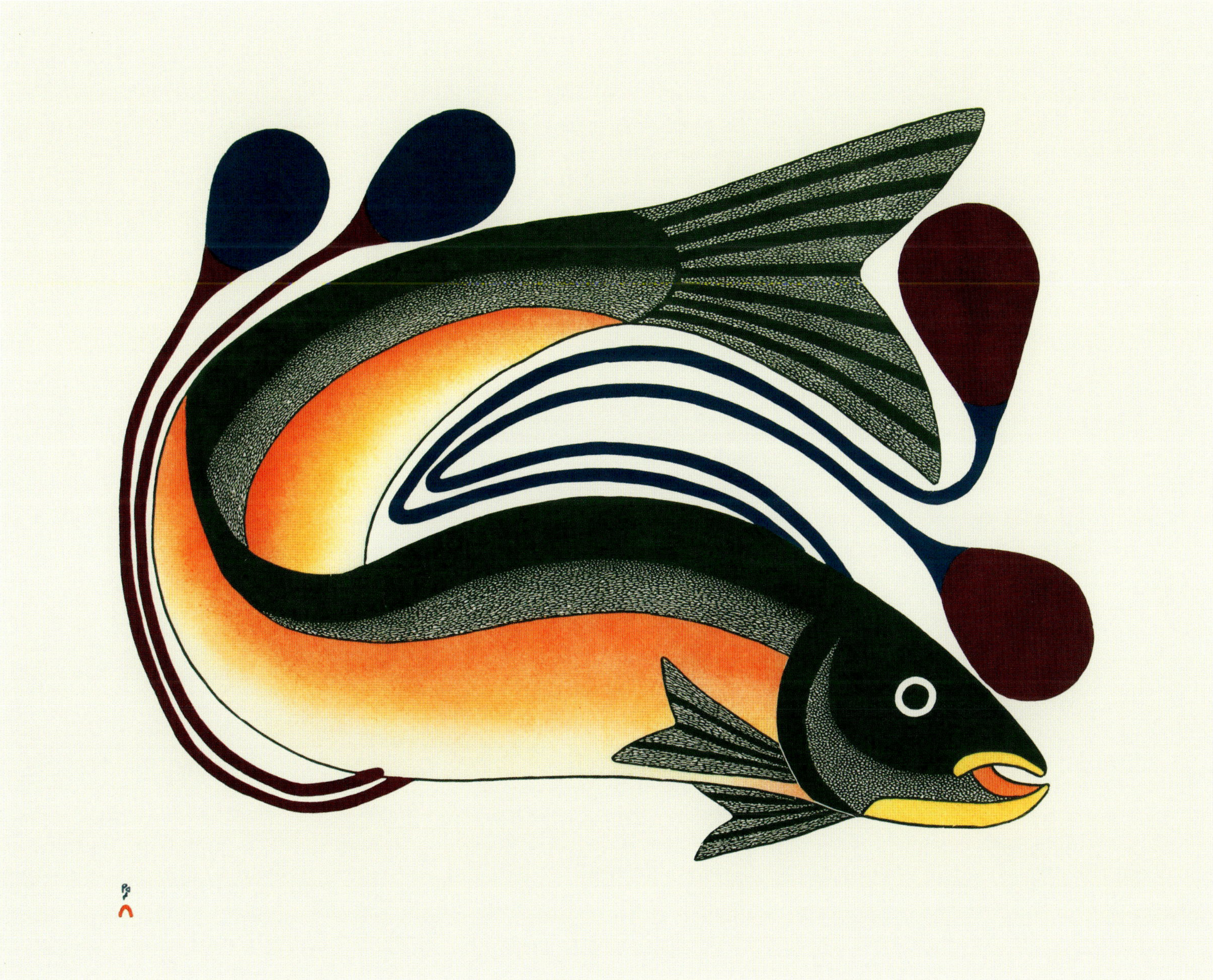

Iqalutsiavak (Beautiful Fish), 2005, stonecut and stencil

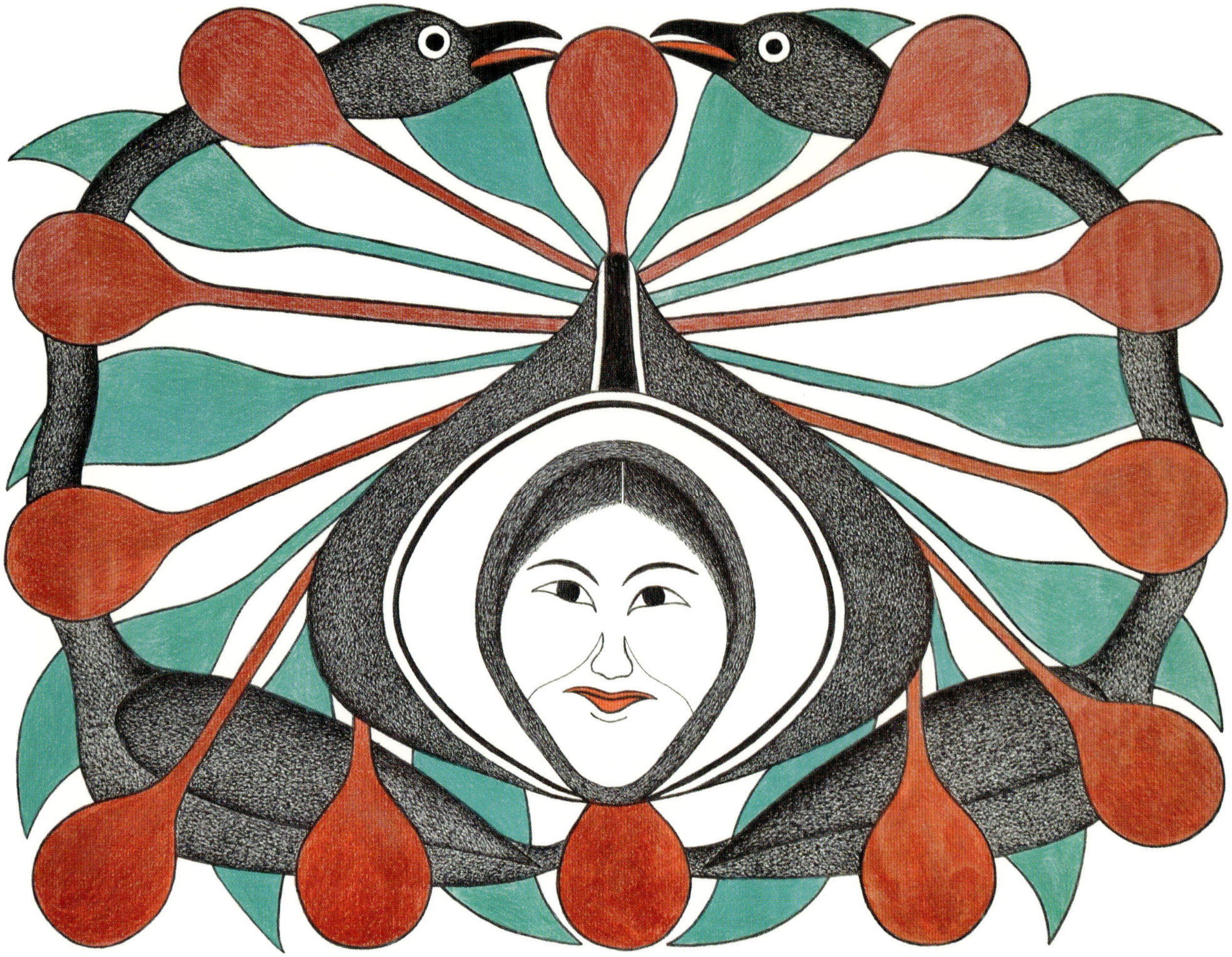

Untitled (Wisdom of the Elders), 2009, ink and colored pencil

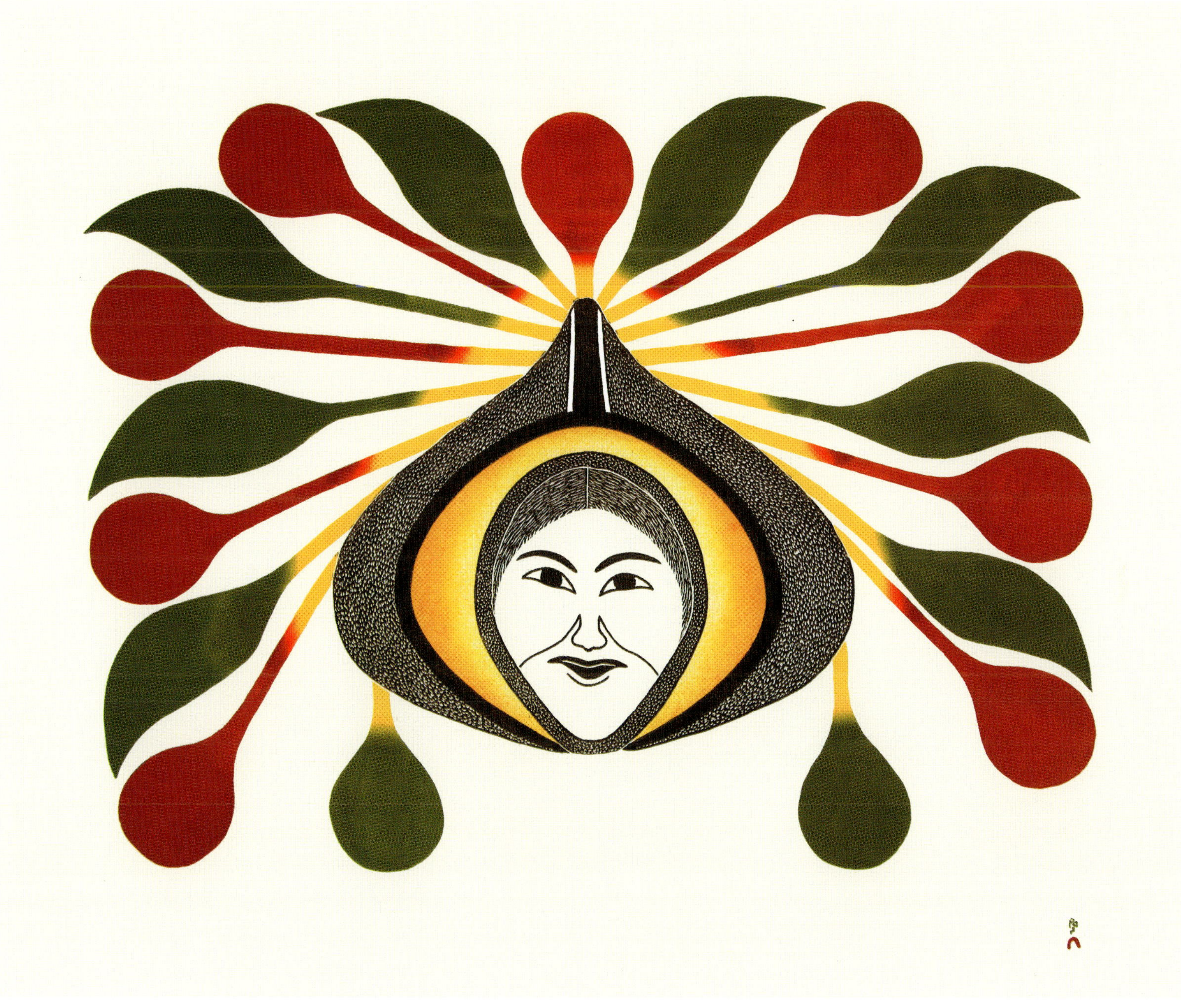

Wisdom of the Elders, 2009, stonecut and stencil

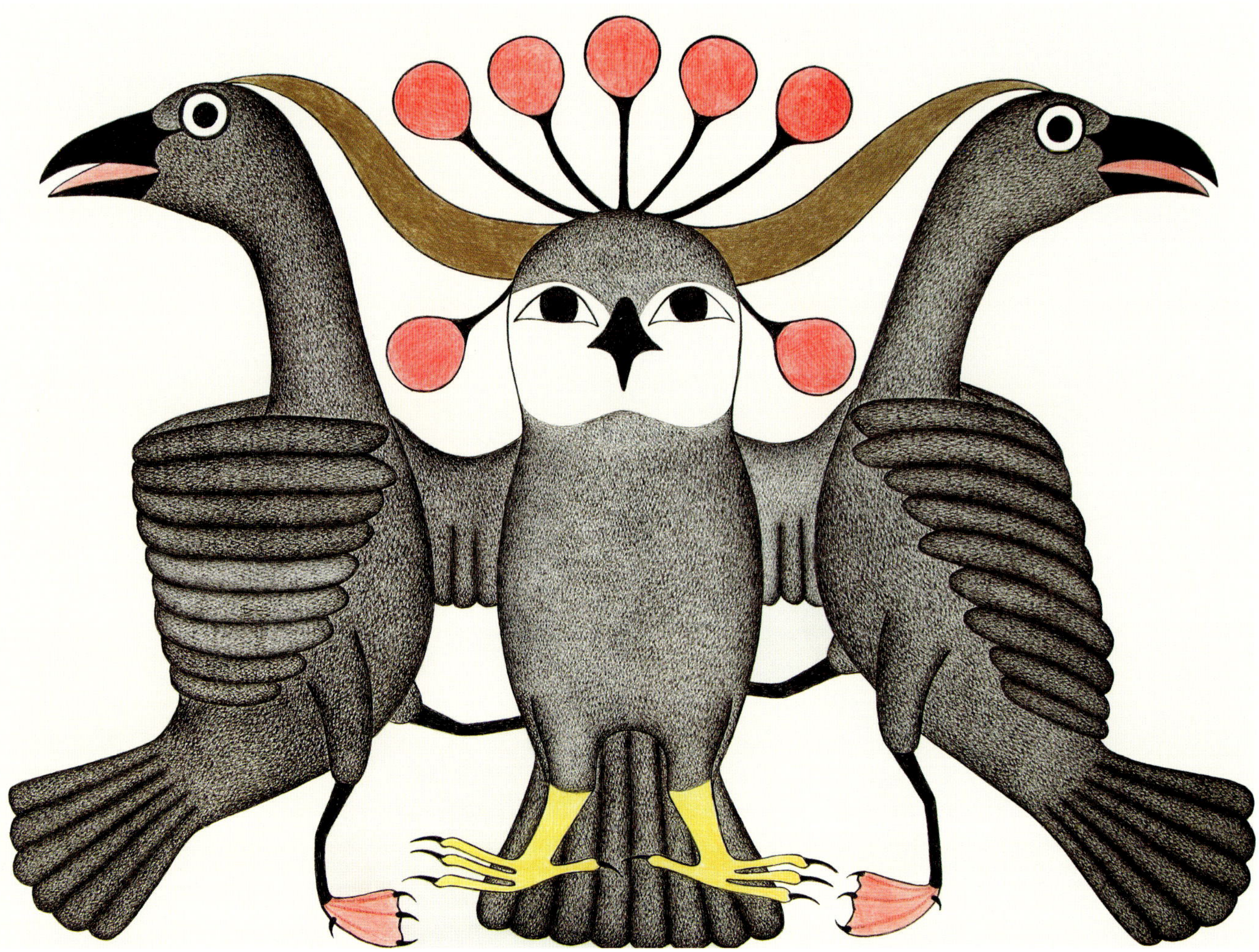

Untitled (Between Friends), 2010, ink and colored pencil

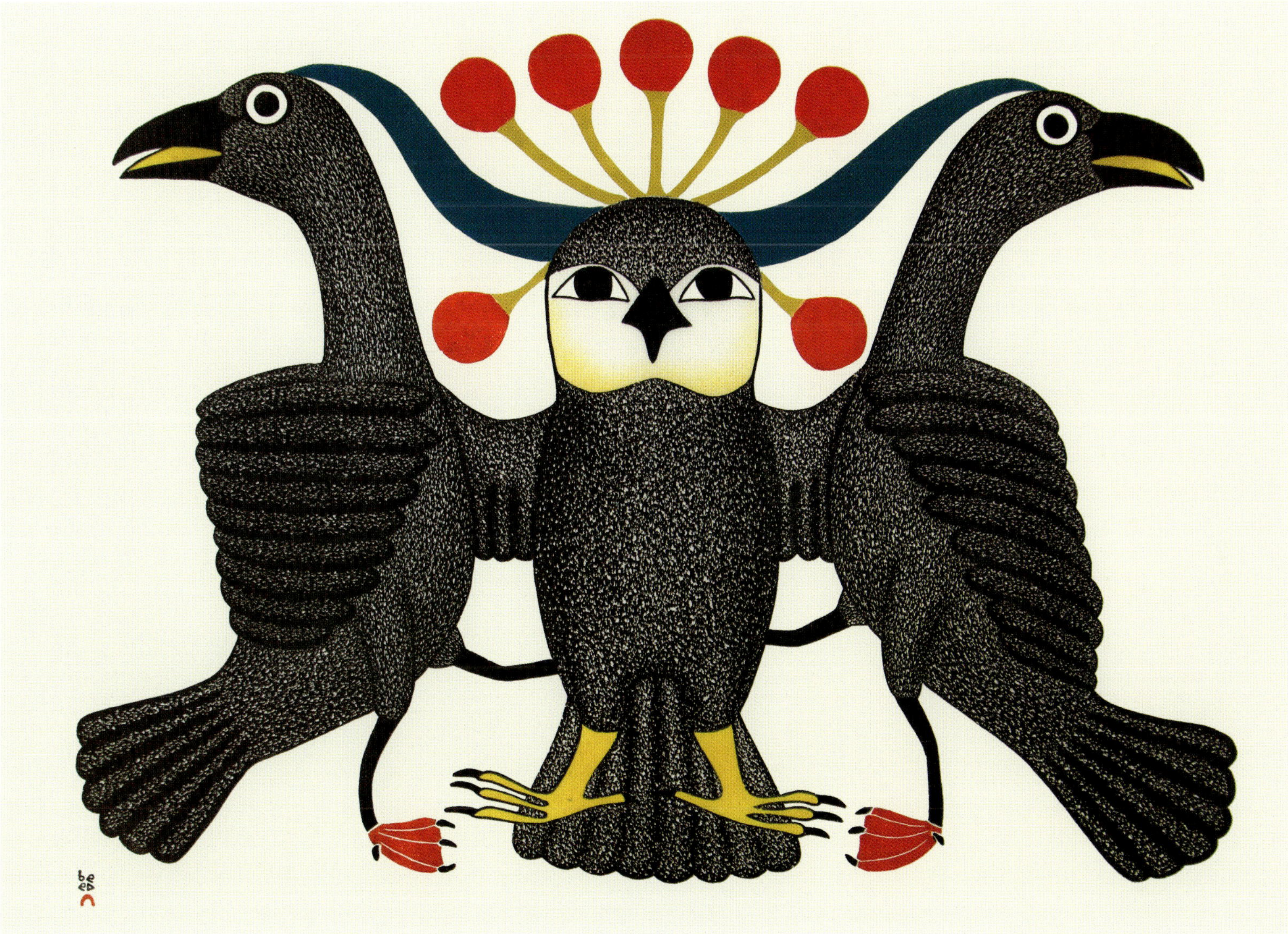

Between Friends, 2010, stonecut and stencil

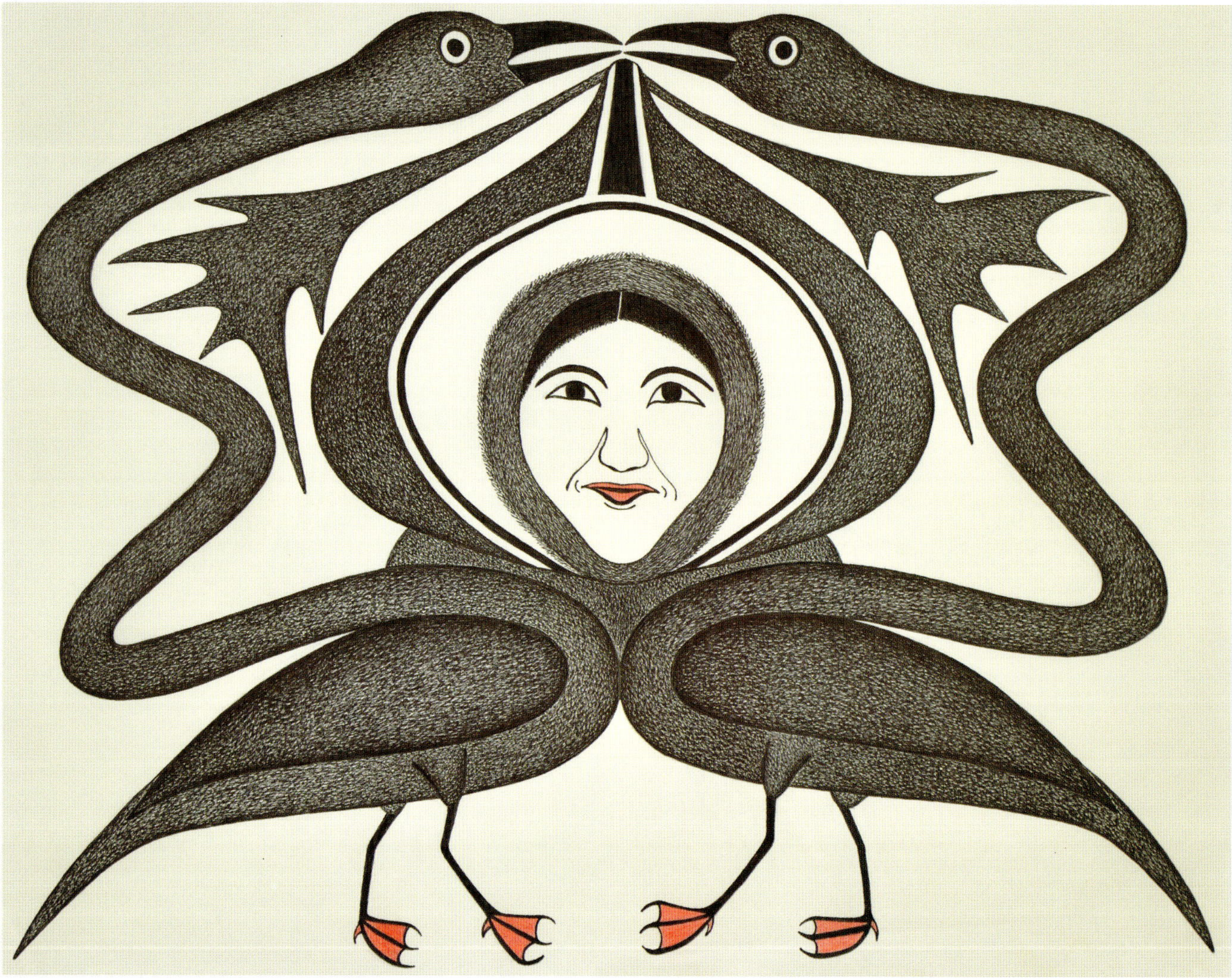

Untitled (Eternal Spirit), 2011, ink and colored pencil

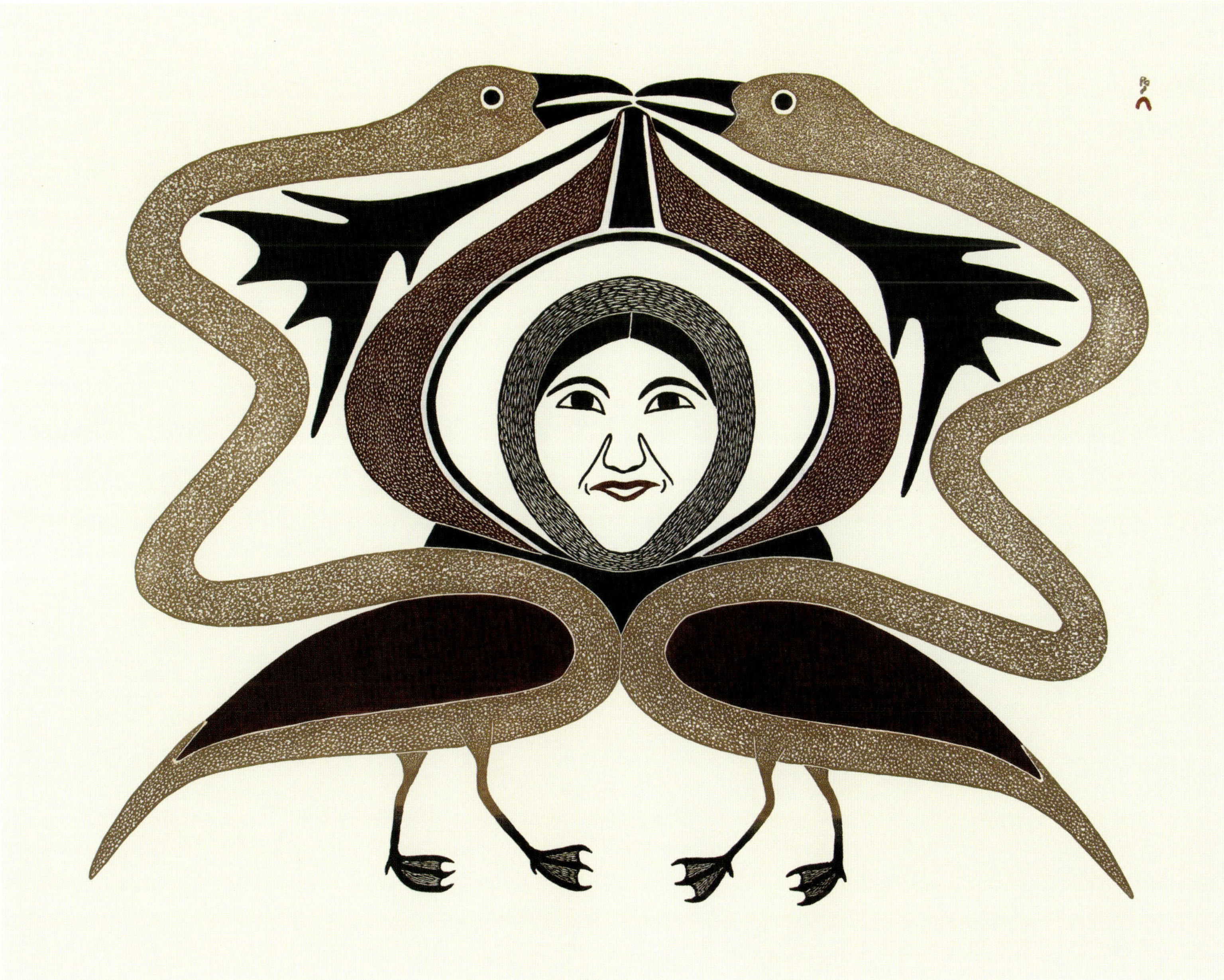

Eternal Spirit, 2011, stonecut

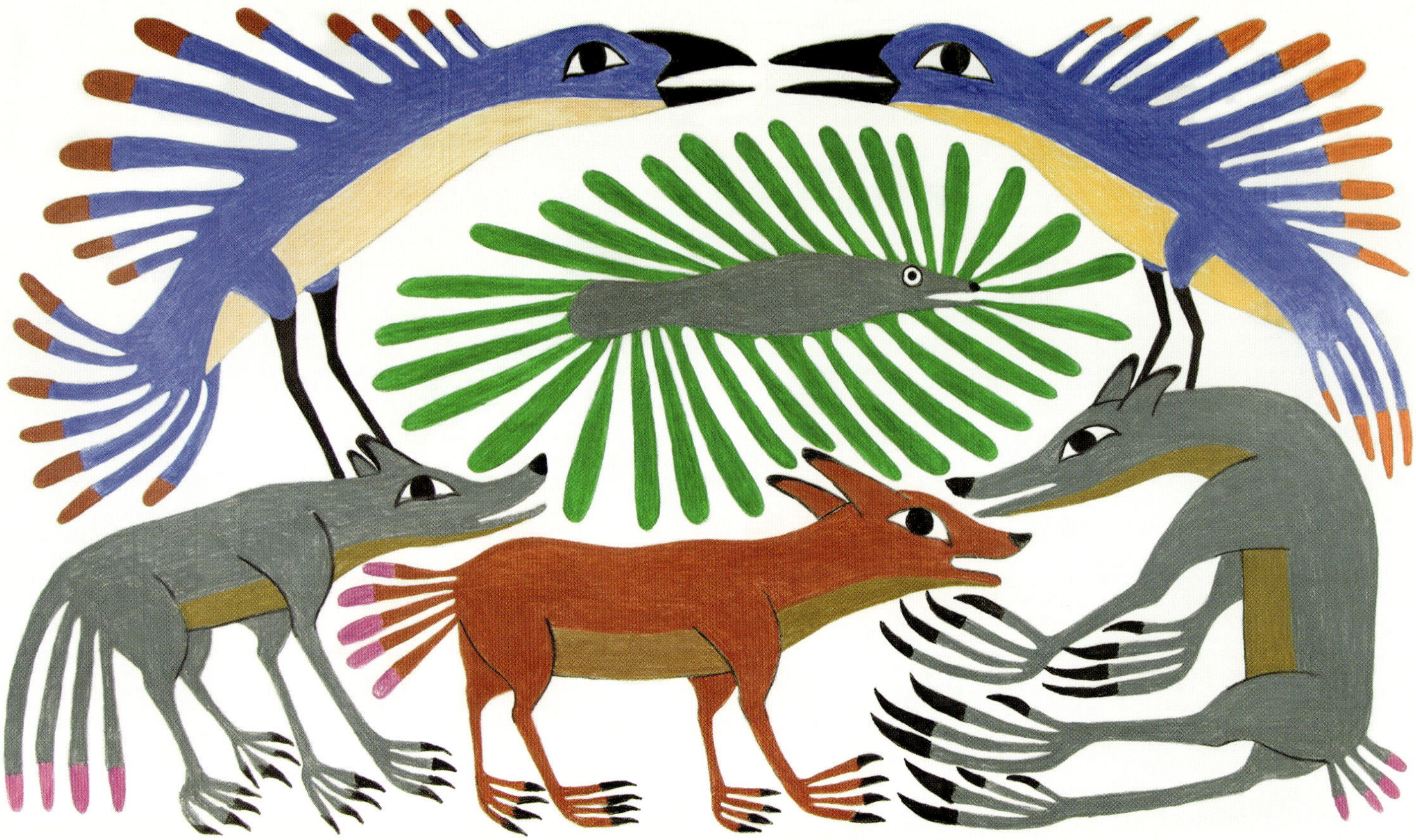

Untitled (Six-Part Harmony), 2011, ink and colored pencil

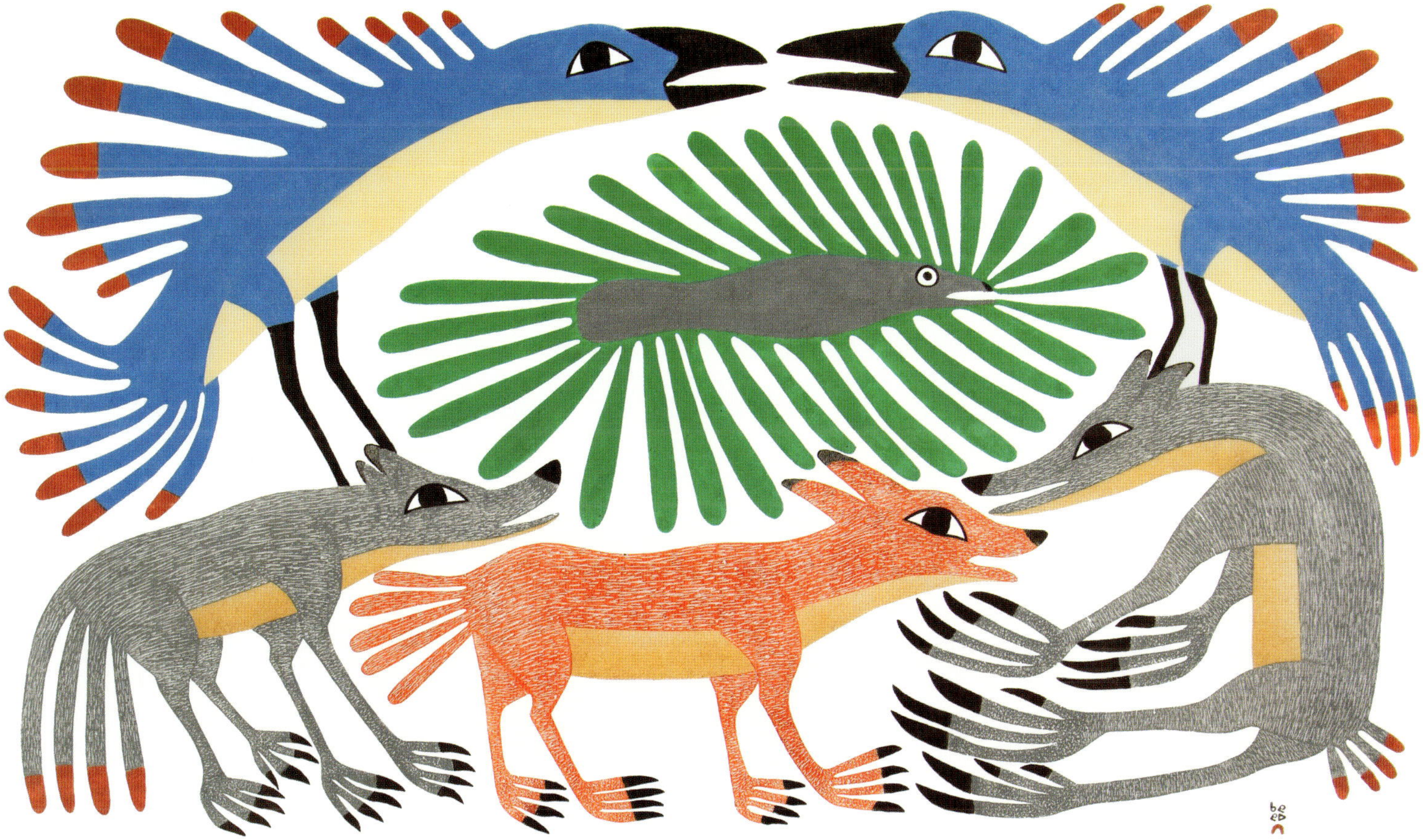

Six-Part Harmony, 2011, stonecut and stencil

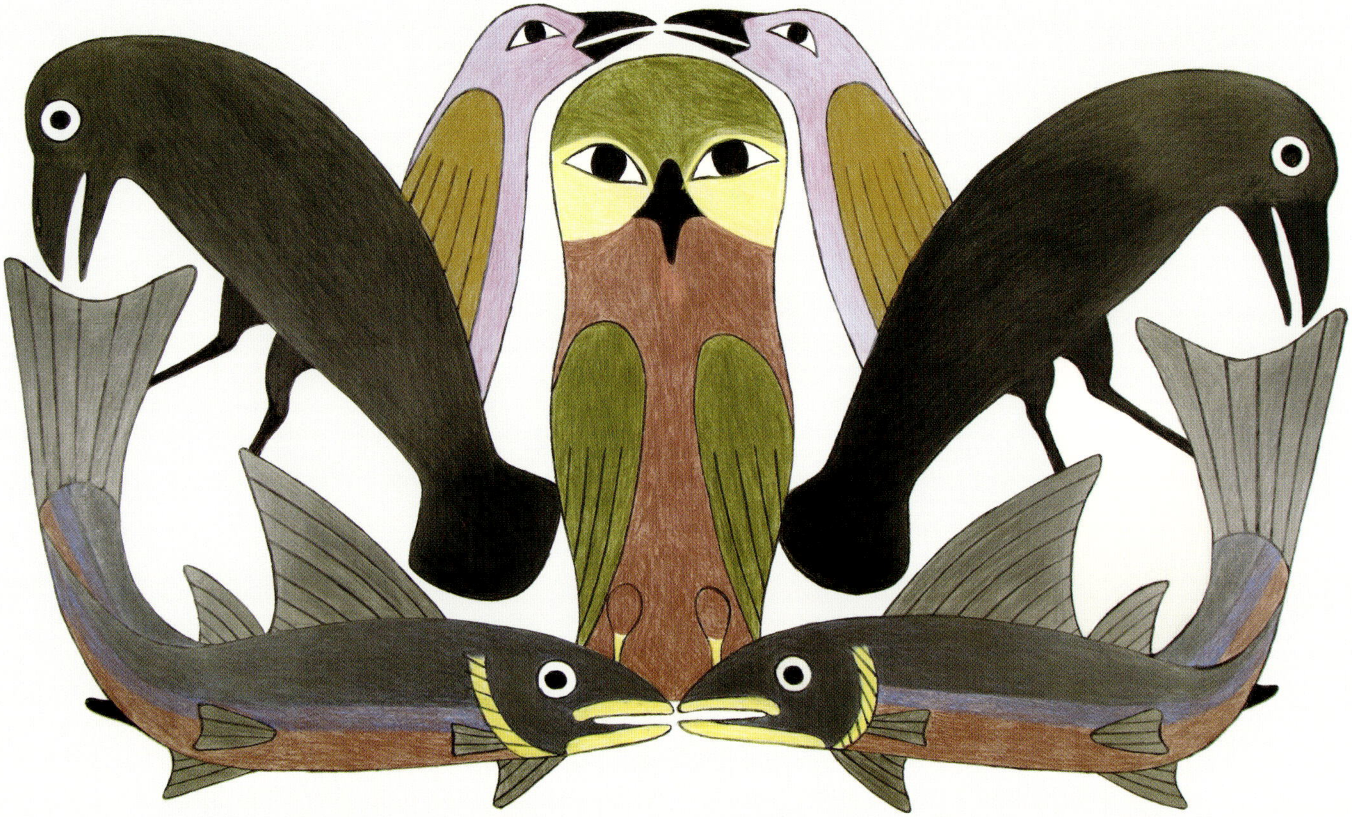

Untitled (Owl's Consort), 2012, ink and colored pencil

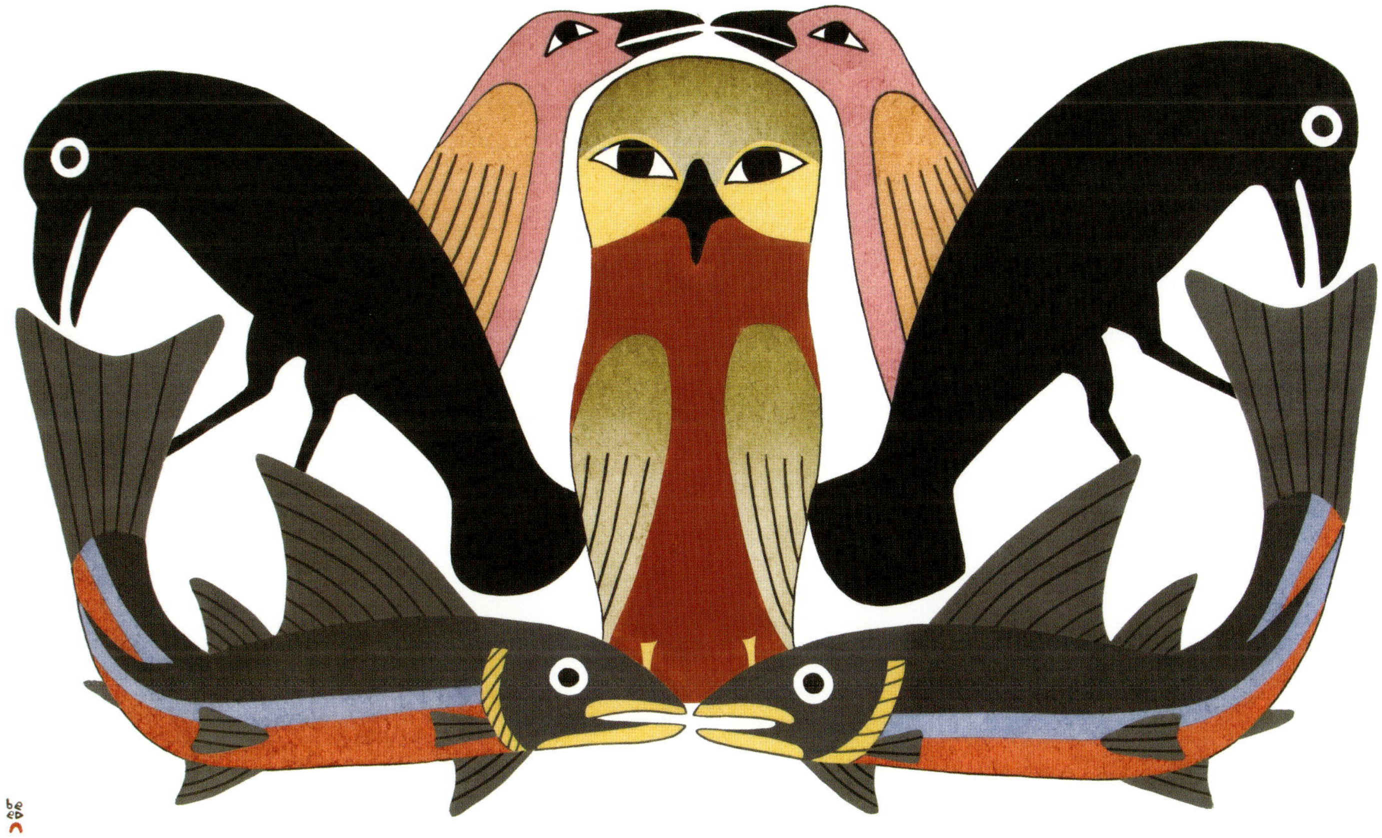

Owl's Consort, 2012, stonecut and stencil

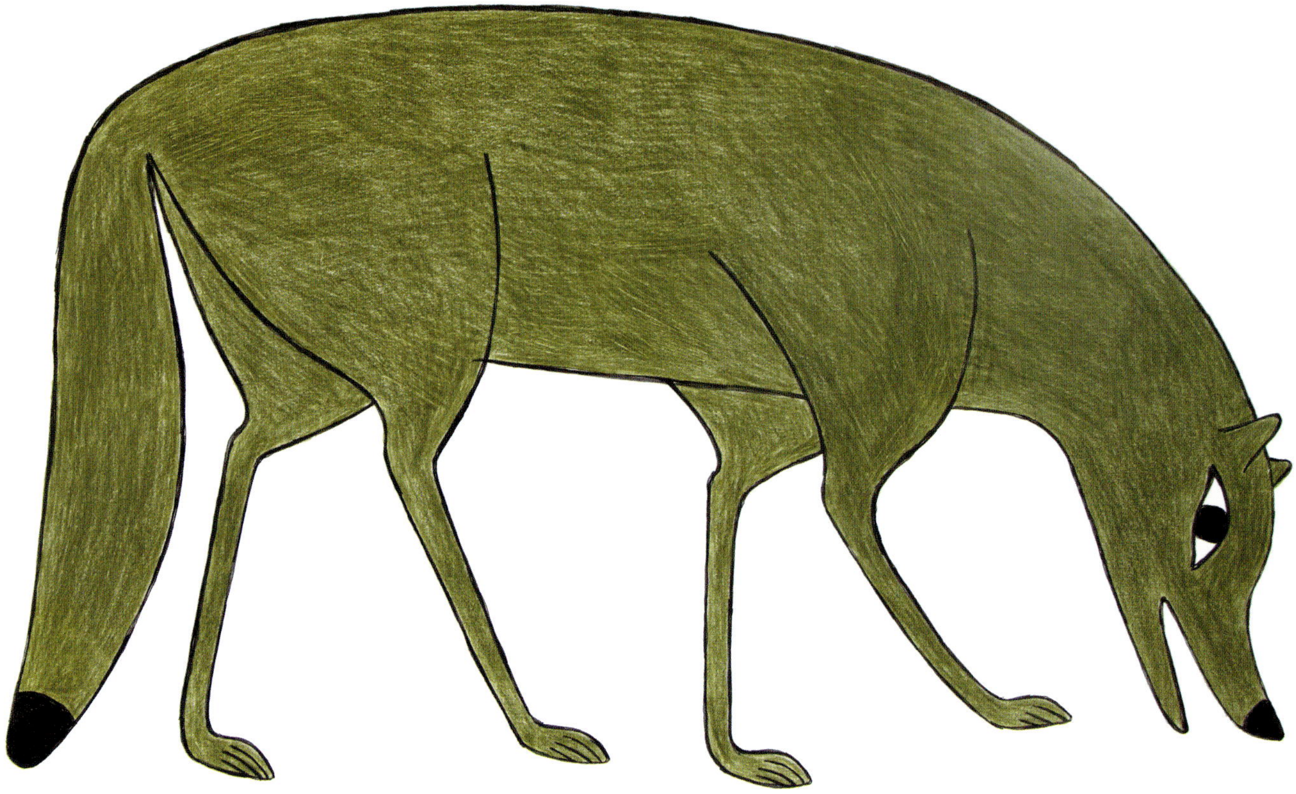

Untitled (Red Fox), 2012, ink and colored pencil

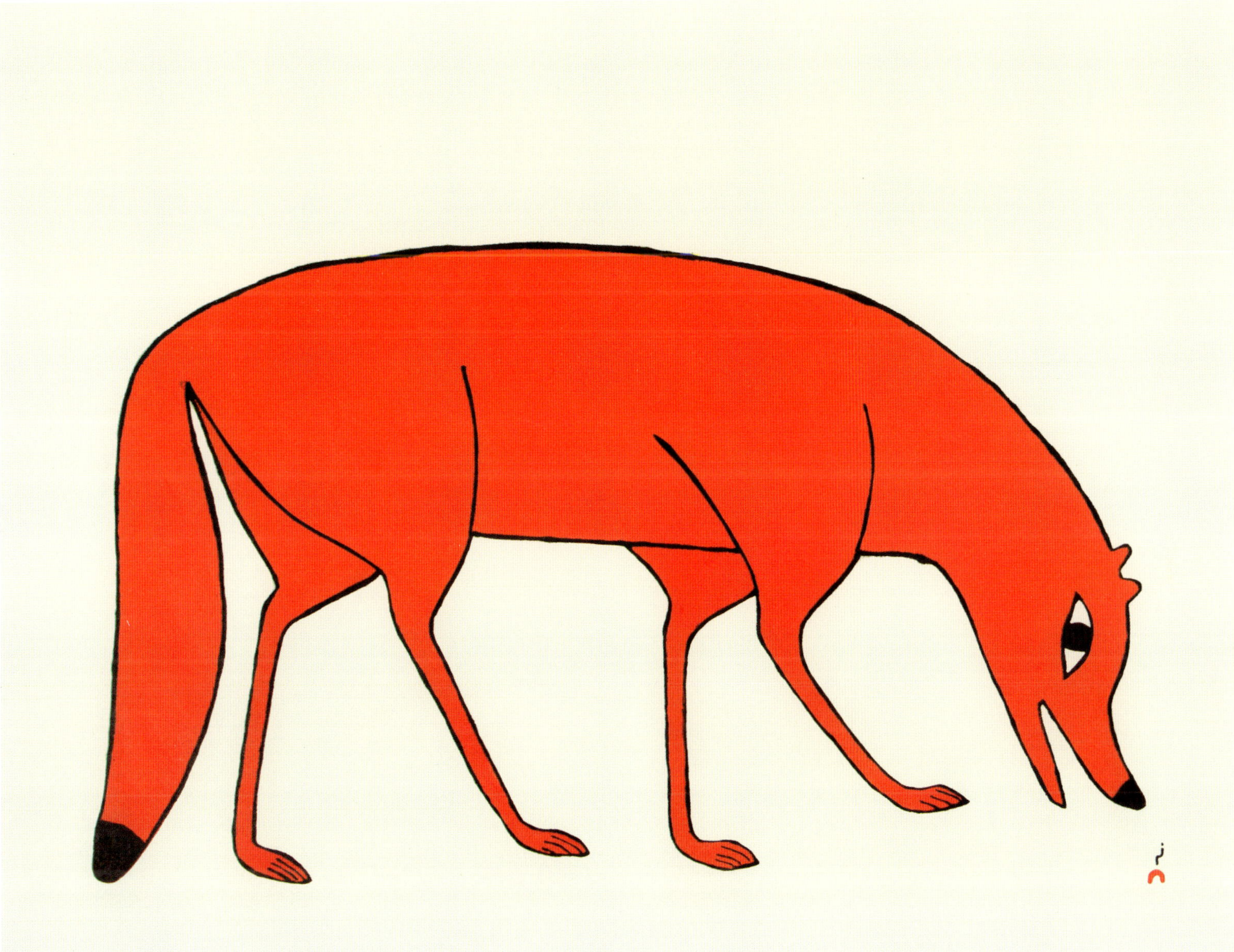

Red Fox, 2012, stonecut

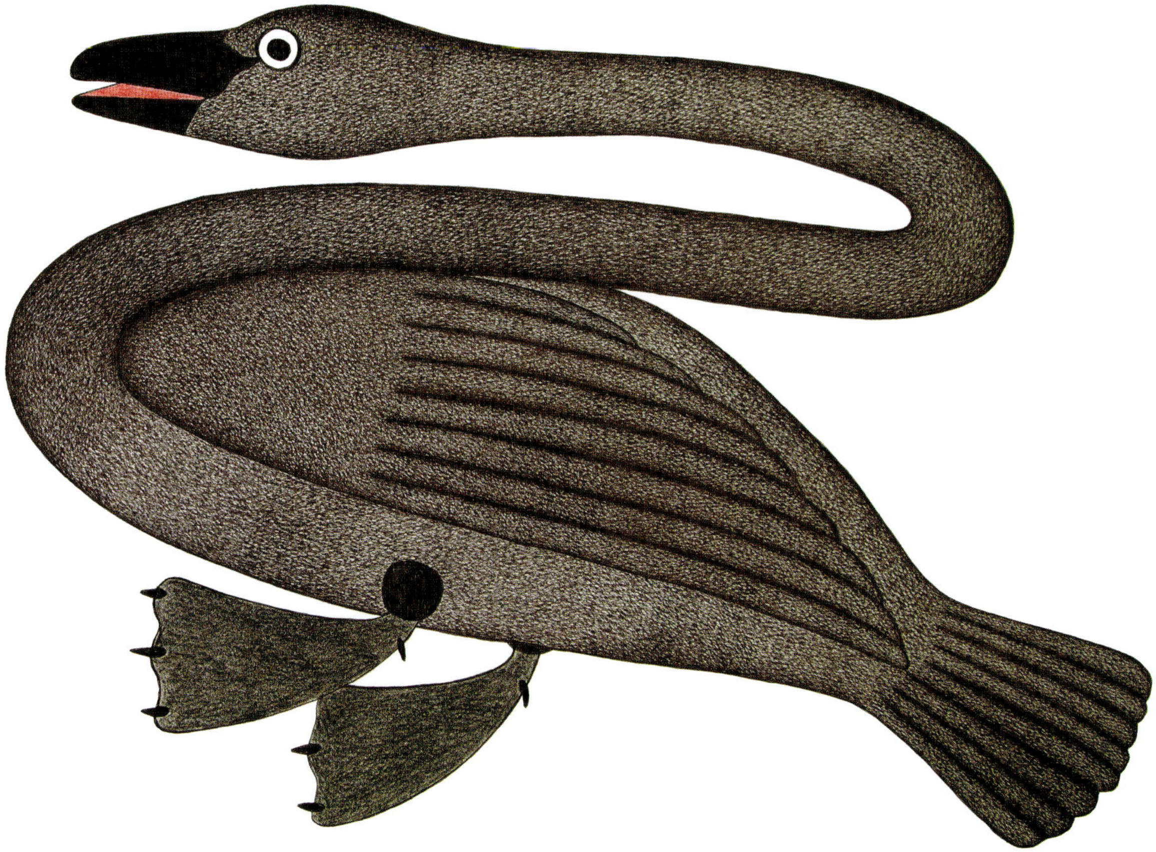

Untitled (Long Necked Goose), 2013, ink and colored pencil

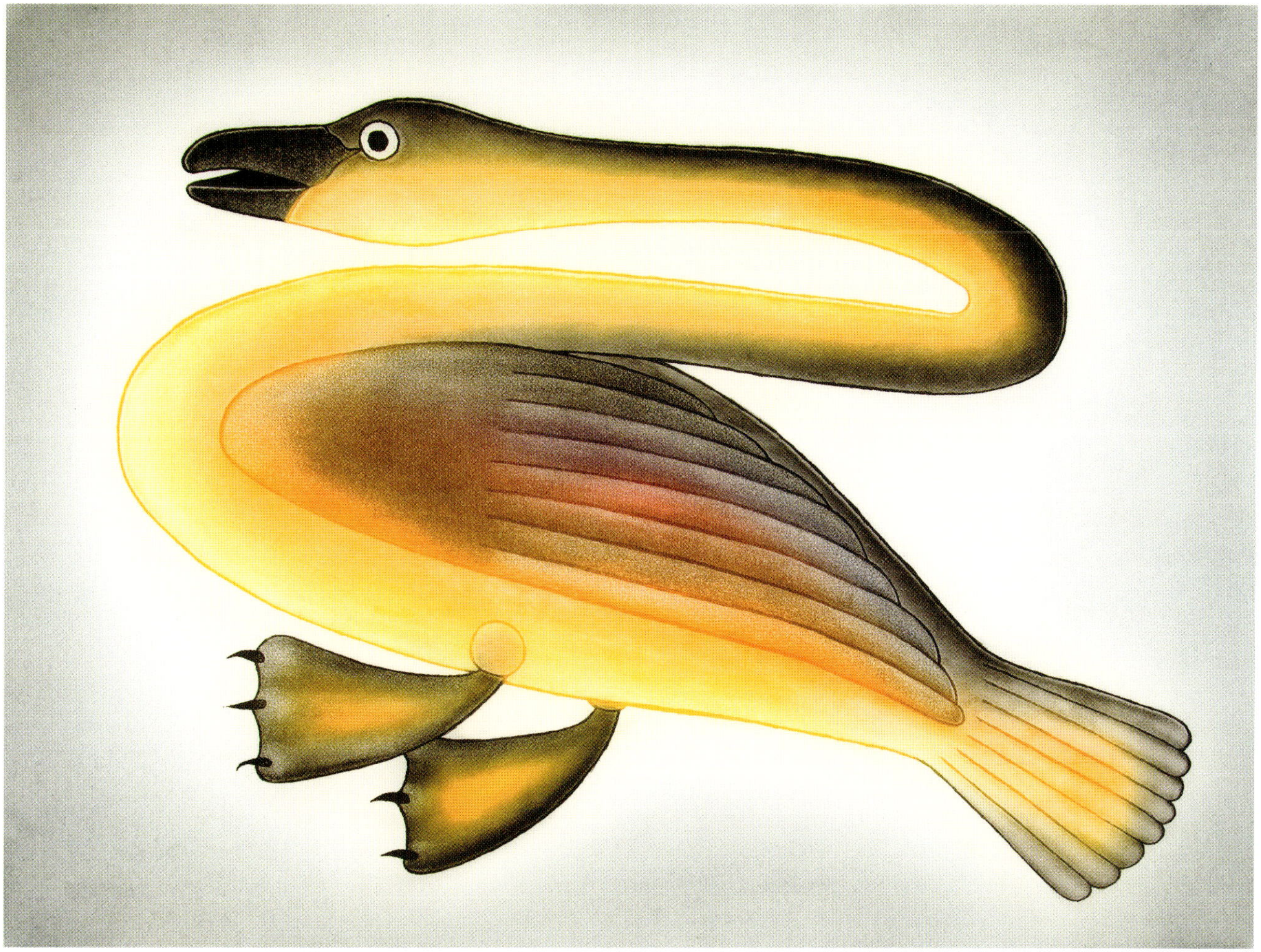

Long Necked Goose, 2013, etching and aquatint

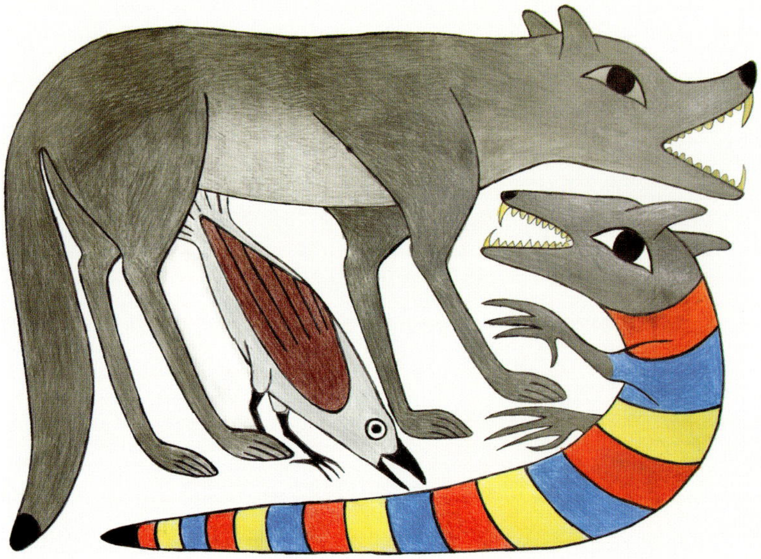

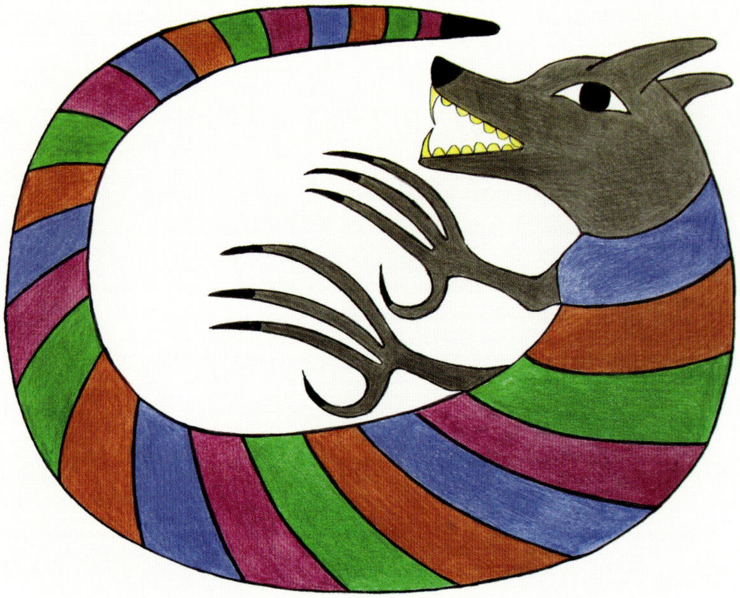

Left: *Untitled (Serpentine Wolf)*, 2010, ink and colored pencil
Right: *Untitled (Serpentine Wolf II)*, 2013, ink and colored pencil

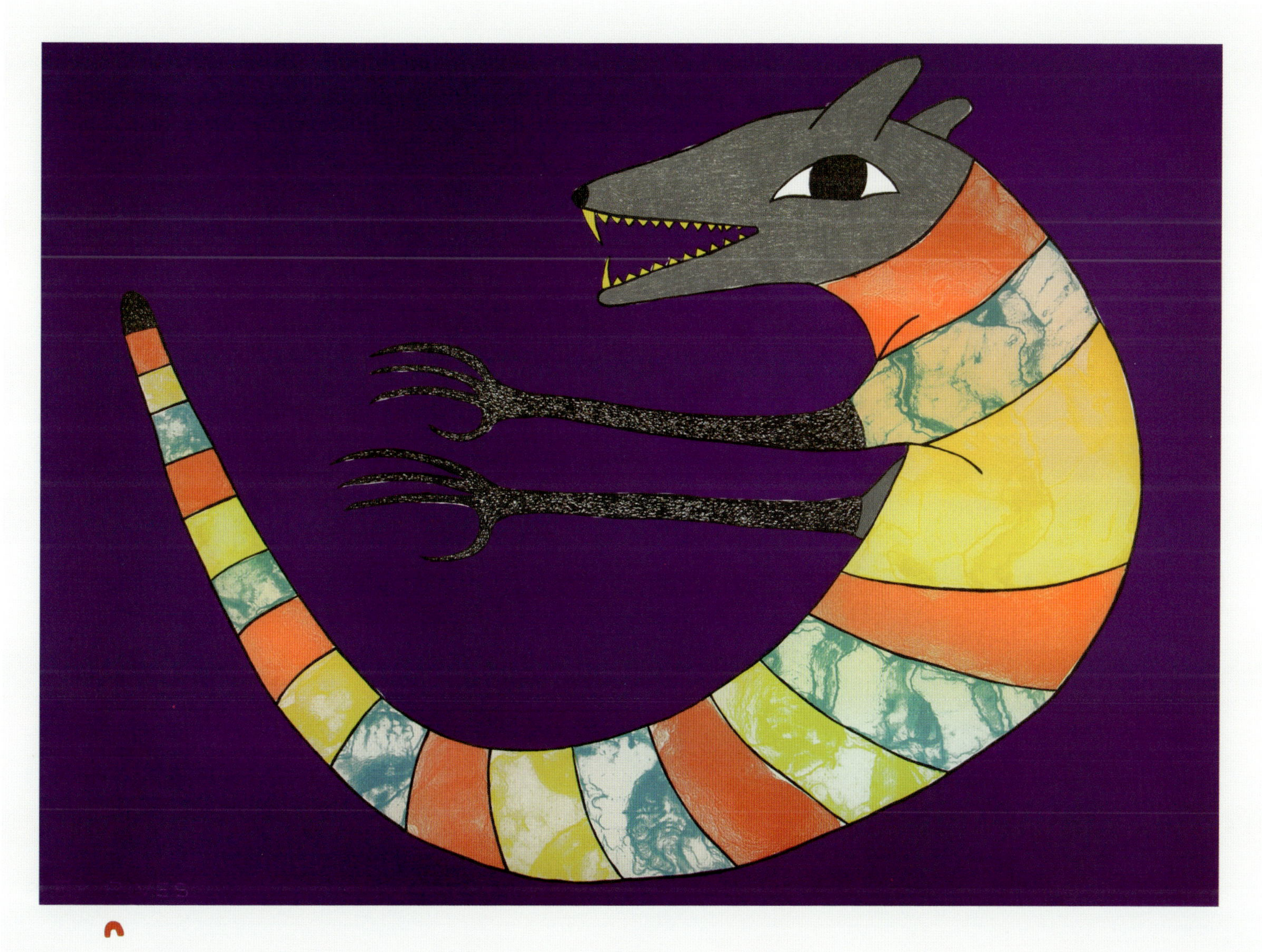

Serpentine Wolf, 2013, lithograph

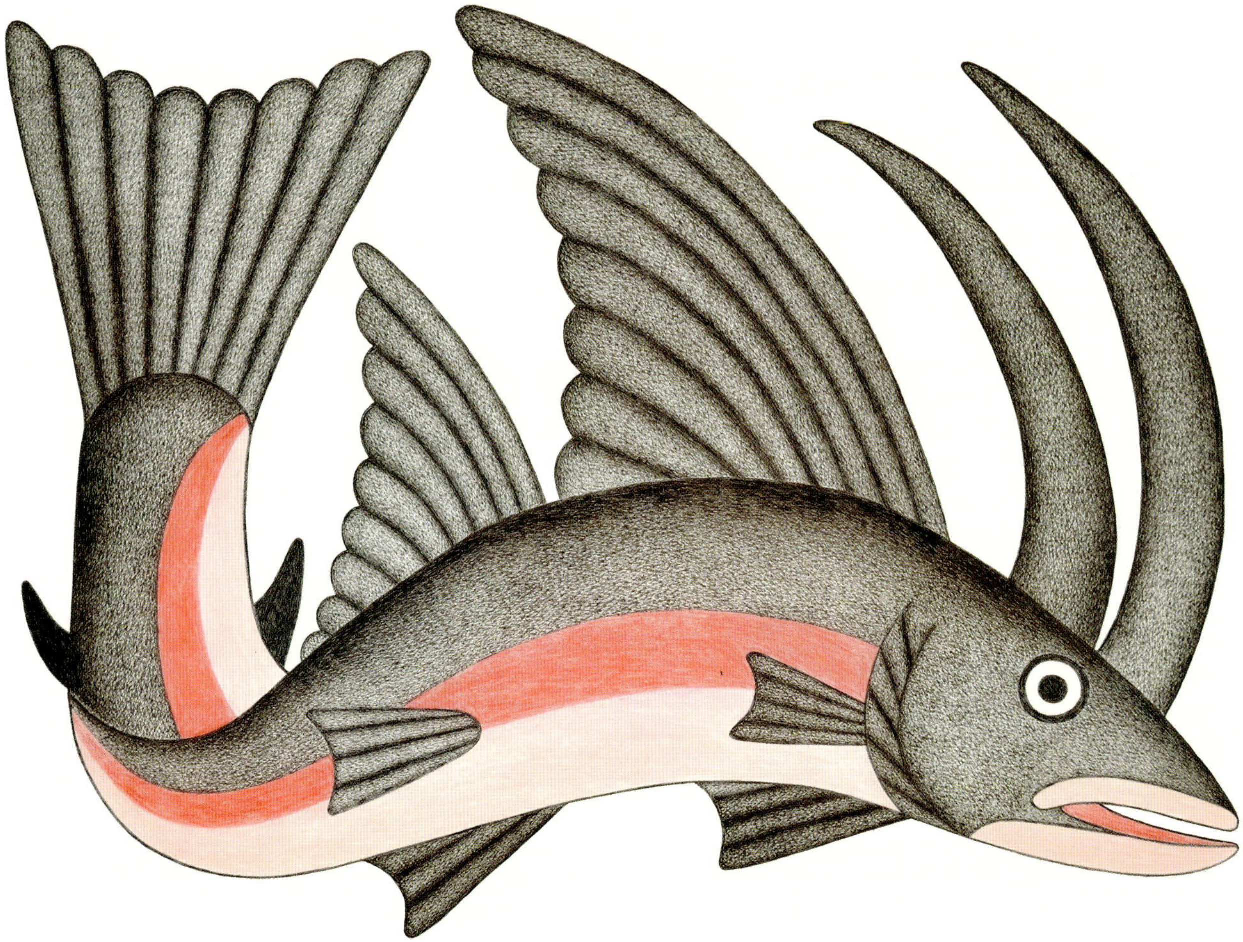

Untitled (Great Big Fish), 2011, ink and colored pencil

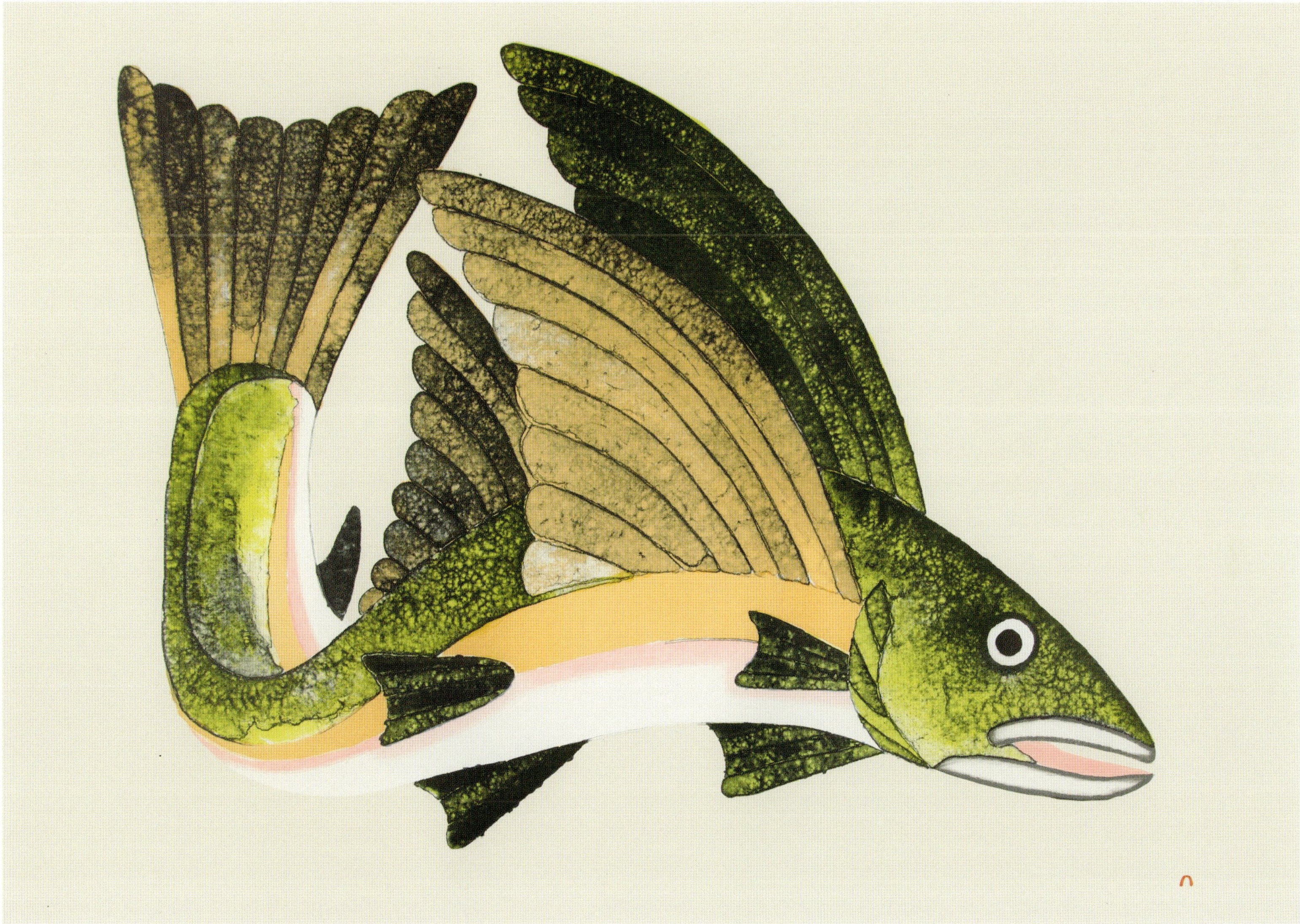

Great Big Fish, 2011, lithograph

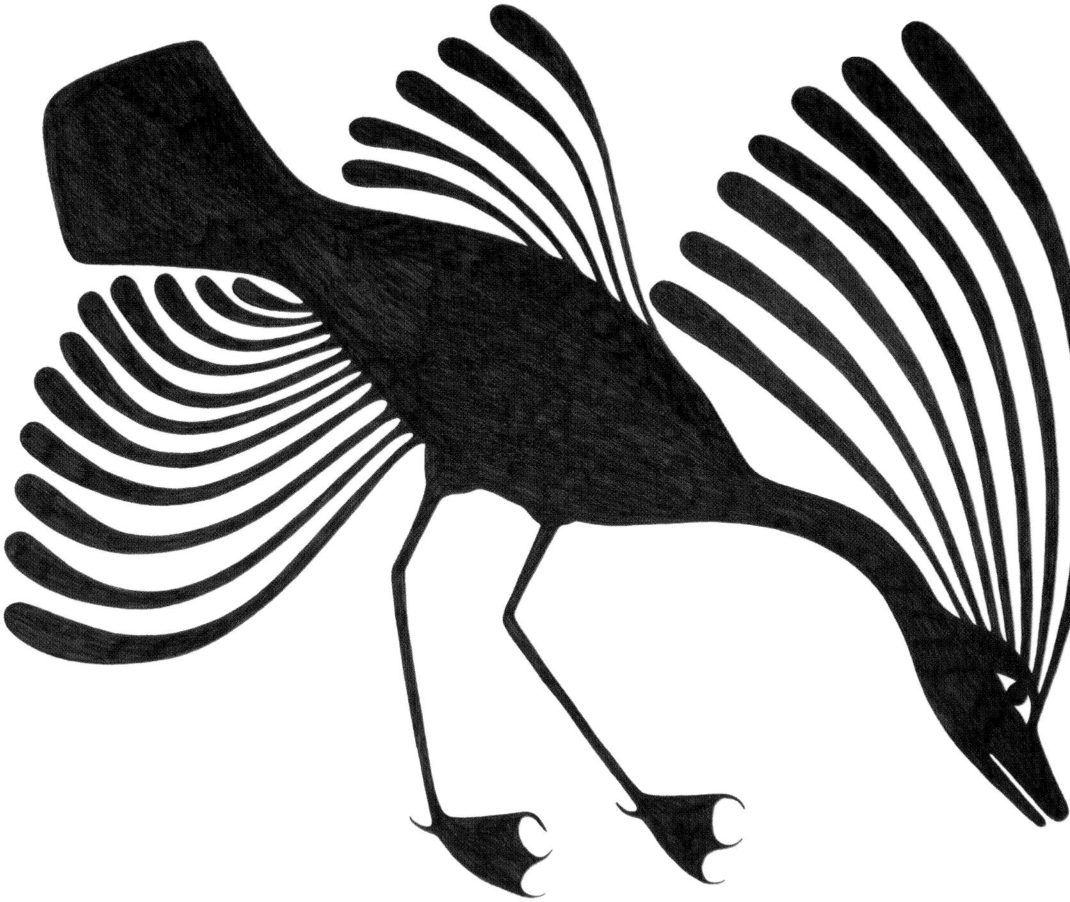

Untitled (Inquisitive Bird), 2001, ink

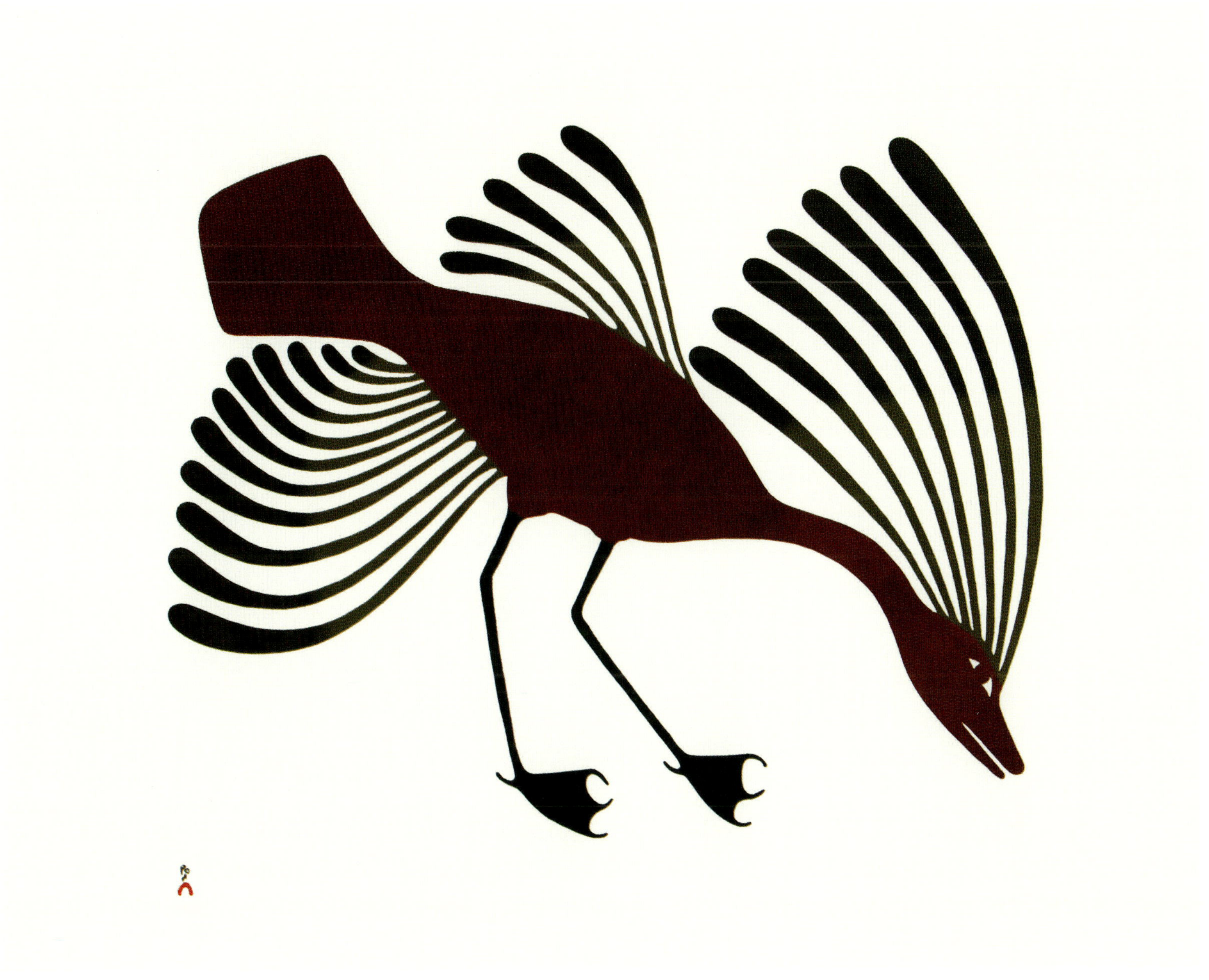

Inquisitive Bird, 2001, stonecut

AVANT-PROPOS

J'ai voyagé pour la première fois avec ma mère en 1991. L'Université Queen's à Kingston, Ontario allait lui conférer un doctorat honorifique et elle m'avait demandé de l'accompagner et d'être son interprète. Pour moi, c'était une expérience incroyable. J'avais l'impression de rêver! J'étais jeune, j'avais à peine 21 ans, et j'ignorais que tant de gens connaissaient ma mère: elle avait beaucoup d'amis.

Debout sur la scène avec elle, j'étais sûre d'être plus nerveuse qu'elle ne l'était. Elle était vraiment fière. Elle n'avait jamais pensé qu'elle allait recevoir un doctorat honorifique, et elle était fière de cet honneur. L'université était fantastique. Avant de venir à Kingston, j'étais loin de penser que j'allais visiter un endroit d'une telle grandeur! Pendant notre visite, j'ai demandé à mère: « Maman, lorsque tu voyages, est-ce que tu visites ce genre de lieux? » Elle m'a répondu qu'elle avait déjà visité beaucoup de grands établissements comme Queen's.

Je pense que ma mère avait un goût de l'aventure, et moi je l'ai aussi. Nous avons vraiment aimé notre voyage à Kingston. Nous avons exploré la campagne, par exemple l'île Wolfe et les Mille-Îles, et aux champs nous avons vu des vaches, des moutons et des chevaux. Le paysage en été était vraiment beau.

J'ai été aussi frappée par notre séjour à Toronto en 2001, quand ma mère a reçu une étoile dans l'Allée des célébrités canadiennes. C'était incroyable de voir ma mère défiler sur le tapis rouge, et de savoir que j'étais là avec elle. Une fois de plus, lorsque nous étions sur scène avec tous ces personnes célèbres, j'étais tellement nerveuse, et après son discours j'ai dit à ma mère: « Maman, on dirait que tu n'étais pas nerveuse du tout! » Elle m'a répondu: « Je ne m'énerve jamais. J'imagine les autres comme une personne, dans le même sens que moi je suis une personne, et c'est ça. »

J'ai voyagé beaucoup avec ma mère, et j'ai aimé chaque voyage. Elle aimait voyager aussi. Des fois elle se sentait fatiguée, mais elle était toujours une voyageuse contente, et elle appréciait l'occasion de sortir de chez elle pour un bout de temps. La célébration de son quatre-vingtième anniversaire à la galerie de la Collection McMichael d'art canadien a été très spéciale. Elle n'a pas voulu trancher le gâteau parce qu'il était tellement beau. Nous sommes allées au McMichael de nombreuses fois, et je me souviendrai pour toujours d'une dame qui est venue à ma mère lors d'une de ces visites, les larmes dans les yeux. J'ai été époustouflée. C'était la première fois que j'ai vu quelqu'un tellement content de rencontrer ma mère. J'ai dit: « Maman, elle pleurait même! » Elle m'a répondu: « Ça se passe souvent, et avec beaucoup de gens. » À mon avis, des fois les gens pleuraient en rencontrant ma mère parce qu'ils adoraient son art. Ils qualifiaient leurs maisons de plus lumineuses et plus joyeuses avec une de ses estampes montée au mur.

J'ai grandi entourée de ses oeuvres, et pour moi elles sont toutes belles. Lorsque j'en aimais une beaucoup, je lui disais: « Vends pas ça au co-op! Garde-la et monte-la au mur! » Mais elle ne s'intéressait jamais à garder ses dessins, sauf *Le Hibou enchanté*. Elle disait que c'était son oeuvre préférée, même si au moment de la créer elle était loin d'imaginer la renommée immense que l'oeuvre allait obtenir. *Le Hibou enchanté*, c'est à moi maintenant. J'habite toujours la même maison, et l'estampe est toujours là au mur, à côté d'une sélection de ses prix.

Elle travaillait tout le temps, à la maison. Je me levais tôt, et elle était déjà là, travaillant sur ses dessins. Lorsque je rentrais du travail, elle dessinait toujours. Je lui disais qu'elle devait avoir tant de patience, étant donné qu'elle dessinait tout le temps, et elle me répondait: « Je l'adore. J'y suis habituée et ma main ne veut pas s'arrêter. Son seul désir, c'est de continuer de bouger avec le crayon. »

Elle parlait peu souvent de sa renommée. Elle disait que, au début, lorsqu'elle commençait sa carrière et avait peur, elle était loin de s'imaginer la renommée internationale qu'elle allait acquérir. Mais elle en avait une, et elle disait d'être choisie par Dieu. La célébrité ne l'a pas changée, pas tellement. Elle était toujours gentille et amicale. Chaque fois qu'elle remarquait qu'il y avait quelqu'un en difficulté, elle essayait d'aider d'une façon ou d'une autre.

Nous étions très proches. J'étais la plus jeune, et je crois que de tous ses enfants j'avais la relation la plus étroite avec elle. Elle me manque chaque jour. Cela me manque de me lever et de la trouver au salon déjà au travail sur un dessin.

Silaqi Ashevak

KENOJUAK ASHEVAK

Sa vie et son héritage artistique

Kenojuak Ashevak, la première dessinatrice de Cape Dorset, est l'artiste inuite la plus renommée au Canada. Sa carrière s'est étendue sur plus de cinq décennies, de la publication de sa première estampe en 1959 jusqu'à sa mort en 2013, à l'âge de 85 ans. Pendant ce temps, ses images ont été publiées dans plus de trois cents éditions originales imprimées, et elle a laissé une archive de plus de deux mille dessins originaux. Elle est née et a passé sa jeunesse sur le vaste territoire du sud de l'île de Baffin. Alors, elle pratiquait le mode de vie traditionnel des Inuits. C'était une existence nomadique répartie entre des camps éloignés: les *haumuqs*, igloos et tentes estivales lui servaient de logement, et elle dépendait des animaux et des plantes de la mer pour sa nourriture et pour sa survie. À sa mort, elle vivait dans une maison modeste mais moderne à Cape Dorset (nom inuit: Kinngait), une communauté isolée dans le territoire arctique du Nunavut, et jouissait d'une immense réputation en tant qu'artiste et icône culturelle majeure du Canada. Son histoire éclaire un mode de vie disparu, et les profonds changements qui ont mené à sa transformation créative.

LES PREMIÈRES ANNÉES

Kenojuak naquit en 1927 à Ikerrasak, une zone de camp traditionnelle au sud de l'île de Baffin[1]. Deuxième enfant de Seelaki et Ushuakjuk, elle devait son nom à son grand-père maternel déjà décédé. Dans son autobiographie, publiée en 1985, elle explique que « Chez les Inuits, nous croyons qu'un enfant qui porte le nom de quelqu'un d'autre s'assure de toute l'amour et de tout le respect dont le mort jouissait en vie. Une relation spirituelle prend forme entre les deux[2]. » [Traduction. Tous les passages cités dans ce document ont été traduits de l'anglais. NDLR.] La coutume s'appelle *atikulu*, ou « nom d'âme ».

Les aïeuls de Kenojuak venaient de la côte nord de la péninsule d'Ungava, la région la plus septentrionale du Québec. Le territoire est connu aujourd'hui sous le nom de Nunavik; le détroit d'Hudson le sépare du sud de l'île de Baffin. Mais les Inuits de la génération de Kenojuak ne prêtaient guère attention à ces divisions territoriales: ils passaient d'un côté du détroit à l'autre selon les saisons, les mouvements de la faune et la volonté de la Compagnie de la Baie d'Hudson. Les premiers souvenirs de Kenojuak étaient d'une traversée du détroit d'Hudson dans le bateau Peterhead de son grand-père. Elle fut frappée par les cris agités et aigus des *akpa* (guillemots) qui nichaient sur les falaises tout le long de la côte.

Ce voyage la menait à Pujjunaq (l'île Mansel), une île aujourd'hui inhabitée au large de la péninsule Ungava au bout septentrional de la baie d'Hudson. La Compagnie de la Baie d'Hudson y avait établi un poste de traite de fourrure en 1929, et plusieurs familles inuites avaient été encouragées à se délocaliser et faire la trappe pour la compagnie. Kenojuak et sa famille y passaient du temps dans la première moitié des années 1930, mais selon elle, les conditions étaient oppressives. Dans ses mémoires, elle raconte que plusieurs membres du camp se sont noyés lors d'une tempête qui avait enfoncé leur petit bateau de bois contre les roches, sous les yeux de ceux sur terre qui étaient incapables de les aider. Les prix de fourrures étaient alors très à la baisse à cause de la Grande Dépression, et les disputes entre les chasseurs et les marchands étaient par conséquent fort communes. Le père de Kenojuak, Ushuakjuk, était souvent au centre de ces querelles. De nombreux habitants du camp le craignaient, puisqu'il menaçait d'autres chasseurs et générait tension au sein du camp. « Seelaki exprimait de la peur — elle croyait qu'il avait complètement perdu la tête », Kenojuak écrivit plus tard[3].

Ushuakjuk devenait de plus en plus instable pendant leur séjour à Pujjunaq. Éventuellement, trois hommes décidèrent d'intervenir et lui tendirent un guet-apens. Comme il sortait de sa maison de neige, ils tirèrent sur lui, le tuèrent, et jetèrent son corps dans la mer avec ses biens et ses chiens. Kenojuak reconnaît que la mort de son père peut sembler incompréhensible pour plusieurs, mais à cette époque-là, « Les Inuits administraient la justice uniquement pour maintenir l'harmonie et la stabilité du groupe. Quiconque se faisait trop belliqueux, ou qui manquait d'autocontrôle, ou qui peut-être aurait volé de la cache d'autrui, devenait une menace pour toute la communauté. Quand cela arrivait, une personne ou plusieurs, soit autoproclamée soit désignée par le groupe, éliminait la menace[4]. »

Seelaki et ses enfants quittèrent Pujjunaq cet été-là et n'y revinrent jamais. Ils voyagèrent à Ivujivik, où ils attendirent l'arrivée annuelle du navire de ravitaillement *Nascopie*, opéré par la Compagnie, qui les ramenèrent à Cape Dorset où leurs parents et amis leur offrirent du réconfort. Le meurtre d'Ushuakjuk fit l'objet d'une enquête officielle mais la police ne porta jamais d'accusation.

Kenojuak passa les années qui lui restaient de sa jeunesse dans divers camps traditionnels au sud de l'île de Baffin. Elle restait souvent chez sa grand-mère, Koweesa. Elle avait de beaux souvenirs de cette époque de sa vie : de « la poursuite interminable de petits oiseaux et animaux dans l'espoir de finalement en capturer un » ; des petits jouets en bois flotté gravés par son oncle, Niviaqsi ; et comment sa grand-mère lui apprenait l'art de coudre du tendon de caribou et faire des coutures imperméables[5].

Sa maison permanente était un *haumuq* — une construction robuste avec une structure et un plancher en bois, couverte de toile en coton et isolée avec de la mousse. On augmentait l'isolation avec des blocs de neige empilés autour du mur extérieur. « À l'intérieur nous étions au chaud et à l'aise, juste avec la chaleur de notre *qulliq* », une lampe en pierre qui brûle de l'huile de phoque. En été, ils déménageaient dans une tente en toile cousue par les femmes, puis de nouveau dans le *haumuq* en automne. « Pour notre subsistance, nous n'avions aucune autre option que de dépendre des produits de la mer et de la terre[6]. »

En 1946, Kenojuak devint la femme, selon la coutume inuite, d'un homme du nom de Johnniebo. Leur mariage fut arrangé par leurs familles. Un jour, le frère de Johnniebo, Towkie, et sa femme, Elisapee, rendirent visite en tant qu'ambassadeurs à la mère et aux oncles de Kenojuak pour parler d'une union possible entre les deux familles. Kenojuak faisait semblant de dormir pendant les pourparlers et admit avoir peur, mais elle se souvenait aussi de rencontrer Johnniebo à Cape Dorset — en particulier, « comment il me taquinait amicalement, et sa grande taille », dit-elle. « Pendant les premières semaines de notre mariage, je ressentais une profonde réticence dans la présence de Johnniebo. Je lui lançais des roches chaque fois qu'il venait vers moi. Il riait jovialement et ne lâchait pas la poursuite. Éventuellement, j'ai appris à apprécier énormément cet homme gentil et tendre », raconte Kenojuak[7].

Kenojuak et Johnniebo commencèrent leur vie ensemble à Sukbuk, un camp situé au long de la côte sud de l'île de Baffin, mais avant la fin de l'année, Peter Pitseolak leur demanda de le rejoindre à son camp, Keatko, juste à l'est de Cape Dorset[8]. C'était une belle époque pour les deux et leur premier fils, Jamasie, y naquit en 1947. Keakto était un bel endroit, protégé mais près de la mer et à seulement quelques kilomètres de Cape Dorset. Les renards étaient nombreux. L'année 1947 fut favorable d'une autre manière, parce que cette année-là, le navire de ravitaillement

Nascopie coula au large de Cape Dorset — un événement capital qui marque encore les imaginations des artistes de la communauté. La perte était triste, mais le navire resta suspendu sur les roches pendant assez de temps pour permettre aux gens de récupérer ce qu'ils pouvaient. Peter érigea une maison en bois à Keakto, ce qui renforçait sa position de leader déterminé et important. Les premières photos identifiables de Kenojuak et Johnniebo furent prises par Peter durant cette époque.

Kenojuak et Johnniebo passèrent les années suivantes à Keatko et connurent une sécurité relative. En 1949, un missionnaire anglican qui prêchait dans les camps du sud de l'île de Baffin les maria. La même année vit la naissance de leur deuxième enfant, Mary[9]. Ensemble, ils vécurent la multitude de changements qui commençait à miner le mode de vie traditionnel des Inuits, y compris la campagne d'envergure contre l'épidémie de tuberculose qui envahissait la région. En 1951, Kenojuak apprit que des radiographies prises en 1950 montraient qu'elle avait contracté la maladie, et elle fut amenée en avion à Québec pour une convalescence à l'Hôpital Parc Savard.

Kenojuak passa trois années à l'hôpital, et en 1955, elle se sentit assez bien pour rentrer. Avant de son retour, elle avait appris le décès de ses deux enfants en 1953. Dans son autobiographie, elle réfléchit sur cette période tragique : « Dans une lettre m'étant adressée, Johnniebo me priait de ne pas pleurer nos deux enfants mais de m'occuper de ma récupération afin d'accélérer mon retour à Cape Dorset. Avec tout le chagrin qui m'envahissait, je ne voulais plus jamais avoir d'enfants. Les Inuits à l'hôpital priaient pour moi[10]. »

Cependant, dans les années suivantes, Kenojuak allait être la mère de quatorze enfants. Sa famille était composée de ses enfants naturels et d'autres enfants qu'elle adopta de diverses familles. Par exemple, en 1956, peu après son retour à Cape Dorset, elle adopta Annago. En plus, selon la coutume inuite et les circonstances, elle donna en adoption quelques-uns de ses enfants naturels. Sept de ses enfants ne parvinrent pas à l'âge adulte. À cette époque-là, les territoires inuits avaient le taux de mortalité infantile le plus élevé au pays. Ce taux a beaucoup baissé grâce aux améliorations des conditions de vie et des services santé, mais la mortalité infantile reste toujours trois fois plus élevée chez les Inuits que chez la population non-autochtone du Canada[11].

UNE ARTISTE S'AFFIRME

Lors de sa convalescence à l'Hôpital Parc Savard, Kenojuak cousait pour passer le temps. Elle était déjà une couturière accomplie, et ses produits attirèrent l'attention du sculpteur canadien Harold Pfeiffer, qui travaillait en tant qu'ergothérapeute à l'hôpital[12]. Il fut particulièrement frappé par la beauté et par l'exécution parfaite de ses poupées de chiffons et de ses vêtements traditionnels, qui présentaient des coutures minuscules et précises. En 1955, Pfeiffer accompagna Kenojuak et d'autres Inuits pendant leur voyage de retour à Cape Dorset sur le navire de ravitaillement médical du gouvernement fédéral, le *C.D. Howe*.

Kenojuak avait beaucoup de temps à consacrer à la couture pendant sa convalescence, mais elle remarque dans son autobiographie qu'elle a dû réapprendre à coudre avec du tendon de caribou après son retour de l'hôpital. Une fois refamiliarisée avec les matériaux traditionnels, elle fit des poupées, des *kamiks* (bottes en peau de phoque), des tapisseries en peau de phoque, et des sacs à main ornés de découpés. C'était avec ces créations que son instinct inné pour la conception et le design s'annonçait. Son talent attira l'attention d'Alma Houston qui établit le premier centre d'artisanat à Cape Dorset en 1956 avec son mari, James Houston. Les revenus tirés de la traite de fourrure étaient désormais insuffisants pour être le seul gagne-pain des Inuits, et par conséquent le gouvernement du Canada encourageait la gravure et d'autres métiers d'artisanat en guise de remplacement. Tandis que James travaillait avec les hommes sur divers projets, Alma monta un programme d'artisanat avec les femmes. « Arnakotak, le nom que nous donnions à Alma Houston, qui veut dire "femme grande", encourageait les femmes Inuites à coudre et à faire ce qu'elles voulaient », dit Kenojuak. « Essayant de nous aider à devenir indépendantes, elle nous consacrait son temps, ses capacités, et son expertise d'une manière énergique et enthousiaste. Je commençais à créer des appliqués en peau de phoque, que j'apportais à Arnakotak pour les vendre[13]. »

Un de ces dessins est à l'origine de la première image de Kenojuak, *Le lapin qui mange des algues*, qui figure maintenant parmi ses plus célèbres. Elle la dériva d'un appliqué en peau de phoque qu'elle avait utilisé dans un sac à main. Impressionnée par le talent pour la conception de Kenojuak, Alma lui suggéra de dessiner. Kenojuak était réticente au début; à cette époque les hommes étaient ceux qui dessinaient. Mais elle accepta quand même le papier bond grand format que James (qui portait le nom Saumik, qui veut dire "gaucher") lui offrit, et rapporta des dessins à crayon qui furent qualifiés de beaux et cohérents par Alma.

Kenojuak était la première femme à Cape Dorset à dessiner. Selon elle, les premiers pas ont été difficiles. « J'avais peur de commencer parce que je ne savais pas ce que j'allais dessiner », rappelle-t-elle[14]. « La première fois que Saumuk m'a donné une feuille de papier et m'a demandé de dessiner, je lui ai demandé de me donner une idée. Mais il m'a dit tout simplement de dessiner ce qui me viendrait à l'esprit — ça pourrait être n'importe quoi », dit-elle[15]. « J'ai détruit le premier dessin que j'ai fait à Keatko, mais j'ai apporté d'autres dessins à Saumuk lors de mon prochain voyage à Cape Dorset. J'étais satisfaite avec sa valorisation de mes oeuvres. Je savais que j'allais continuer[16]. »

LA DESSINATRICE ET SON STYLE

Les premiers dessins de Kenojuak montrent une forte influence de son expérience comme couturière. Empruntant une pratique employée dans la couture, elle utilisait souvent des patrons en carton et traçait des images sur le papier. Les motifs qui se répètent dans un dessin ont souvent été dessinés à l'aide d'un modèle; elle a fait beaucoup de dessins qui présentent des images reflétées arrangées symétriquement autour d'un sujet central. Kenojuak dit que l'idée d'employer des patrons lui est venue quand elle a vu qu'une autre femme, Sheouak Petaulassie, les utilisait. Elle s'est rendue compte que si elle faisait de même, « alors toutes les lignes seraient droites[17]. »

En même temps, elle développait sa propre démarche intuitive; elle disait que dans ce processus sa main quittait sa pensée[18]. Gauchère, elle commençait au coin gauche de la page, puis elle la remplissait lentement et systématiquement d'oiseaux, d'animaux, de figures humaines et de combinaisons fantastiques de tous les trois. Il était rare qu'elle ait une idée préconçue de ce qu'elle voulait dessiner ou de l'état final de la composition, mais elle savait par instinct ce qu'il fallait. « Je regarde la page pour un bout de temps, puis de nouvelles idées me viennent à l'esprit pour remplir l'espace et pour embellir davantage l'image, pour intensifier l'image, et ainsi je continue à y ajouter des éléments, dit-elle. Au fur et à mesure que mon imagination fait son travail [...] je dessine et je dessine, puis tout d'un coup je la regarde et je me dis, bien, c'est complété; et c'est ça[19]. »

Tandis que l'approche de Kenojuak était fluide, sa palette de couleurs était prédéterminée. Au fur et à mesure que des matériaux nouveaux devenaient disponibles, elle échangeait le graphite pour les crayons de couleur et les stylos feutres. Avant de se mettre à dessiner, elle étalait les couleurs qu'elle voulait utiliser. Une fois le dessin commencé, le choix de couleurs ne changeait pas. « J'arrange les couleurs d'une certaine façon, je leur donne une cohérence. [...] Je pose l'une à côté de l'autre deux couleurs qui, je crois, s'accorderaient bien [...] arrangées d'une manière qui plaît à mon sens de la couleur », explique-t-elle. « C'est peu probable que des idées soudaines en termes de couleur me viennent à l'esprit, par contre c'est possible avec la forme ou la taille[20]. »

Kenojuak aimait des combinaisons brillantes et agréables de couleurs primaires, et les utilisait avec la même précision et la même limpidité qu'elle apportait à ses formes fluides et entrelacées. Une fois terminé, le dessin était une image riche, complexe et agréable qui liait tous les éléments dans une apothéose d'harmonie visuelle.

Pour Kenojuak, le choix de sujet était un moyen d'arriver à une fin — dessiner de belles images. Au contraire de plusieurs de ses contemporains, elle n'était pas une raconteuse ou une narratrice. L'esthétique était toujours sa préoccupation majeure. Parmi les artistes provenant de Cape Dorset, elle est considérée comme hors-pair dans la représentation d'oiseaux — toutes les collections annuelles d'estampes de Cape Dorset sauf deux incluent des oiseaux dessinés par Kenojuak ; les hiboux et les corneilles y sont fortement représentés. Ceux-ci étaient ses sujets favoris, mais il était rare qu'elle ait l'intention explicite de les dessiner avant de commencer une image. Lorsqu'un membre du Conseil canadien des arts esquimaux lui demanda d'expliquer ce que le hibou lui signifiait, elle répondit que le hibou n'avait pas d'importance particulière, mais que chaque fois qu'elle commençait à dessiner, un hibou lui venait à la tête[21]. Ses oeuvres ne représentaient pas d'une façon directe les mythes et légendes traditionnelles des Inuits, mais elle comprenait par instinct l'interconnectivité de la vie et de tous les êtres vivants qui figure au coeur de la mythologie et la cosmologie de son peuple. Les thèmes de la lumière et de la noirceur étaient représentés par le soleil et la lune, le hibou et la corneille et, dans ses oeuvres plus tardives, par le visage d'une femme tranquille au centre du tout.

DU DESSIN À LA GRAVURE

Kenojuak est connue pour ses estampes, mais elle n'était pas elle-même graveuse. Au début du programme de gravure, c'étaient les hommes qui apprenaient le nouveau métier, et pour la plupart, ils tiraient les oeuvres d'autres artistes. Ce système se développa pour des raisons d'ordre pratique. Lors du début du programme de gravure, la plupart des Inuits vivaient toujours dans leurs camps traditionnels et venaient à la communauté pour visiter et échanger. Ceux qui s'intéressaient à dessiner — les hommes autant que les femmes — se procuraient du papier et des crayons, rentraient dans leurs camps, et revenaient pour vendre leurs dessins complétés. Les femmes trouvaient — ou consacraient — plus de temps à dessiner tout en s'acquittant de leurs autres responsabilités, tandis que leurs hommes chassaient, des fois absents pendant plusieurs jours de suite. D'autre part, les graveurs étaient des hommes qui acceptaient de rester dans ou près de la communauté et de travailler de longues heures dans l'atelier. Cette division du travail permettait à l'artiste de travailler à la maison et de voyager, et donnait au graveur une plus grande liberté de choix à l'égard de l'image. Éventuellement, les graveurs devenaient très compétents et capables de prendre des décisions techniques et esthétiques. Chaque estampe publiée par l'atelier depuis 1960 porte une marque de graveur estampillée en reconnaissance de l'importance de leur rôle.

Kenojuak connaissait bien les procédés de gravure, mais elle n'était généralement pas présente lors du tirage de ses estampes. Elle signait ses éditions après leur tirage et donnait rarement des commentaires là-dessus. La gravure sur cuivre, qui fut introduite en 1962, faisait exception. Kenojuak fabriqua plusieurs plaques de cuivre et maîtrisa éventuellement comment manier le burin, mais elle n'aimait pas ce genre de travail. Il lui fatiguait le poignet et la main, et elle avait peur de se couper[22]. Elle n'était pas la seule dans son impression de la gravure sur cuivre ; de nombreux artistes la qualifiaient de difficile et pénible après l'avoir essayée, et le programme ne dura pas longtemps.

Les éditions originales des estampes de Kenojuak sont maintenant complètement épuisées. Elles surviennent aux enchères de temps en temps. Leur valeur ne cesse d'augmenter. Son oeuvre de 1960 *Le Hibou enchanté* a été vendue en 2018 pour 216 000 $ — battant le record du montant le plus élevé versé pour une estampe d'un artiste canadien.

LA CÉLÉBRITÉ

Le monde fit connaissance de Kenojuak en 1963 par le moyen d'une production de l'Office national du film intitulée *Kenojuak : artiste esquimau*. Durant les années 60, son monde — l'Arctique canadien — était une région lointaine et mystérieuse, connue du reste du pays seulement pour son climat inhospitalier et pour le peuple autochtone, les « Esquimaux », qui arrivaient à y survivre. Ce film extraordinaire exposa aux yeux du reste du monde la vie riche et l'art captivant de cette jeune femme, et une connexion durable s'établit. Les collections annuelles d'estampes de Cape Dorset publiées « dans le Sud » rendirent le nom de Kenojuak synonyme du mystère, de la richesse et de la beauté du Grand Nord du Canada.

Le monde tomba amoureux de Kenojuak quatre années plus tard, en novembre 1967, quand Johnniebo et elle voyagèrent à Ottawa. Elle reçut la Médaille pour services éminents de l'Ordre du Canada présentée par le gouverneur général Roland Michener à l'occasion de l'investiture inaugurale de la nouvelle distinction honorifique du Canada. Dans la presse, Kenojuak fut qualifiée de « tout simplement magnifique[23]. » Kenojuak et Johnniebo revinrent à Ottawa deux années plus tard pour travailler ensemble durant deux mois sur une murale destinée au pavillon canadien de l'Expo '70 à Suita, Osaka, Japon. Pendant leur séjour, le focus médiatique se concentra sur eux en tant que couple artistique : une manchette annonça que « Ces artistes partagent un lit et une planche à dessin[24]. » Deux années plus tard, ils furent de nouveau dans le Sud, à Halifax, pour la première d'une exposition majeure à la St. Mary's University Art Gallery qui venait d'ouvrir ses portes. Ce serait, malheureusement, leur dernière opportunité de voyager et d'être fêtés ensemble. Johnniebo mourut en 1972 d'une crise d'appendicite. Un avion fut appelé pour l'évacuer à Iqaluit (connu alors comme Frobisher Bay) pour une opération, mais il ne put pas atterrir en raison des mauvaises conditions météorologiques. Ce fut un événement tragique, et pour Kenojuak, la perte fut lourde.

La carrière florissante de Kenojuak multipliait ses opportunités de voyager en Europe, aux États-Unis, et bien sûr aux autres parties du Canada. Elle assumait souvent le rôle d'ambassadeure culturelle et servait de modèle pour des femmes, ouvrant la voie pour d'autres artistes inuites, tant de sa propre génération que pour celles à venir. Plus tard dans sa carrière elle parlait plus franchement d'elle-même en tant qu'artiste professionnelle qui maintenait sa famille avec les revenus tirés par la vente de ses oeuvres. Elle se hérissait si l'on demandait quand elle allait cesser de dessiner : « Souvent les gens traitent l'art comme s'il était complètement différent de n'importe quel autre métier et ils me demandent, pourquoi souhaites-tu continuer avec ça ? Mais c'est mon métier et mon amour. Je ne puis pas imaginer la vie sans l'art[25]. »

Kenojuak est aussi devenue une célébrité dans sa propre terre. Elle marqua la création du territoire inuit, Nunavut, avec une oeuvre majestueuse — *Siilavut, Nunavut (Notre environnement, notre terre)*. En 2003, à l'âge de 76 ans, elle fut invitée par Adventure Canada à rejoindre leur croisière Arctic Art à travers la baie d'Hudson. Pour la grande artiste, ce voyage fut l'occasion de fêter et d'être fêtée. Un journaliste décrit l'arrivée du navire de croisière à Cape Dorset ainsi : « C'est comme si la Reine elle-même est arrivée. [...] Des parents, des admirateurs et des pêcheurs se rassemblent le long de la côte rocheuse. Des artistes s'arrêtent pour serrer la main de Kenojuak[26]. » En 2009, elle assista à sa première exposition en solo au Nunavut au Musée Nunatta Sunakkutaangit Museum à Iqaluit, et en 2012, elle fut nommée à l'Ordre du Nunavut, la plus haute distinction honorifique du territoire.

L'HÉRITAGE DE KENOJUAK

Le Kenojuak Cultural Centre a été officiellement ouvert à Cape Dorset en septembre 2018 après une longue attente. Des plans pour un centre culturel à Cape Dorset existaient depuis 20 ans, mais le projet avait été reporté indéfiniment dû aux velléités de la politique et aux difficultés financières. Mais il n'avait jamais été oublié. Cape Dorset est la communauté artistique la plus célèbre au Nunavut, et les raisons pour y construire un centre culturel — célébrer son héritage artistique — n'ont jamais changés, et en fait sont devenues de plus en plus fortes grâce à une nouvelle génération d'artistes qui figurent parmi les meilleurs du Nord.

La cérémonie tant attendue, en présence de dignitaires invités, de donateurs et de plus de 600 membres de la communauté, a été une célébration remplie d'émotion. Après que la corde en peau de phoque à l'entrée a été coupée par un couteau de neige traditionnel, la foule a été introduite dans le centre pour admirer les ateliers de gravure de pointe, des espaces pour les artistes, un espace de réunion pour les anciens et d'autres groupes communautaires, et un espace d'exposition — le premier espace construit expressément pour l'exposition des oeuvres sur papier au Nunavut. Aux murs pendaient 31 dessins et trois estampes de Kenojuak, dont le centre culturel porte le nom.

Les dessins présentés dans l'exposition d'ouverture proviennent des archives de la West Baffin Eskimo Co-operative. La collection de la coopérative rassemble des oeuvres de plus de 200 Inuits de la région de Cape Dorset (Kinngait) qui se sont essayés à la création de dessins au fil des années. Quelques-uns ont laissé tomber, dû au manque de talent ou d'intérêt (ou des deux), mais plusieurs ont continué et ont posé les fondations pour le programme de gravure et les éditions annuelles d'estampes à Cape Dorset. Mais le total des dessins achetés par la coopérative excède de loin ceux qui ont été publiés dans les éditions imprimées, et éventuellement un trésor de plus de 100 000 oeuvres originales s'est accumulé. La plupart de celles-ci font l'objet d'un prêt à long terme chez la Collection McMichael d'art canadien à Kleinburg, Ontario, et les autres sont entreposées par la coopérative à Cape Dorset et à Dorset Fine Arts à Toronto.

Malgré la renommée mondiale des artistes de Cape Dorset, avant l'inauguration du centre culturel la triste réalité était que les résidents locaux avaient un accès minimal, voire inexistant, à leur propre patrimoine artistique. L'archive de dessins et d'estampes de la coopérative avait été transférée ailleurs pour raisons de sécurité, c'est-à-dire par crainte d'incendie, qui avait détruit des oeuvres valables à Pangnirtung et à Baker Lake. Heureusement, avec l'ouverture du Kenojuak Cultural Centre les membres de la communauté peuvent désormais profiter de l'espace d'exposition pour admirer les oeuvres créées par leurs aïeuls et leurs parents pour la première fois.

Cette exposition — *Kenojuak Ashevak: Sa vie et son héritage artistique* — est la première exposition provenant de l'Arctique canadien à aller en tournée à l'échelle nationale. Louisa Parr du Kenojuak Cultural Centre et William Huffman de la West Baffin Eskimo Co-operative en sont les co-commissaires, et elle inclut des dessins, ici exposés au public pour la première fois, qui ont inspiré des estampes sur pierre, des lithographies et des gravures d'eau-fortes emblématiques. La communauté de Cape Dorset a aussi été invitée à contribuer avec des objets personnels, des pensées et des anecdotes aussi bien que des oeuvres sur papier qui éclairent davantage le rôle essentiel qu'a joué Kenojuak dans le développement et l'appréciation de l'art et de la culture inuits.

Si Kenojuak était encore en vie pour admirer l'hommage représenté par cette exposition, elle serait particulièrement contente de voir que les nouvelles générations ont désormais l'occasion d'apprécier leur propre culture et de tirer les leçons des efforts que faisaient leurs grand-parents et leurs arrière-grand-parents pour raconter leurs histoires au moyen de l'art. Elle avait toujours la nouvelle génération en tête, et elle pensait constamment à ses enfants, au futur et à sa responsabilité de s'occuper d'eux au mieux de ses capacités. Elle a toujours été reconnaissante de l'opportunité de devenir une artiste professionnelle et de « faire quelque chose de beau. » Après avoir été nommée compagnon de l'Ordre du Canada en 1982, on lui a demandé ce qu'elle pensait de l'honneur : « Je ne penserai pas qu'à moi-même, je penserai aussi à mes enfants. [...] Je ne penserai pas qu'au présent, mais aussi à la signification que cette médaille aura dans le futur, et à ce qu'elle représente, et je me souviendrai que Dieu l'a voulu. C'est ainsi que j'y penserai[27]. »

NOTES

1 Ce nom renvoie à un pont ou une voie qui relie une île au continent à marée basse.

2 Patricia Ryan, « The Autobiography of Kenojuak, » dans *Kenojuak*, Jean Blodgett (Toronto : Firefly Books, 1985), 7.

3 Ryan, « Autobiography of Kenojuak, » 8.

4 Ryan, 8.

5 Ryan, 10.

6 Ryan, 11.

7 Ryan, 12.

8 Peter Pitseolak était un leader dans les camps et était connu comme documentariste et photographe à Cape Dorset. L'histoire de sa vie, *People from Our Side*, fut publiée en 1975 (Edmonton : Hurtig Publishers).

9 Les Inuits commencèrent à se convertir au christianisme au début du vingtième siècle, et aux années 20 le taux d'alphabétisation des adultes était près de 100 %.

10 Ryan, « Autobiography of Kenojuak, » 18.

11 Inuit Tapiriit Kanatami. *Inuit Statistical Profile 2018*, 2018, 11, https://www.itk.ca/wp-content/uploads/2018/08/Inuit-Statistical-Profile.pdf.

12 Le frère d'Harold Pfeiffer, Walter Pfeiffer, était médecin et soignait des patients à l'hôpital.

13 Ryan, « Autobiography of Kenojuak, » 20.

14 West Baffin Eskimo Co-operative, *Dorset 77: Cape Dorset Annual Graphics Collection 1977* (Toronto : M. F. Feheley Publishers, 1977), 48.

15 West Baffin Eskimo Co-operative, *Dorset 79: Twentieth Annual Cape Dorset Graphics Collection* (Toronto : M. F. Feheley Publishers, 1979), 37.

16 Ryan, « Autobiography of Kenojuak, » 20.

17 Jean Blodgett, « The Art of Kenojuak, » dans *Kenojuak* (Toronto : Firefly Books, 1985), 39.

18 Blodgett, « Art of Kenojuak, » 38.

19 Blodgett, 38.

20 Blodgett, 41.

21 Blodgett, 37.

22 Blodgett, 52.

23 Charles Lynch, « Our Brightest Lights, » *Ottawa Citizen*, 25 novembre, 1967.

24 « These Artists Share Bed and Drawing Board, » *Star Weekly* (Toronto), 28 juin, 1969.

25 Marina Jimenez, « Art Is My Job and My Love, » *Globe and Mail* (Toronto), 20 octobre, 2003.

26 Jimenez, « Art Is My Job. »

27 « Inuktitut Asks Kenoajuak [sic] About Her Life as an Artist and Mother, » *Inuktitut Magazine*, janvier 1983, 13.

ᓇᓄᓇᐃᓯᐃᔾᔪᑏᑦ

ᓯᕗᓪᓕᖅᐹᒥ ᐊᓈᓇᒐ ᐊᐅᓪᓚᖅᑲᑎᒋᒋᐅᓚᐅᖅᓯᒪᔪᖅ ᑭᖕᔅᑕᓐ, ᐋᓐᑎᐅᕆᐅᒧᑦ 1991-ᒥ. ᐃᓕᑕᕆᓯᐅᔾᔪᑎᑖᖅᑎᓪᓗᒍ ᐃᓕᓯᒪᔪᕐᔪᐊᖑᒍᑎᒥᒃ ᑯᐃᓐ ᓯᓚᑦᑐᓴᕐᕕᔾᔪᐊᖓᓂᒃ, ᐅᕙᓐᓄᑦ ᒪᓕᑦᑕᐅᒍᒪᓚᐅᖅᓯᒪᔪᖅ ᐊᐃᑉᐸᖅᑲᐳᒪᑦᓯᓂ ᑑᓵᐳᖅᑲᖅᓯᓐᓈᑦ. ᑕᐸᐃᑦᓯᐊᓚᐅᖅᓯᒪᔪᖓ—ᓲᕐᓗ ᓯᓐᓇᑦᑑᒪᔪᖓ! ᐅᕝᕙᐅᑦᓱᖓ, 21-ᑐᐃᓐᓇᕐᓂᒃ ᐅᑭᐅᖅᑲᖅᓱᖓ, ᖃᐅᔨᕆᐅᓚᐅᖅᓯᒪᑦᓱᖓᓗ ᐊᓈᓇᒐ ᐊᒥᓱᐊᓗᓐᓄᑦ ᖃᐅᔨᒪᔭᐅᕆᐊᖓ; ᐊᒥᓱᐊᓗᓐᓂᒃ ᐱᖃᑎᖃᖅᓯᒪᔪᖅ.

ᓇᖏᖅᑲᑎᕆᑦᓱ ᑕᐸᐹᓂ, ᕿᑲᖕᖏᓂᖅᓴᐅᓕᖅᐸᓪᓚᐃᓚᐅᖅᓯᒪᔪᖓ ᐋᓈᓐᓂᒃ. ᐱᒃᑯᕆᑦᓯᐊᓚᐅᖅᓯᒪᔪᖅ. ᐃᓱᒪᓚᐅᖅᓯᒪᙱᑦᑐᖅ ᑕᐃᒪᐃᑦᑐᒥᒃ ᐃᓕᑕᕆᓯᐅᔾᔪᑎᑖᕐᓴᕆᐊᑦᓴᖅ, ᓂᕈᐊᕐᑦᓴᓕᐊᖑᓐᓂᕐᒥ ᖁᕝᕙᐊᓚᐅᖅᓯᒪᔪᖅ. ᓯᓚᑦᑐᓴᕐᕕᔾᔪᐊᖅ ᑕᐸᐃᕐᓇᑦᓯᐊᓚᐅᖅᓯᒪᔪᖅ—ᑕᐃᑦᑐᒧᑦ ᓯᓚᑦᑐᓴᕐᕕᔾᔪᐊᕐᒧᑦ ᐃᑎᓚᐅᖅᓯᒪᓂᐊᖅᑐᓇᓚᐅᖅᓯᒪᙱᑦᑐᖓ, ᐅᖃᖏᓐᓇᓕᓚᐅᖅᓯᒪᔪᖓ, “ᐊᓈᓈ, ᐊᐅᓪᓚᕈᐃᒐᕝᕕᑦ ᑕᐃᒪᐃᑦᑐᒑᓗᓐᓂᒃ ᐅᐸᖅᑲᑦᑕᓲᖑᕕᑦ?” ᑭᐅᑦᑕᖅᑯᖅ ᐅᕙᓐᓄᑦ ᖃᓄᐃᑦᑐᑐᑦᓯᐊᓄᑦ ᐅᐸᖅᑲᑦᑕᖅᓯᒪᓂᖅᓯᓂ.

ᐊᓈᓇᒐ ᓇᒧᑐᐃᓐᓈᓇᐊᑦᓴᖅ ᖁᕝᕙᐊᕆᔭᖅᐸᓪᓚᐃᓚᐅᖅᓯᒪᔪᖅ, ᐅᕙᖓᓕᑦᑕᐅᖅ. ᑭᖕᔅᑕᓐᓕᐊᖅᓯᓄᒃ ᖁᕝᕙᐊᖅᑎᕇᓗᐊᓚᐅᖅᓯᒪᔪᒍᒃ. ᐆᓪᕗ ᕿᑭᖅᑕᖕᒐᓅᓚᐅᖅᓯᒪᔪᒍᒃ ᐊᕙᑖᓂᓗ ᑕᐅᓴᓐ ᕿᑭᖅᑕᐃᑦ, ᐳᓚᕐᑎᑕᐅᑦᓯᑕᓗ ᓄᓇᑏᑦ ᓯᓚᑖᓐᓄᑦ, ᑕᑯᑦᓯᑕ ᐃᒻᒧᑦᓯᐅᕙᕐᓂᒃ, ᓄᕐᕋᐅᓯᕐᓂᒃ ᐊᒻᒪᓗ ᕿᒧᑦᓯᐅᑎᓂᒃ ᓄᓇᒥ. ᐊᐅᓯᐅᓚᐅᖅᓯᒪᒻᒪᑦ, ᑲᔾᔩᓇᖅᑐᐹᓗᒃ.

ᑭᖑᓪᓕᕐᒥ ᐃᖅᑲᐅᒪᕆᒻᒥᔭᖅ ᐊᓚᒡᒐᐃᕆᓯᒪᑦᓱᒍ ᑐᓵᓐᑐᓕᐊᖅᓱᓄᒃ, ᐋᓈᓇᒐ ᐅᓪᓗᓂᐊᖅᑖᖅᑎᑕᐅᑎᓪᓗᒍ ᑲᓇᒥ ᐱᓯᕝᕕᒻᒥ ᐃᓕᑕᕆᓯᐅᓯᒪᔪᕐᔪᐊᓄᑦ, 2001-ᖑᑎᓪᓗᒍ. ᐃᓱᒪᖅᑲᓚᐅᖅᓯᒪᙱᓐᒥᔪᖓ ᖃᖓᓕᒫᑦᓯᐊᖅ ᐋᓈᓇᒐ ᑕᐃᑰᓇ ᐊᐅᐸᖅᑐᒃᑯᑦ ᓇᑎᖅᑯᑦ ᐱᓱᒐᔭᕆᐊᖓ, ᐊᐃᑉᐸᕆᒐᔭᕆᐊᖓᓗ. ᓱᓛᓛᒃ, ᓇᖏᖅᓱᓄᒃ ᑕᐸᐹᓂ ᐊᑯᖕᒐᓐᓂ ᖃᐅᔨᒪᔪᕐᔪᐊᑦ ᐃᓄᐃᑦ, ᕿᑲᐳᓐᓇᑦᓯᓚᐅᖅᓯᒪᙱᑦᑐᖓ, ᐅᖅᑲᓕᒫᕐᒪᓪᓗ, ᐅᖅᑲᐅᑎᑦᓯᒍ, ᐊᓈᓇ ᓱᔪᕐᔫᓯᑲᐃᓐᓇᖏᑦᑐᑎᑦ!” ᑭᐅᑦᑕᖅᑯᖅ, “ᕿᑲᐳᓐᓇᐃᑦᓲᖑᙱᑦᑐᖓ. ᐃᓱᒪᕆᓲᒃᑲ ᐃᓄᑐᐃᓐᓇᐅᕆᐊᖏᑦᑕᐅᖅ, ᑕᐃᒫᑦᑕᐅᖅ ᐃᓄᑐᐃᓐᓇᐅᒐᒪ.”

ᐊᐅᓪᓚᖅᑎᕆᖅᑲᑦᑕᖅᓯᒪᔪᖅ ᐋᓈᓇᒐ ᐊᒥᓱᐊᖅᑎᖅᓱᒍ, ᖁᕝᕙᐊᕆᔭᐃᓐᓇᓇᓯᒪᑦᓱᕆᑦᓗ. ᐊᐅᓪᓚᖅᑲᑦᑕᓇᐊᑦᓴᖅ ᖁᕝᕙᐊᕆᔭᖅᑲᖅᐸᔪᒻᒥᔪᖅ. ᐃᓚᖓᓂ ᑕᖅᑲᔪᐸᔾᔫᖅᑲᑦᑕᔪᔪᖅ, ᑭᓯᐊᓂ ᖁᕝᕙᐊᕆᔭᖅᑲᐃᓐᓇᖅᑰᔭᔪᔪᖅ ᐊᐅᓪᓚᖅᑲᑦᑕᓇᐊᑦᓴᖅ, ᐊᖏᕐᕋᒥᓂᒃ ᓅᓯᒪᑲᐃᓐᓇᓇᐊᖅᓴᖅ. ᓇᓪᓕᐅᓂᖅᓯᐅᓚᐅᖅᓯᒪᔪᖅ 80-ᓂᒃ ᐅᑭᐅᖅᑖᖅᓱᓂ ᒪᒃᒪᐃᑯᑦ ᑕᑯᔭᒐᖅᑲᖅᕕᖓᓂ ᐊᔾᔨᐅᓚᐅᖅᓯᒪᙱᓐᒥᔪᖅ. ᐊᖑᐃᒍᒪᓚᐅᖅᓯᒪᙱᑦᑐᖅ ᑮᓪᒥᒃ ᐱᐅᓗᐊᕐᓂᑯᖓᓄᑦ. ᐊᒥᓱᐊᖅᑎᖅᓯᓄ ᒪᒃᒪᐃᑯᓪᓕᐊᖅᓯᒪᔪᒍᒃ, ᐃᖅᑲᐅᒪᐃᓇᓲᑎᓚᖓᔭᕆᓗ ᑕᐃᓐᓇ ᐊᕐᓇᖅ ᖁᕝᕙᐅᖅᓯᓂ ᐊᓈᓐᓅᓚᐅᖅᓯᒪᔪᖅ. ᑕᐸᐃᑦᓯᐊᓚᐅᖅᓯᒪᔪᖓ; ᑕᑯᒥᐅᓚᐅᖅᓯᒪᔪᖓ ᖁᕝᕙᐊᓪᓚᑎᑦᑐᒥᒃ ᐊᓈᓐᓂᒃ ᑕᑯᒥᐅᕐᒥ. ᐊᓈᓐᓄᑦ ᐅᖅᑲᑦᑕᖅᑯᖓ, “ᐊᓈᓇ, ᕿᐊᒻᒪᓇᓕᖅᑐᖅ!” ᑭᐅᑦᑕᖅᑯᖅ, “ᑕᐃᒪᐃᖁᕕᐅᒐᔪᑦᑐᖓ ᐊᒥᓱᐊᓗᓐᓄᑦ.” ᐃᓄᐃᑦ ᕿᐊᓯᓚᕿᖅᑲᑦᑕᐸᓪᓚᐃᔪᔪᑦ ᑎᑎᖅᑐᒐᖏᓐᓂᒃ ᐱᐅᓴᓗᐊᕐᓂᑯᒧᑦ. ᐅᖅᑲᖅᓯᑎᓪᓗ ᑎᑎᖅᑐᒐᖕᒐᓂᒃ ᓂᐅᕕᖅᑐᒥᓂᐅᓂᖅᓯᑎᒃ ᐊᑭᓐᓇᖅᒨᖅᓯᒍ, ᓲᕐᓗᒨᖅ ᖃᐅᒻᒪᐃᔪᖅ ᐃᓪᓗᓕᒫᒥᒃ.

ᐱᕈᖅᐸᓪᓕᐊᔪᔪᖓ ᑕᑯᓐᓈᖅᓱᒍ ᑎᑎᖅᑐᒐᖅᑐᖅ, ᐅᕙᓐᓄᑦᑐ ᐱᐅᔫᓯᒪᔪᐃᓐᓇᐅᑦᓯᑎᒃ. ᐱᐅᒥᓗᐊᓕᕐᐃᓚᒃᑭᑦ ᐃᓚᖏᑦ ᐅᖅᑲᐅᑎᖅᑲᑦᑕᓚᐅᖅᓯᒪᔪᖅ, “ᓂᐅᕕᐊᖑᒃᑲᑦᑕᐃᓕᐅᒃ ᑯᐊᐸᒃᑯᓐᓄᑦ; ᐱᕆᑐᐃᓐᓇᓕᕈᒃ ᐊᑭᓐᓇᕐᒨᕐᓗᒍ.” ᑭᓯᐊᓂ ᐸᐸᑦᓯᒍᒪᕙᔪᙱᑦᑐᖅ ᑎᑎᖅᑐᒐᕐᒥᓂᒃ ᑎᑎᖅᑐᒐᓕᐊᖑᓯᒪᔪᓂᑦ ᔫᓐᓈᓃᑦ—ᐸᐸᑕᑐᐊᓇᓯᒪᔭᖓ ᐅᐱᔾᔪᐊᖅ. ᐱᐅᒥᓂᖅᐹᓇᓂᖅᐸᔪᔪᖕ ᐃᓱᒪᕆᓚᐅᖅᓯᒪᙱᑦᑲᓗᐊᖅᓯᓂᐅᒃ ᖃᐅᔨᒪᔪᐊᓪᒪᓇᕿᓴᓇᐊᖓ. ᒫᓐᓇ ᐱᒥᓕᖅᑕᖅ ᐅᑉᐱᔾᔪᐊᖅ. ᑕᕝᕙᓂᑦᓴᐃᓐᓇᖅ ᐊᖏᖅᑲᖅᑐᖓ, ᓯᓕᓗ ᐊᑭᓐᓇᕐᒦᑦᓯᓂ, ᐊᒻᒪᓗ ᐃᓚᖏᑦ ᐃᓕᑕᕆᓯᐅᔾᔪᑎᑎᓯᒪᔪᖏᑦ.

ᑎᑎᖅᑐᒐᐃᓐᓇᔪᔪᖅ, ᐅᕙᓂ ᐊᖏᕐᕋᑎᓐᓂ. ᐅᓪᓛᐹᓗᒃᑯᑦ ᒪᑭᒐᐃᒐᒪ, ᑎᑎᖅᑐᓕᓈᖅᑲᑦᑕᔪᔪᖅ. ᐊᖏᕐᕋᕋᐃᕋᒪᓗ ᐃᖅᑲᓇᐃᔭᓈᕋᐃᒪᒪ, ᓯᓕ ᑎᑎᖅᑐᒐᖅᑐᖅ. ᐅᖅᑲᐅᑎᕙᔪᔪᖅ ᕿᓄᐃᑦᑑᒥᐊᕐ, ᐃᓯᕚᖅᑐᖅ ᑎᑎᖅᑐᒐᖅᑐᖅ ᐅᓪᓗᓕᒫᖅ, ᐅᖅᑲᑐᐃᓐᓇᖅᐸᔪᔪᖅ “ᖁᕝᕙᐊᕆᒐᒃᑯ ᑎᑎᖅᑐᒐᓂᕐᒥᓪᓗ ᐊᓪᓚᒃᑲ ᓄᖅᑲᐳᒪᙱᓪᒪᑕ. ᐃᖏᕐᕋᖅᑎᖅᑲᐳᒪᑐᐃᓐᓇᖅᑐᖅ ᑎᑎᖅᑑᑎᒥᒃ.”

ᖃᐅᔨᒪᔪᕐᔪᐊᖑᕆᐊᑦᓴᖅ ᐅᖅᑲᓕᒪᓗᐊᖅᐸᔪᖏᑦᑐᖅ. ᐅᖅᑲᖅᐸᔪᔫᒐᓗᐊᖅ, ᓯᕗᓪᓕᕐᒥ, ᐱᕆᐊᖅᐸᓪᓕᐊᕐᒥ ᑲᑉᐱᐊᓱᑦᓱᓂᓗ, ᐃᓱᒪᖅᑲᓚᐅᖅᓯᒪᓐᓂᖏᑎᐊᑦᓴ ᖃᐅᔨᒪᔪᕐᔪᐊᕈᓴᕆᐊᑦᓴ. ᑭᓯᐊᓂ ᖃᐅᔨᒪᔪᕐᔪᐊᖑᔪᔪᖅ, ᓂᕈᐊᖅᑕᒥᓂᐅᓂᕐᒥᓂᒃ ᔫᑎᒧᑦ ᖃᐅᔨᒪᔪᕐᔪᐊᖑᓗᓂ ᑎᑎᖅᑐᒐᖅᑎᐅᓂᕐᒧᑦ. ᐊᓯᔾᔨᕈᑎᒥᑐᐊᖅᓯᒪᙱᑦᑐᖅ. ᐃᓄᑦᓯᐊᖑᐊᓇᔪᔪᖅ ᐱᖅᑲᓐᓂᖅᑑᑦᓯᓂᓗ. ᖃᐅᔨᕙᐃᕙᒥ ᐃᑲᔪᖅᑕᐅᕆᐊᓕᒻᒥᒃ, ᐃᑲᔪᓇᖅᕕᒥᒍᑦ ᐃᑲᔪᕐᓯᐊᖅᐸᔪᔪᖅ.

ᖃᓂᕇᑦᑐᓪᓚᓇᐅᔪᔪᒃ. ᓄᖅᑲᖅᓯᐸᐅᔪᖓ ᕿᑐᖕᒐᖏᓐᓂ, ᖃᓂᕇᓐᓂᖅᐸᐅᓯᒪᕙᓪᓚᐃᑦᓱᓄᒃ. ᐸᐃᖑᖅᑕᖅ ᖃᐅᑕᒫᑦ. ᐅᓪᓛᒃᑯᑦ ᑐᐸᒍᒪᓪᓕᐸᑦᑐᖓ ᑕᑯᓗᒍᓗ ᐃᑦᓯᕙᔪᖅ ᐅᕙᓂ, ᐳᓛᕐᕕᒻᒥ, ᑎᑎᖅᑐᒐᖅᑐᖅ.

ᓯᓚᖅᑭ ᐋᓯᕙᒃ

ᕿᓐᓄᐊᔪᐊᖅ ᐋᓯᕙᒃ

ᐃᓅᓯᖓ ᕿᒪᐃᔾᔪᑎᖏᑦᓗ

ᕿᓐᓄᐊᔪᐊᖅ ᐋᓯᕙᒃ, ᓯᕗᓪᓕᖅᐸᐅᓯᒪᔪᖅ ᑭᙵᕐᓂ ᐊᕐᓇᓂᒃ ᑎᑎᖅᑐᕐᓂᕐᒥᒃ, ᑲᓇᑕᒥ ᐃᓕᑕᕆᔭᐅᓯᒪᓂᖅᐸᐅᑦᑐᓂ ᐃᓅᑦᑐᓂ ᑎᑎᖅᑐᒐᖅᑎᐅᓯᒪᔪᖅ. ᐊᕐᕌᒍᐃᑦ 50 ᐅᖓᑖᓄᑦ ᑎᑎᖅᑐᒐᖅᑎᐅᓯᒪᔪᖅ, ᑎᑎᖅᑐᒐᖅᑕᒥᓂᖓ ᑎᑎᖅᑐᒐᓕᐊᖑᕆᐊᙳᓚᐅᖅᓯᒪᒻᒪᑦ 1959-ᒥ ᑎᑭᐅᑎᑦᓯᓂ ᐃᓅᓯᖓᑕ ᐃᓱᐊᓄᑦ 2013-ᒥ, ᐊᕐᕌᒍᖅᑲᓕᖅᓯᓂ 85-ᓂᒃ. ᑕᐃᑦᓱᒨᓇ, ᑎᑎᖅᑐᖅᓯᒪᔭᖏᑦ ᑎᑎᖅᑐᒐᓕᐊᖑᕆᓯᒪᔪᑦ ᐅᖓᑖᓂᑦᑐᑦ 300, ᐊᒻᒪᓗ ᖃᒪᐃᑦᓯᓂ ᐅᖓᑖᓃᑦᑐᓂᒃ 2000 ᑎᑎᖅᑐᕐᓂᒃ ᑎᑎᖅᑐᒐᓕᐊᖑᕆᓯᒪᙱᑦᑐᓂᒃ. ᐃᓅᓕᖅᓯᒪᔪᖅ ᐱᕈᖅᓴᓯᒪᑦᓯᓂᓗ ᑕᖅᑳᓂ ᐊᓯᓂ ᐃᓄᑦᑎᑐᑦ ᐱᖅᑯᓯᖅᑲᖅᓯᑎᒃ, ᓄᑦᑕᐸᑦᓯᑎᒃ ᕿᑭᖅᑖᓘᑉ ᓂᒋᐊᓂ; ᐊᖏᕐᕋᖅᑲᖅᓯᑎᒃ ᖃᕐᒪᓂᒃ, ᐃᓪᓗᐃᑦ. ᐊᐅᔭᖅᓯᐅᑏᑦᓗ ᑐᐲᑦ; ᓯᖏᖅᑑᑎᖅᑲᖅᐸᑦᓯᑎᑦᓗ ᐆᒪᔪᕐᓂᒃ ᐱᕈᖅᑐᓂᑦᓗ ᐃᒪᕐᒥᒃ ᓄᓇᒥᑦᓗ ᐆᒪᔾᔪᑎᑦᓴᓂᒃ ᐊᓐᓇᒍᑎᑦᓴᓂᑦᓗ. ᐃᓅᓯᖓ ᐃᓱᓕᒻᒪᑦ, ᐊᖏᕐᕋᐸᖅᑲᔭᔪᖅ ᐅᓪᓗᓯᒥᐅᑎᒥᒃ ᐃᓪᓗᒥ ᑭᙵᕐᓂ, ᐅᖓᓯᑦᑐᒦᑦᑐᑦ, ᐅᑭᐅᖅᑕᖅᑐᒥ ᓄᓇᑖᑦ ᑲᓇᑕᐅᑉ ᐅᑭᐅᖅᑕᖅᑐᖑᓂ ᓄᓇᕗᒻᒥ, ᐃᓕᑕᕆᔭᐅᓯᒪᑦᓯᓂᓗ ᑲᓇᑕᒥ ᐊᓚᖕᒐᐃᓂᖅᐸᐅᖅᑕᐅᕆᐊᖑ ᑎᑎᖅᑎᒐᖅᑎᓂ ᐊᒻᒪᓗ ᐱᖅᑯᓯᕐᒨᖑᔪᓄᑦ ᐃᓕᑕᕆᔭᐅᔾᔪᑎᓂ. ᐅᓂᒃᑳᖓ ᑕᑯᑦᓴᐅᑎᑦᓯᔪᖅ ᐃᓅᓯᐅᕙᓚᐅᖅᑐᒥᒃ ᐊᑐᖅᑕᐅᒍᓐᓃᖅᑐᒥᒃ, ᐊᓯᔾᔨᕐᓂᒻᒪᓇᐅᓯᒪᔪᓂᑦᓗ ᐃᓅᓯᕐᒨᖑᔪᓂᒃ ᓴᓇᑐᓂᕐᒧᑦ ᓯᕗᒧᑎᕆᓯᒪᔭᖏᑦ.

ᑕᐃᑦᓯᒪᓂᒋᐊᖅ ᐊᕐᕌᒍᐃᑦ

ᕿᓐᓄᐊᔪᐊᖅ ᐃᓅᓕᓚᐅᖅᓯᒪᔪᖅ 1927-ᒥ ᐃᑭᖅᓴᒻᒥ, ᓄᓇᑖᑦ ᓂᒋᐊᓃᑦᑐᖅ ᕿᑭᖅᑖᓘᑉ.[1] ᓄᖅᑲᖅᓯᕐᑯᑎᒋᔭᐅᔪᖅ ᓯᓚᖅᑭᑰᓐᓄᑦ ᐅᓯᐊᕐᔪᑰᓐᓄᑦ, ᐊᑦᓯᖅᑕᐅᓯᒪᑦᓯᓂ ᐃᓅᒍᓐᓃᖅᑐᒥᒃ ᐊᑖᑕᑦᓯᐊᒥᓂᒃ ᐊᓈᓇᖓᑕ ᐊᑖᑕᖓᓂᒃ. ᐅᖃᓚᐅᖅᓯᒪᔪᖅ, ᑎᑎᕋᖅᑕᐅᓯᒪᔪᓂ 1985, "ᐃᓄᐃᑦ ᐅᐸᐱᕈᓯᒻᒪᑕ ᐱᐊᕋᖅ ᐊᑦᓯᖅᑕᐅᔪᖅ ᐃᓄᒻᒥᒃ ᑕᐃᓖᑦᓴᐃᓐᓇᖅ ᓇᑦᓕᕆᔭᐅᓂᐊᖅᑐᖅ ᑕᐃᓐᓇᑎᑐᑦ ᐊᑦᓯᖅᑕᐅᔾᔪᑎᖑᒐᑎᑐᑦ. ᒪᖄᒃ ᑕᕐᓂᒃᑯᑦ ᑲᔫᒪᓂᖅᑲᓕᖅᓯᑎᒃ."[2] ᐱᖅᑯᓯᖅᑎᒧᑦ ᑐᓯᖅᕋᐅᓯᖅ ᐊᑎᑯᓗᒃ, ᑕᕐᓂᖓᑕᓐᓄᓂᑦ ᐊᑎᖓ.

ᕿᓐᓄᐊᔪᐊᑉ ᓯᕗᓕᖏᑦ ᐅᐊᓐᓇᖅᐸᓯᖓᓂᙵᓖᖅᓯᒪᔪᑦ ᓯᓈᖅᐸᓯᖓᓂᒃ ᐅᖓᕙᐅᑉ, ᐅᐊᓐᓇᖅᐸᓯᓐᓂᖅᐹᖅ ᐊᕙᑦᑐᖅᓯᒪᓂᖅᔪᐊᖓᓂᒃ ᑯᐸᒃ. ᒫᓐᓇ ᖃᐅᔨᒪᔭᐅᕙᓕᕐᒥᔪᖅ ᓄᓇᕙᒻᒥᒃ, ᐃᒻᒥᒃᑰᖓᑦᓯᓂ ᓂᒋᐊᓂᒃ ᕿᑭᖅᑖᓘᑉ, ᓄᓇᕗᒻᒥ, ᑕᓯᐅᔭᕐᔪᐊᑉ ᐃᑭᓯᖓᓂ. ᑖᒃᑯᐊ ᐊᕙᑦᑐᖅᓯᒪᓂᐅᔪᑦ ᐊᑑᑎᖃᓗᐊᖅᓯᒪᙱᑦᑐᓐᓄᑦ ᐃᓅᖃᑎᒌᓐᓂᖃᖅᑎᑦᑐᒥ ᕿᓐᓄᐊᔪᐊᒃᑯᑦ, ᑭᓯᐊᓂᓕ, ᐅᑎᖅᑕᖁᔭᐸᓐᓂᕐᒪᑕ ᓯᓚᐅᑉ ᖃᖓᐅᓕᕐᓂᖓ ᑐᙵᕙᐅᑦᓯᓂ ᐆᒪᔪᐃᑦᓗ ᐊᒻᒪᓗ ᑎᓕᓯᔾᔪᑎᖏᑦ ᓂᐅᕕᖅᑎᒃᑯᑦ. ᕿᓐᓄᐊᔪᐊᖅ ᐊᐅᓚᔨᒋᐊᙳᖅᑐᖅ ᐃᑳᖅᓯᑎᒃ ᑕᓯᐅᔭᕐᔪᐊᑉ ᐃᑭᓯᖓᓂᒃ ᐊᑖᑕᑦᓯᐊᖓᑕ ᐅᒥᐊᒻᒪᓇᖑᒍᑦ, ᑐᓴᕐᓈᖅᓯᒋᑦ ᖃᑕᐃᑦᑐᐹᑐᐃᑦ ᐊᒃᐸᖅᑯᓗᐃᑦ ᐃᓐᓈᕈᐊᓗᓐᓂᒃ ᐅᑦᑐᑏᑦ ᓯᓈᓂ.

ᐃᖏᖅᖃᑕᐅᖅᓯᒪᔪᑦ ᐳᔾᔪᓇᓕᐊᖅᐸᑦᑕᐊᑦᓯᑎᒃ, ᒫᓐᓇ ᐃᓄᖅᑲᖅᐸᒍᓐᓃᖅᑐᖅ ᕿᑭᖅᑕᖅ ᓯᓈᖓᓂ ᐅᖓᕙᐅᑉ ᑲᖏᖅᓯᖓᑕ ᐅᐊᓐᓇᖅᐸᓯᖓᓂ ᓯᓈᓂ ᑕᓯᐅᔭᕐᔪᐊᑦ. ᓂᐅᕕᖅᑎᒃᑯᑦ ᒪᑐᐃᖅᓯᓚᐅᖅᓯᒪᒻᒪᑕ ᓂᐅᕕᕐᕕᒻᒥᒃ 1929-ᒥ, ᖃᑦᓯᓖᑦᑐ ᐃᓄᐃᑦ ᐃᓚᒌᑦ ᓄᑦᑎᕐᑯᔭᐅᓕᖅᓯᑎᒃ ᒥᑭᒋᓐᓂᐊᖅᑎᐅᕐᑯᔭᐅᑦᑐᑎᒃ ᓂᐅᕕᖅᑎᒃᑯᓐᓄᑦ. ᕿᓐᓄᐊᔪᐊᒃᑯᑦ ᑕᐃᑲᓃᑲᐃᓐᓇᖅᓯᒪᔪᑦ ᐃᓚᒌᑦ 1930-ᖏᓐᓂ, ᐃᖅᑲᐅᒪᔭᖑᑎᒍᑦᑐ, ᐊᑦᓯᕈᕐᓇᖅᑑᓯᒪᔪᖅ. ᐃᖅᑲᐅᒪᓂᖃᖅᑐᖅ ᖃᑦᓯᐅᓖᒻᒪᓂᑦ ᓄᓇᖓᓐᓂ ᐃᐱᔪᒥᓂᐅᕆᐊᖏᑦ ᐅᒥᐊᓵᕈᓗᐊᑦ, ᕿᔪᒃ ᑎᔾᔭᕐᓗᕈᖅᑐᐊᓘᒻᒪᑦ ᐊᖅᑯᑯᓇᖅᑐᐊᓘᑎᓪᓗᒍ ᑖᒃᑯᐊ ᓄᓇᒦᑦᑐᑦ ᑕᐅᑦᑎᓪᓗᒋ ᓱᒋᐊᓪᓚᕝᕙᖅᑲᖅᑎᒃ. ᐊᒦᑦᓗ ᐊᑭᑭᑦᓕᓯᒪᔪᐊᓘᑦᓯᑎᒃ,

ᓄᓇᓕᕐᔪᐊᓕᒫᓪᓗ ᐊᑦᓯᕈᕐᓇᖅᑐᒦᓚᐅᖅᓯᒪᒻᒪᑕ ᓱᓇᓕᒫᑦ ᑲᑦᓯᒪᑎᓪᓗᒋᑦ. ᓈᒻᒪᒋᐅᑎᕙᒐᑎᓪᓗ ᐊᖑᓇᓱᑦᑏᑦ ᓂᐅᕕᖅᑏᓪᓗ, ᐊᑖᑕᖓ ᕿᓐᓄᐊᔪᐊᑦ, ᖃᓄᐃᓕᐅᕈᑎᖅᑕᐅᓚᔪᑉᐸᑦᑐᒥᓂᐅᑦᓯᓂ. ᐊᒥᓱᓄᓪᓗ ᑲᑉᐱᐊᒋᔭᐅᔫᔭᓕᖅᓯᓂ, ᓯᕗᕋᓵᕆᖅᑲᑦᑕᕐᓂᑯᖓᓂᒃ ᐊᓯᕙᖅᑎᐅᖅᑲᑎᒥᓂᒃ ᖃᐅᔨᓵᖓᔭᐅᓕᖅᓯᓂ ᓄᓇᓕᓐᓂ. "ᓯᓚᖅᑭ ᐅᖃᓚᐅᖅᓯᒪᔪᖅ ᑲᐲᐊᓱᓐᓂᕋᖅᓯᓂ—ᑐᑮᕈᓕᕐᓂᕋᖅᓱᒍ." ᕿᓐᓄᐊᔪᐊᖅ ᐃᖅᑲᐅᒪᔭᖅ.[3]

ᐅᓱᐊᖅᔫᕐ ᐃᓱᒪᖓ ᓈᒻᒧᓐᓃᑉᐸᓪᓕᐊᑐᐃᓐᓇᓕᓚᐅᖅᓯᒪᔪᖅ ᐳᔾᔪᓇᕐᒦᑦᓱᑎᒃ. ᐅᑉᐸᑦᑕᐅᓕᕋᑕᓚᐅᖅᓯᒪᔪᖅ, ᐱᖓᓱᓄᑦ ᐊᖑᑎᓄᑦ ᓇᒻᒥᓂᖅ ᐱᔭᐅᓕᖅᓱᓂ ᐅᑉᐸᓚᔭᐅᑦᓱᓂ ᐊᓂᕙᓪᓕᐊᑎᓪᓗᒍ ᐃᓪᓗᒥᓂᒃ. ᖁᑭᖅᑕᐅᑦᓱᓂ ᑐᖁᑕᐅᓯᒪᔪᖅ ᑎᒥᖓᓗ ᐃᒫᓄᑦ ᐃᕆᑕᐅᑦᓱᓂ, ᐱᖁᑎᓕᒫᑦᓯᐊᖏᓐᓄ ᕿᒻᒥᖏᓐᓄ. ᐃᓅᓯᕐᒥ ᐃᓚᖓᓂ, ᕿᓐᓄᔪᐊᖅ ᓇᓗᓇᐃᖅᓯᓯᒪᔪᖅ ᐊᑖᑕᖓᑕ ᐃᓅᒍᓐᓃᕐᓂᒥᓂᖓ ᑐᑭᓯᓇᖅᑐᑦᓴᐅᖏᑦᑑᓪᓗᐊᖅ ᐃᓚᖏᓐᓄᑦ, ᑭᓱᐊᓂᓕ ᑕᐃᑦᓱᒪᓂ, "ᐃᓄᐃᑦ ᒪᓕᒐᖏᑦ ᐊᑐᖅᑕᐅᕙᔪᒻᒪᑕ ᓴᐃᒪᓂᖅᑲᖅᑯᔭᐅᑦᓯᑎᒃ ᒪᑭᒪᑦᓯᐊᕈᓐᓇᖅᑯᓐᓄᑎᓐᓄ ᓄᓇᖅᑲᑏᑦ. ᑭᓇᑐᐃᓐᓇᖅ ᐊᑭᕋᖅᑐᖅᓂᐅᓴᓗᐊᖅᑐᖅ, ᓇᒻᒥᓂᕐᔫᓐᓃᑦ ᓇᔪᒻᒥᒍᓐᓇᐃᓪᓕᔪᖅ, ᐊᓯᐊᑕᔫᓐᓃᑦ ᕿᓐᓂᖏᓐᓂᒃ ᑎᒍᐃᓐᓇᖅᓯᒪᔪᖅ, ᐅᓗᕆᐊᓇᖅᓱᒍᓐᓇᕐᒪᑦ ᓄᓇᓕᓕᒫᑦᓯᐊᓄᑦ. ᑕᐃᒪᐃᑦᑐᖅᑲᕋᐃᒻᒪᑦ, ᐃᓄᒃ ᐊᑕᐅᓯᖅ ᐊᑕᐅᓯᐅᙱᑦᑐᕐᔫᓐᓃᑦ, ᓇᒻᒥᓂᖅ ᐊᐅᓚᑦᑐᖅ ᐅᕝᕙᔫᓐᓃᑦ ᓇᓗᓇᐃᖅᑕᐅᓯᒪᔪᖅ ᓄᓇᖅᑲᑎᒌᓄᑦ, ᑲᒪᒋᐊᖅᑲᑦᑕᖅᓯᒪᔪᑦ ᐅᓗᕆᐊᓇᖅᓯᓯᒪᔪᓂᒃ".[4]

ᓯᓚᖅᑭᒃᑯᑦ ᕿᑐᕐᖓᓖᑦ ᐊᐅᓪᓛᓕᓚᐅᖅᓯᒪᔪᑦ ᐳᔾᔪᓇᕐᒥᒃ ᑕᐃᑲᓂ ᐊᐅᔭᖓᓂ ᐅᑎᕐᓵᕋᑎᓪᓗ. ᐃᒡᓗᕕᓕᐊᖅᓱᑎᒃ ᐅᑕᖅᑭᓚᐅᖅᓯᒪᔪᑦ ᐊᕐᖌᑕᒫᑦ ᑎᑭᑉᐸᑦᑐᒥᒃ ᓂᐅᕕᖅᑎᒃᑯᑦ ᐅᒥᐊᕐᔪᐊᖓᓐᓂᒃ ᓇᒡᑯᐱᒥᒃ, ᑕᒡᕗᓇ ᐅᑎᓕᓚᐅᖅᓯᒪᑦᓱᑎᒃ ᑭᙵᕐᓄᑦ ᐃᓚᒥᓂ ᐊᑲᕐᓂᓕᖅᓱᑎᒃ ᐱᖃᓇᕐᓂᔭᒥᓂᓗ. ᑐᑭᓯᓂᐊᖅᑎᒻᒪᕐᓄᑦ ᑐᑭᓯᐊᕈᑕᐅᓯᒪᕗᓚᓗᐊᖅ ᐃᓄᐊᖅᑕᐅᓂᒥᓂᖅ ᐳᔾᔪᓇᕐᒥ ᑭᓱᐊᓂ ᐃᖅᑲᖅᑐᕋᑦᓴᔭᕈᖅᑐᖃᓚᐅᖅᓯᒪᙱᑦᑐᖅ.

ᕿᓐᓄᐊᔪᐊᖅ ᓂᕕᐊᖅᓯᐊᖑᑦᓯᓂ ᐱᕈᖅᓴᓕᓚᐅᖅᓯᒪᔪᖅ ᓇᒥᑐᐃᓐᓇᖅ ᓄᓇᓂ ᐊᓯᓂ ᓂᕆᐊᓂ ᕿᑭᖅᑖᓗᐸ, ᐊᓈᓇᑦᓯᐊᒥᓃᕙᔪᑦᓯᓂ ᓇᓪᓕᑦᑕᒥᓂ, ᖃᐅᔨᓵᕐᒥ. ᑲᔾᔭᓇᔾᔭᖃᓗᐊᖅᑐᖅ ᑕᒪᑦᓯᒥᖓ ᐃᖅᑲᐅᒪᕆᐊᑦᓴᖅ: "ᑎᓪᓕᐊᕋᓵᖅᓯᐅᖅᑲᑦᑕᕐᓂᖅ ᐆᒪᔪᕐᓂᓪᓗ ᐱᑕᕋᑕᕋᒪᒐᓗᐊᖅᓱᑎᑦ;" ᐱᙳᐊᖅᑲᕐᓂᖅ ᐱᙳᐊᓪᓚᑑᑎᕈᓗᐊᓂᒃ ᓴᓇᓯᒪᔪᓂᒃ ᑎᔅᓯᓗᑯᓂᒃ ᕿᔪᓐᓂᒃ, ᓴᓇᐅᒐᖕᓂᐊᓂᒃ ᐊᖓᖓᑕ, ᓂᕕᐊᖅᓯᐅᑉ; ᐃᓕᓐᓂᐊᐸᑦᓯᓂᓗ ᐊᓈᓇᑦᓯᐊᒥᓂᒃ ᒥᖅᓱᕐᓂᕐᒥᒃ ᐊᑐᖅᓱᑎᒃ ᑐᑦᑐᔾᔭᓂᒃ ᐃᕐᓗᓂᒃ ᒥᖅᓱᑕᖅᑲᖏᓐᓄ ᐃᓪᓚᑦᑕᔅᔭᐃᖅᓯᒪᑦᓱᑎᒃ ᑭᓗᖏᑦ.[5]

ᐊᖏᕋᖅᑲᐃᓐᓇᓚᐅᖅᓯᒪᔪᖅ ᖄᒪᒥᒃ—ᐊᑦᓇᑕᐃᑦᑐᕌᓗᒃ ᓇᐸᖅᓯᒪᔪᖅ ᕿᔪᒥᒃ ᐊᕙᓗᖅᑲᖅᓯᓂ ᓇᑎᖅᑲᖅᓯᓂᓗ, ᖄᓕᖅᓯᒪᑦᓯᓂ ᑐᐱᖕᓴᔭᒥᒃ ᓂᕈᒻᒪᖅᑯᓯᖅᓯᒪᑦᓯᓂ ᐃᕕᑦᓯᑲᖅᓂᒃ. ᓯᒃᑭᑦᑕᓕᐊᓇᓯᒪᔪᑦ ᐊᐳᑏᑦ ᐊᕙᑖᓃᑦᓯᑎᒃ ᓯᓚᑖᓂ ᓂᕈᒻᒪᖅᑯᑎᒃᑲᓐᓂᐅᑦᓯᑎᒃ. "ᐃᓗᐊᓂ ᐆᓇᑐᐊᒥᒃ ᐊᑲᖅᑎᓇᖅᑐᖅ, ᐅᖅᑯᓴᐅᑎᑦᑎᓐᓃᙯᕙᓪᓗᑦᑐᖅ ᖁᓪᓕᖅᒥᒃ" ᐅᔭᕋᖅᒥᒃ ᓴᓇᓯᒪᔪᖅ ᖁᓪᓕᖅ ᓇᑦᓯᖅᒧᑦ ᐅᖅᓱᖅᑐᖅᑐᖅ. ᐊᐅᔭᒃᑯᑦ ᓄᑎᐸᑦᓯᑎᒃ ᑐᐱᑦᓴᔭᒥᒃ ᑐᐱᓕᐊᕆᓯᒪᔭᖕᖏᓄᑦ ᐊᖅᓇᐃᑦ, ᐅᑎᖅᐸᑦᓯᑎᒃ ᖃᖅᒪᒧᑦ ᐅᑭᐅᒃᑯᑦ. "ᐆᒪᕙᓯᐊᕈᑎᓕᒫᒍᑦ ᐱᔭᓇᐊᖅᑲᑦᑕᖅᓯᒪᕙᑦᑎᒍ ᐃᒪᖅᒥᒃ ᓄᓇᒥᓪᓗ"[6]

1946-ᒥ, ᕿᓐᓄᐊᔪᐊᖅ ᓄᓕᐊᖅᑖᖑᓚᐅᖅᓯᒪᒐᖅ, ᑐᓴᕝᕙᐅᑦᓯᓂ ᐃᓄᐃᑦ ᐱᖅᑯᓯᖓᑦ, ᐊᖑᒻᒧᑦ ᐊᑎᓕᒻᒧᑦ ᔫᓂᐆ. ᐊᐃᑉᐸᖅᑖᕐᓵᖅᑯᔭᐅᔫᓪᓕ ᐃᓚᖏᓐᓄᑦ ᓇᒻᒥᓂᖏᓐᓄᑦ ᔫᓂᐆᑉ ᐊᖓᔪᐊ, ᑕᐅᑭ, ᓄᓕᐊᖓᓗ ᐃᓕᓴᐱ, ᐅᖃᓕᐊᖅᑐᖅᑎᑕᐅᓚᐅᖅᓯᒪᒻᒪᑎᑦ ᕿᓐᓄᐊᔪᐊᑉ ᐊᓈᓇᖓᓄᑦ ᐊᖓᖏᓐᓄᓪᓗ. ᕿᓐᓄᐊᔪᐊᖅ ᓯᓂᙳᐊᓚᐅᖅᓯᒪᔪᖅ ᑲᑎᒪᑎᓪᓗᒋᑦ ᑲᐱᐊᓱᑦᑐᒥᓂᐅᓂᕋᖅᓯᓂ, ᑭᓱᐊᓂ ᐃᖅᑲᐅᒪᒋᓪᓗᓂ ᔫᓂᐆᒥᒃ ᑕᑯᒋᐅᖅᓯᓂ ᑮᓐᓂᖅᓂ—ᐱᓗᐊᖅᑐᒥᒃ "ᖁᕕᐊᓱᐊᑦᑕᕋᓗᐊ ᑕᑉᐸᑦᑕᐅᓂᖓ, ᑕᑭᔪᐊᓘᒥᐊᖓ," ᐅᖃᖅᑐᖅ ᕿᓐᓄᐊᔪᐊᖅ. "ᐱᓇᓱᐊᕈᓯᕐᓂᒃ ᖃᑦᓯᓕᑳᓂᒃ ᑲᑎᒪᓕᖅᓱᖓ, ᑲᑦᓱᖓᔪᐸᕐᔫᓚᐅᖅᓯᒪᔪᖓ ᐅᕙᒃᑳᖑᓪᓗᖓ ᔫᓂᐆ ᐊᐃᑉᐸᕆᒋᐊᖓ. ᖃᐃᓯᑐᐊᕋᐃᒻᒪᑦ ᐅᔭᕋᕐᓄᑦ ᒥᓪᓗᖅᐸᓚᐅᖅᓯᒪᔭᕋ. ᐃᔪᕋᓚᓯᑐᐃᓐᓇᐸᑦᓯᓂ, ᓴᐱᓕᙵᑦᑐᖅ. ᐅᖓᕆᓕᕐᔫᒥᓕᓚᐅᖅᓯᒪᔭᕋ ᐃᓄᑦᓯᐊᐸᕐᔫᑦᓯᓂᓗ,"
ᕿᓐᓄᐊᔪᐊᖅ ᐃᖅᑲᐅᒪᒐᖅ.[7]

ᕿᓐᓄᐊᔪᐊᒃᑯᒃ ᔫᓂᐆᒃᑯᒃ ᓄᓇᖅᑲᓕᓚᐅᖅᓯᒪᔫᒃ ᓴᕐᕕᒥ, ᓯᓕᑦᑕᐅᖅ ᓄᓇᕆᔭᐅᓚᔪᑦᑐᒥ ᓂᕆᐊᓂ ᕿᑭᖅᑖᓗᐸ ᓯᓈᖓᑕ, ᑭᓱᐊᓂ ᐊᕋᒍᐸ ᐃᓗᐊᓂ, ᖃᐃᖅᑯᔭᐅᓚᐅᖅᓯᒪᔫᒃ ᐲᑕ ᐱᑦᓯᐅᑳᕐᒧᑦ ᓄᓇᖅᑲᑎᒋᒍᒪᓪᓗᓂᒋᑦ ᓄᓇᒥᓂ, ᕿᐊᒃᑑᕐᒥ, ᑲᓇᓐᓇᖅᐸᓯᖓᓐᓂ ᑮᖓᐃᑦ.[8] ᖁᕕᐊᓇᖅᑐᕌᓘᓚᐅᖅᓯᒪᔪᖅ, ᐃᕐᓂᑖᕆᐅᕈᑎᖓᓪᓗ, ᔭᐃᒥᓯ ᐃᓅᓕᓚᐅᖅᓯᒪᔪᖅ ᑕᐃᑲᓂ 1947-ᒥ. ᑭᐅᒃᑑᖅ ᑲᔾᔭᓇᖅᑐᕌᓗᒃ, ᓴᐳᑎᔭᐅᓯᒪᑦᓯᐊᖅᑐᖅ ᖃᓂᑦᑐᕌᓘᑦᓯᓂᓗ ᑕᕆᐅᕐᒧᑦ, ᐅᖓᓯᑦᑑᒻᒥᒐᓂᓗ ᑮᖓᕐᓂᒃ. ᑎᕆᒐᓐᓂᐊᓕᕌᓘᑦᓯᓂᓗ. 1947 ᐊᔾᔨᐅᖏᑦᑑᓚᐅᖅᓯᒪᒻᒥᔪᖅ ᐊᓯᐊᒍᑦ, ᓂᐅᕕᖅᑎᒃᑯᑦ ᐅᒥᐊᕐᔪᐊᖓᑦ ᓇᒡᑯᐱ ᑭᕙᓚᐅᖅᓯᒪᒻᒪᑦ ᓯᓈᖓᓂ ᑮᖓᐃᑦ—ᐊᑑᑎᓚᔪᐃᒧᑦ ᐃᖅᑲᐅᒪᔭᕙᓐᓃᑦ ᐃᓚᖏᓐᓄᑦ ᓯᓚ ᑎᑎᖅᑐᓚᖅᑏᑦ. ᔭᓚᓐᓂᖓ ᖁᕕᐊᓇᓚᐅᖅᓯᒪᙱᑦᑑᓪᓗᐊᖅ, ᑭᓱᐊᓂ ᐃᑲᕈᒦᑲᐃᓐᓇᑎᓪᓗᒍ ᐃᓄᐃᑦ ᓇᐆᖅᑖᕆᒍᓐᓇᖅᑕᒥᓂᒃ ᓇᐆᖅᑕᔪᒻᒪᑕ. ᐲᑕ ᐃᓪᓗᓕᐅᓕᖅᓱᓂ ᕿᔪᒻᒥᒃ ᑭᐊᒃᑑᒥ, ᓱᓕᓗ ᐊᓚᒃᑲᐃᓕᒃᑲᓐᓂᖅᓱᓂ ᐊᖓᔪᖅᑳᐅᓵᖑᓂᖓ

ᓯᕗᓕᖅᑎᒪᓇᐅᓂᖓᓗ. ᐊᔾᔨᓕᐅᖅᑕᐅᑎᐊᙳᖅᓯᒪᔫᒃ ᕿᓐᓄᐊᔪᐊᒃᑯᒃ ᔫᓂᕝᕘᒃᑯᒃ ᐲᑕᒧᑦ ᑕᐃᑦᓯᒨᓇ.

ᕿᓐᓄᐊᔪᐊᒃᑯᒃ ᔫᓂᕝᕘᒃᑯᒃ ᖃᑦᓯᓚᖀᓂᒃ ᐊᕐᕋᒍᓂᒃ ᑭᐊᒃᑑᒥᓚᐅᖅᓯᒪᔫᒃ ᐊᑲᕐᓇᑦᓯᐊᖅᓯᑎᒃ. 1949–ᒥ ᑲᑎᑎᑕᐅᓚᐅᖅᓯᒪᔫᒃ ᐋᖓᓕᒃᑲᒃᑯᑦ ᐊᔪᓂᖅᑐᐃᔾᔭᖓᓐᓄᑦ ᑎᑭᑲᐃᓐᓇᑉᐸᑦᑐᒧᑦ ᓄᓇᓕᓐᓄᑦ ᐊᔪᓂᖅᑐᐃᓕᐊᖅᑐᖅᓯᓂ ᑲᑎᑎᑦᓯᓕᐊᖅᑐᖅᓯᓂ ᕖᖅᑎᑦᓯᓕᐊᖅᑐᖅᓯᓂᓗ, ᕿᑐᕐᖓᖅᑖᖓᓪᓗ ᓄᑲᖅᓯᖅ, ᒥᐊᓕ, ᐃᓅᓕᑦᑕᖅᑯᖅ.[9] ᑕᒪᓐᓇᐅᑎᓪᓗᒍ ᖃᓄᑐᐃᓐᓇᑦᓯᐊᖅ ᐊᓱᐃᑉᐸᓪᓕᐊᓂᒃᑰᓚᐅᖅᓯᒪᔪᑦ ᐊᑦᑐᖅᑕᐅᕙᓪᓕᐊᓕᖅᓯᓂ ᐱᖅᑯᓯᖅᑎᒍᑦ ᐃᓅᓯᑐᖃᖅ, ᐱᖃᓯᐅᑎᑦᓯᓂ ᐳᕙᓪᓗᓐᓂᖅ ᐃᓄᐃᑦ ᓄᓇᖓᓐᓃᑦᑐᖅ. 1951–ᖑᑎᓪᓗᒍ, ᕿᓐᓄᐊᔪᐊᖅ ᖃᐅᔨᓕᓚᐅᖅᓯᒪᔪᖅ ᐳᕙᖏᑦᑕ ᐊᔾᔨᓕᐅᖅᑕᐅᔾᔪᑎᒥᓂᖏᑦ 1950–ᒥ ᖃᐅᔨᔭᐅᒍᑎᒋᓐᓂᓇᐊᖏᑦ ᐳᕙᓪᓗᑦᑐᖅ, ᐊᐅᓪᓚᖅᑎᑕᐅᓕᖅᓯᓂᓗ ᐸᒃ ᓴᕖᖅᑦ ᐋᓐᓂᐊᕙᒻᒧᑦ ᑯᐸᐃ ᓯᑎᒥ.

ᕿᓐᓄᐊᔪᐊᖅ ᐋᓐᓂᐊᕙᒻᒦᓚᐅᖅᓯᒪᔪᖅ ᐊᕐᕋᒍᓂᒃ ᐱᖓᓱᓂᒃ, ᐊᖏᕐᕋᕈᓐᓇᖅᓯᔫᒥᕐᕋᑕᖅᓯᓂ 1955–ᒥ. 1953–ᖑᑎᓪᓗᒍ ᑐᓴᓚᐅᖅᓯᒪᔪᖅ ᕿᑐᕐᖓᖏᑦ ᒪᕐᕉᒃ, ᔭᐃᒥᓯᒃᑯᒃ ᒥᐊᓕᒃᑯᒃ, ᐃᓅᒍᓐᓃᕐᓂᓇᐊᖏᑦ. ᐃᒻᒥᓅᖓᔪᓂᒃ ᐅᓂᒃᑳᖏᓐᓂ, ᐅᖃᖅᓯᒪᔪᖅ ᐊᑦᓯᕋᕐᓇᖅᑑᓯᒪᔪᒥᒃ ᐃᓅᓯᕐᒥᓂ: "ᔫᓂᕝᕘ, ᑎᑎᕋᖅᓯᓂ ᐅᕙᓐᓄᑦ, ᐊᔪᐃᓐᓇᓚᐅᖅᓯᒪᔪᖅ ᑭᑦᓵᖑᑐᐃᓐᓇᕐᑯᔨᒐᓂ ᒪᕐᕉᓐᓂᒃ ᕿᑐᕐᖓᕕᓐᓂᒃ ᑭᓯᐊᓂ ᐅᕙᓐᓂᒃ ᐃᒻᒥᓂᒃ ᐃᓱᒪᖅᑲᖢᕐᑯᔨᑦᓯᓂ ᖃᓄᐃᒍᓐᓃᕐᑯᔨᒻᒧᑦ ᐅᑎᕈᓐᓇᖅᓯᕐᑯᔨᓪᓗᓂ ᑭᙵᕐᓄᑦ. ᐊᑦᓯᕋᕐᓇᖅᑐᒃᑰᓕᓇᓕᐅᖅᓯᒪᓗᒍ ᑕᒪᑦᓯᒧᖓ, ᕿᑐᕐᖏᐅᓕᐅᖅᓯᒪᒍᒪᐃᓕᐅᖅᓯᒪᔪᖓ. ᐃᓄᐃᑦ ᐋᓐᓂᐊᕕᒦᑦᑐᑦ ᐅᕙᓐᓂᒃ ᑐᑦᓯᐅᔾᔨᓕᐅᖅᓯᒪᔪᑦ."[10]

ᕿᓐᓄᐊᔪᐊᖅ ᕿᑐᕐᖏᐅᑲᓐᓂᓚᐅᖅᓯᒪᔪᖅ ᑎᒍᐊᖅᓯᒪᑦᓯᓂᓗ ᐊᒥᓯᒃ, 14 ᑲᑎᑦᓯᑎᒃ. ᐅᑎᕋᑖᑦᓯᐊᖅᓯᓂ ᑭᙵᕐᓄᑦ ᑎᒍᐊᓚᐅᖅᓯᒪᔪᖅ ᐊᕐᓇᖅᑯᕐᒥᒃ, 1956–ᖑᑎᓪᓗᒍ. ᑕᐃᒫᑦᑕᐅᖅ ᐃᓄᐃᑦ ᐱᖅᑯᓯᓕᒪᒍ ᖃᓄᐃᓐᓂᐅᔪᓪᓗ ᑐᙵᕙᐅᑦᓯᑎᒃ, ᐃᓚᖏᑦ ᕿᑐᕐᖓᖏᑦ ᑎᒍᐊᖅᑖᓕᓯᒪᔭᖏᑦ, ᐃᓚᖏᑦ ᑎᒍᐊᖅᑖᖑᓯᒪᔪᑦ, ᐃᓚᖏᓪᓗ ᐸᐸᑦᓯᓂᒋᑦ ᕿᓐᓄᐊᔪᐊᒃᑯᒃ ᔫᓂᕝᕘᒃᑯᒃ. 7 ᕿᑐᕐᖓᖏᑦ ᐱᐊᕋᐅᑦᓯᑎᒃ ᐃᓅᒍᓐᓃᖃᑦᑕᖅᓯᒪᔪᑦ ᓄᑕᕌᐱᐅᑦᓯᑎᓪᓘᓐᓃᑦ. ᑕᐃᑦᓯᒨᓇ ᐃᓄᐃᑦ ᓄᓇᖏᓐᓂ ᐃᓅᑯᑖᙳᓂᖅᐸᐅᖃᑦᑕᓚᐅᖅᓯᒪᓪᓚᑕ ᐱᐊᕋᐃᑦ ᑲᓇᑕᒥ. ᒫᓐᓇᓕ ᐊᐸᐸᑦᓕᖅᓯᒪᓕᖅᑐᖅ, ᐃᓅᓇᓱᐊᕐᓂᖅ ᐱᕖᓪᓕᖅᓯᒪᓪᓚᑦ ᐋᓐᓂᐊᖅᑐᓕᓴᐅᓂᕐᓗ, ᑭᓯᐊᓂ ᓱᓕ ᐱᐊᕋᐃᑦ ᐃᓅᒍᓐᓃᖃᑦᑕᕐᓂᖏᑦ ᓱᓕ ᐱᖓᓱᐊᖅᑎᓪᓗᐊᖅᑐᒥᒃ ᖁᕝᕙᓯᓐᓂᖅᓴᐃᑦ ᐃᓄᐃᑦ ᑕᑯᓈᖅᓱᒋᑦ ᐃᓅᙱᑦᑐᑦ ᑲᓇᑕᒥᐅᑦ.[11]

ᑎᑎᖅᑐᒐᖅᑎᕈᖅᐸᓪᓕᐊᓂᖅ

ᕿᓐᓄᐊᔪᐊᖅ ᒪᒥᓴᓂᖃᖅᓯᓂ ᐸᖅ ᓴᕖᖅᑦ ᐋᓐᓂᐊᕙᒻᒥ, ᒥᖅᓱᕋᑦᓴᓂᒃ ᐊᐃᑦᑐᖅᑕᐅᓚᐅᖅᓯᒪᔪᖅ ᖄᑐᐃᓐᓇᕐᓂᐊᖏᒻᒪᑦ. ᒥᖅᓱᖅᓯᑎᐅᓕᕇᕋᓗᐊᖅᓯᓂ, ᓴᓇᔭᖏᑦᑐ ᑕᑯᔭᕐᕈᒋᓕᖅᓯᓂᒋᑦ ᑲᓇᑕᒥ ᓴᓇᙳᐊᖅᑎᐅᑉ Hᐃᐅᕈᑦ ᕗᐃᕗ, ᑕᐃᑦᓯᒨᓇ ᐃᖅᑲᐃᓕᓴᖅᑎᑦᓯᔨᐅᑦᓯᓂ ᐋᓐᓂᐊᕙᒻᒥ.[12] ᑕᑯᔭᕐᕈᒋᓚᐅᖅᓯᒪᔭᖏᑦ ᕿᑐᕐᖓᙳᐊᓕᐊᖏᑦ ᐊᓐᓄᕌᙳᐊᕋᓛᓪᓗ, ᒥᖅᓱᖅᓯᒪᔪᑦ ᑭᓗᑦᓚᑐᑦᓯᐊᓇᑦᑐᐊᔫᑦᓯᑎᒃ. 1955–ᖑᑎᓪᓗᒍ, ᕗᐃᕗ ᒪᓕᓚᐅᖅᓯᒪᔪᖅ ᕿᓐᓄᐊᔪᐊᒥᒃ ᐊᓯᖏᓐᓂᓪᓗ ᐃᓄᓐᓂᒃ ᑭᙵᕐᓄᑦ ᑲᕙᒪᑐᖅᑲᒃᑯᑦ ᐅᒥᐊᕐᔪᐊᖓᑦᑎᒍᑦ *ᒪᑦᑖᕝᕕᒃ ᓰᑏ Hᐊᐅ*.

ᕿᓐᓄᐊᔪᐊᖅ ᒥᖅᓱᕈᓐᓇᑦᓯᐊᖅᑦᑕᖅᓯᒪᓚᐅᓗᐊᖅᓯᓂ ᒪᒥᓴᕐᓗᓂ, ᐅᖃᖅᓯᒪᔪᖅ ᐃᒻᒥᓅᖓᔪᓂᒃ ᐅᓂᒃᑳᓕᐊᖏᓐᓂ ᐃᓕᓐᓂᐊᒐᓐᓂᓚᐅᖅᓯᒪᓕᕐᓂᐊᖅᑲᕐᓂᕋᖅᓯᓂ ᒥᖅᓱᓇᐊᑦᓴᖅ ᐊᑐᕐᓗᓂ ᑐᑦᑐᔭᓂᒃ ᐃᕗᓗᓂᒃ ᐅᑎᕋᒥ ᐋᓐᓂᐊᕙᒻᒦᓚᐅᖅᓯᓂ. ᒥᖅᓱᖅᑦᑕᖅᑲᓐᓂᓯᒪᒥ ᓄᓇᖅᑲᖅᑳᖅᓯᒪᔪᑦ ᓴᓇᓲᖏᓐᓂᒃ, ᐃᓄᙳᐊᓕᐅᖅᓯᓂ, ᑲᒦᑦ, ᓇᑦᓯᕋᔭᐃᑦ ᐊᑭᓐᓇᕐᒥᐅᑕᐃᑦ ᓂᕈᒥᐊᒐᐃᑦᓗ ᐅᑭᑦᓯᒪᔪᓂᒃ ᑕᖅᓴᖅᑲᐅᖅᓯᑎᒃ, ᑖᒃᑯᑎᒨᓇ ᓴᓇᔭᖏᑦᑎᒍᑦ ᐃᓱᒪᓯᓇᒍᓐᓇᖅᑕᖏᑦ ᑎᑎᖅᑐᒐᕈᓐᓇᖅᑕᖏᑦᓗ ᓵᖅᑭᓇᐊᙳᓚᐅᖅᓯᒪᔪᑦ. ᓴᓇᖅᑦᑕᕐᓂᖓ ᐃᐸᐱᕆᔭᐹᓗᕆᑦᑕᖅᑲᐅᒃ ᐃᐅᓪᒪ Hᐃᐅᔅᑕᓐ, ᐅᐃᕇᒃ ᔭᐃᒻᔅ Hᐃᐅᔅᑕᓐᑯᒃ, ᐱᕆᐊᖅᑎᑦᓯᓚᐅᖅᓯᒪᔫ ᓯᕗᓪᓕᖅᐹᒥᒃ ᓴᓇᐅᒐᐃᔭᕝᕕᒥᒃ ᑭᙵᕐᒥ 1956–ᖑᑎᓪᓗᒍ. ᒥᑭᑦᐊᕐᓂᐊᕐᓂᖅ ᓱᖏᖅᑰᑎᑦᓴᐅᒍᓐᓂᓚᐅᖅᓯᒪᓪᓚᑦ ᑮᓇᐅᔭᓕᐅᕋᓱᐊᕈᑎᑐᐊᓇᓗᒍ, ᓴᓐᖑᐊᖅᑕᖅᓂᖅ ᐊᓯᖏᓐᓂᓪᓗ ᓴᓇᖅᑦᑕᖅᓂᖅ ᑎᓕᐅᓇᔾᔭᑕᐅᓕᓚᐅᖅᓯᒪᔪᖅ ᑲᓇᑕᐅᑉ ᒐᕙᒪᑐᖅᑲᒃᑯᖏᓐᓄᑦ ᒥᑭᑦᐊᕐᓂᐊᕐᓂᕐᒥᒃ ᐃᓇᖏᑎᑕᐅᑦᓯᓂ. ᔭᐃᒻᔅ ᐊᖑᑎᓂᒃ ᓯᓕᓐᖅᑎᖅᑲᖅᑎᓪᓗᒋᑦ ᓯᓇᑐᐃᓐᓇᕐᓂᒃ, ᐱᖅᑯᓯᐅᑎᑦᓯᑎᒃ ᐆᑦᑐᕋᓇᐊᙳᐊᕆᑦ ᑎᑎᖅᑐᒐᓕᐅᕐᓂᕐᒥᒃ, ᐃᐅᓪᒪ ᓴᓇᐅᒐᓕᐅᕝᕕᒥᒃ ᐱᕆᐊᖅᑎᑦᓯᓚᐅᖅᓯᒪᔪᖅ ᐊᕐᓇᓄᑦ. "ᐊᕐᓇᑯᑖᒃ, ᐊᑦᓯᐅᑎᕆᓚᐅᖅᓯᒪᔭᕗᑦ ᐃᐅᓪᒪ Hᐃᐅᔅᑕᓐᒧᑦ, ᑐᑭᓕᒃ 'ᐊᕐᓇᖅ ᑕᑭᔪᖅ', ᑎᓕᐅᓇᓚᐅᖅᓯᒪᓪᓚᑦ ᐃᓄᓐᓂᒃ ᐊᕐᓇᓂᒃ ᒥᖅᓱᖅᑦᑕᖅᑯᔨᑦᓯᓂ ᓴᓇᒍᒪᔭᑐᐃᓐᓇᕐᒥᒃ," ᕿᓐᓄᐊᔪᐊᖅᑐᖅ ᐅᖃᖅᑐᖅ. "ᐃᑲᔪᕋᓯᐊᖅᓯᓂ ᐅᕗᑦᑎᓐᓂᒃ ᓇᒻᒥᓂᖅ ᒪᑭᒪᓇᓯᐊᕈᑎᑦᓴᓄᑦ, ᐆᒪᓇᓐᓂᖅᑲᑦᓯᐊᖅᓯᓂ ᑲᑦᓯᖓᐃᑦᓯᐊᖅᓯᓂᓗ ᑲᒪᓚᐅᖅᓯᒪᔪᖅ ᐱᔪᓐᓇᖅᑕᒥᓂᓪᓗ ᖃᐅᔨᒪᔭᒥᓂᓪᓗ ᐃᓕᓐᓂᐊᑎᑦᓯᑦᓯᓂ. ᓴᓇᖅᑦᑕᓕᓚᐅᖅᓯᒪᔪᖓ ᓇᑦᓯᕋᔭᓐᓂᒃ ᐅᑭᑦᓯᒪᔪᓂᒃ, ᐊᕐᓇᑯᑖᒻᒧᑦ ᐋᐸᑦᓯᓂᑦ ᑮᓇᐅᔭᖅᓯᓂᐅᑎᒋᑦᓯᓂᑦ."[13]

ᐃᓚᖓᑦ ᓴᓇᔭᖓᑦᑕ ᑐᙵᕕᐅᓚᐅᖅᓯᒪᔪᖅ ᕿᓐᓄᐊᔪᐊᑉ ᑎᑎᖅᑐᒐᒋᐊᙵᖓᓄᑦ, ᐃᓚᒋᔭᐅᓕᐅᖅᑐᖅ ᐃᓕᑕᕆᔭᐅᓯᒪᔪᕐᔪᐊᓄᑦ, ᐅᑲᓕᖅ ᑯᐊᓐᓂᑐᖅᑐᖅ. ᐱᓯᒪᔪᖅ ᓇᑦᓯᕋᔭᒻᒥᒃ ᐅᑭᑦᑕᒥᓂᖓᓂᒃ ᓴᓇᑦᓯᒍ ᓂᕈᒥᐊᒐᕐᒨᖅᓯᒍ. ᑕᐸᐃᖅᓯᒪᑦᓯᓂ ᕿᓐᓄᐊᔪᐊᑉ ᐱᔪᓐᓇᓂᖓᓂᒃ ᑎᑎᖅᑐᒐᖏᓐᓂᓪᓗ, ᐃᐅᑦᒪᐅᑉ ᐅᖅᑲᐅᑎᓕᓚᐅᖅᓯᒪᔭᖓ ᑎᑎᖅᑐᒐᖅᑯᓪᓗᒍ. ᕿᓐᓄᐊᔪᐊᖅ ᓯᕗᓪᓕᕐᒥ ᑲᑦᓱᖓᓚᐅᖅᓯᒪᔪᖅ; ᑕᐃᑦᓯᒪᓂᓕ ᐊᖑᑏᓐᓇᐃᑦ ᑎᑎᖅᑐᕐᑲᑦᑕᕗᒻᒪᑕ, ᑭᓯᐊᓂ ᒐᕙᒪᒃᑯᓐᓃᙱᖅᑐᒥᒃ, ᑎᑎᖅᑐᕐᕕᑦᓴᔭᑖᓚᐅᖅᓯᒪᔪᖅ ᔭᐃᒻᓴᒥᒃ (ᐊᑦᓯᖅᑕᐅᓯᒪᔪᖅ ᓴᐅᒥᒻᒥᒃ, ᓴᐅᒥᐅᒻᒪᑦ), ᐋᑦᓯᓯᑦᓯᓂ ᐃᐅᑦᒪᐅᑉ ᐅᖅᑲᐅᓯᓕᓯᒪᔭᒐ ᐱᐅᔪᒻᒪᓈᑦ, ᑲᓱᖅᑎᓯᒪᔪᑦ ᑎᑎᖅᑑᑎᒧᑦ ᑎᑎᖅᑐᒐᖏᑦ.

ᕿᓐᓄᐊᔪᐊᖅ ᓯᕗᓪᓕᖅᐸᐅᓚᐅᖅᓯᒪᔪᖅ ᐊᕐᓇᓂ ᑭᙵᕐᓂ ᑎᑎᖅᑐᖅᐸᓪᓕᐊᓕᖅᓱᓂ, ᓯᕗᓪᓕᖅᐹᒥ ᐊᑦᓱᕈᕐᓇᖅᒥᓂᐅᓂᕋᖅᑕᖓ. “ᑲᑉᐱᐊᓱᑦᓯᐊᑲᐃᓐᓇᓚᐅᖅᓯᒪᔪᖓ ᑎᑎᖅᑐᕐᓄᑦ ᓯᕗᓪᓕᖅᐹᓄᑦ, ᓇᒍᑦᓯᐊᓕᖅᓯᒪᒐᒪ ᓱᓇᒥᒃ ᑎᑎᖅᑐᒐᓕᐊᑦᓴᖅ,” ᐃᖅᑲᐅᒪᔪᖅ.[14] “ᓯᕗᓪᓕᖅᐹᒥ ᓴᐅᒥᒃ ᖃᐃᑦᓯᒻᒪᑦ ᑎᑎᖅᑐᕐᕕᑦᓴᒥᒃ ᐸᐃᑉᐹᒥᒃ ᑎᑎᖅᑐᕐᑯᔨᑦᓯᓂ, ᐊᐱᕆᓚᐅᖅᓯᒪᔭᖓ ᓱᓇᒥᒃ ᑎᑎᖅᑐᕐᓂᐊᕐᒪᖔᕐᒪ. ᑭᐅᑐᐃᓐᓇᓚᐅᖅᓯᒪᔪᖅ ᓱᓇᑐᐃᓐᓇᑦᓯᐊᓂᒃ ᑎᑎᖅᑐᕐᑯᔨᑦᓯᓂ ᐃᓯᒪᓅᖅᑐᓂᒃ—ᓱᓇᑐᐃᓐᓇᐅᒍᓐᓇᖅᓯᑎᒃ,” ᐅᖃᖅᓯᓂ.[15] “ᑎᑎᖅᑐᓕᐊᙵᖅᑕᖃ ᓱᖃᑦᑎᓚᐅᖅᓯᒪᔭᖃ ᑭᐊᒃᑑᒥ, ᑭᓯᐊᓂ ᑭᖑᕐᖓᒍᑦ ᑎᑎᖅᑐᕐᓂᒃ ᐋᑦᓯᕕᕆᖅᑲᑦᑕᓯᔪᔭᖃ ᑭᙵᓕᐊᖃᐃᒐᒪ. ᐊᑭᖏᑦ ᖁᕕᐊᕆᖅᑲᑦᑕᔪᒐᒃᑭᑦ ᓴᓇᔭᒪ. ᓇᓗᓇᕈᓐᓃᓚᐅᖅᓯᒪᔪᖅ ᑲᔪᓯᓂᐊᓕᐊᒪ.”[16]

ᑎᑎᖅᑐᒐᕐᓂᖅ

ᕿᓐᓄᐊᔪᐊᑉ ᓯᕗᓪᓕᖅ ᑎᑎᖅᑐᒐᖏᑦ ᐊᑦᑐᐊᖅᑲᓪᓚᓇᓚᐅᖅᓯᒪᔪᑦ ᒥᖅᓱᖅᑲᑦᑕᖅᓯᒪᓂᖓᓄᑦ. ᐊᑐᖃᔪᑉᐸᑦᓯᓂ ᕿᖃᑕᔪᓂᒃ ᐸᐃᑉᐹᓂᒃ ᐊᑐᐊᕈᑎᒋᑦᓯᒋᑦ, ᑕᐃᒪᐃᖅᑲᑦᑕᖅᓯᒪᒻᒥᒐᒥ ᒥᖅᓱᖅᓯᓂ, ᐸᐃᑉᐹᒨᖅᓯᒋᑦ ᐊᑐᐊᕈᑎᒋᓕᖅᓯᒋᑦ. ᑖᒃᑯᐊᓴᐃᓐᓇᐃᑦ ᐊᑐᖅᐸᑦᓯᒋᑦ ᑎᑎᖅᑐᒐᐅᑉ ᐃᓗᐊᓂ, ᓱᕐᓗ ᑕᕐᖃᖅᑰᑎᕇᑦᑐᑦ ᐊᕙᑖᓂ ᕿᑎᖓᓂ ᑎᑎᖅᑐᒐᐅᑉ. ᕿᓐᓄᐊᔪᐊᖅ ᐅᖅᑲᓚᐅᖅᓯᒪᔪᖅ ᐆᑦᑑᑎᓂᒃ ᐊᑐᐊᒐᕐᓂᒃ ᐊᑐᖅᑲᑦᑕᖅᓴᓕᐊᑦᓴᖅ ᑕᑯᒐᒥ ᐊᕐᓇᐅᖅᑲᑎᒥᓂᒃ, ᓯᐅᕋᕐᒥᒃ, ᐊᑐᖅᑎᓪᓗᒍ, ᐃᑉᐱᒍᓱᓕᖅᓯᓂ ᑕᐃᑲᓂ ᑕᐃᒪᐃᓕᐅᕈᒪᖅᑲᐃ “ᑎᑎᖅᑐᖅᑐᑦ ᑐᖃᐃᓐᓇᑦᓯᐊᖅᓯᒪᓚᖓᕙᑦ.”[17]

ᑕᐃᑦᓱᒨᓇᓗ, ᓇᒻᒥᓂᖅ ᑎᑎᖅᑐᒐᕈᓯᖓ ᐱᐊᓪᓕᐊᓕᓚᐅᖅᓯᒪᔪᖅ, ᐅᖅᑲᐅᓯᓕᓯᒪᔪᖓ ᐊᒡᒐᖏᑦ ᓯᕗᓕᖅᑐᑦ ᐃᓱᒪᖓᓂᒃ.[18] ᓴᐅᒥᐅᑦᓯᓂ, ᐱᒋᐊᖃᔪᖅᑲᑦᑕᖅᓯᒪᔪᖅ ᓴᐅᒥᐊᓂᒃ ᑎᓇᖅᑯᐊᓂᒃ ᐸᐃᑉᐹᑉ, ᓱᒃᑲᐃᑦᑐᒥᒃ ᑎᑎᖅᑐᒐᖓ ᐱᕙᓪᓕᐊᓕᖅᓯᓂ ᐸᐃᑉᐹᓕᒫᖅ ᑎᒻᒥᐊᖅᑕᖅᑲᐅᖅᓯᓂ ᐆᒪᔪᕐᓂᓪᓗ ᐃᓄᓐᓂᓪᓗ ᑕᐸᐃᕐᓇᖅᑐᓂᓪᓗ ᐃᓚᒪᑦᓯᑎᒃ ᐃᓘᓐᓇᑎᒃ. ᐃᓱᑦᓴᖅᓯᐅᑯᑖᓗᐊᖅᑲᑦᑕᖅᓯᒪᙱᑦᑐᖅ ᓱᓇᒥᒃ ᑎᑎᖅᑐᒐᕈᒪᒻᒪᖔᕐᒥ ᖅᑲᓄᖅ ᐱᔭᓈᕈᓂ ᑕᐅᑦᑐᖅᑲᕐᓂᐊᕐᒪᖔᖅ, ᑭᓯᐊᓂ ᓇᓗᖅᑲᑦᑕᖅᓯᒪᙱᑦᑐᖅ ᖅᑲᓄᐃᓕᐅᕐᓂᐊᕐᒪᖔᕐᒥ. “ᑕᑯᓐᓈᑲᐃᓐᓇᖅᓯᒍ ᐃᓱᒪᓐᓂᓪᓗ ᐊᓚᒃᑲᖅᑐᖅᑲᓕᖅᓯᓂ ᓄᑖᓂᒃ ᑎᑎᖅᑐᕐᓂᐊᖅᑕᓐᓂᒃ ᐱᐅᓯᕆᐊᒃᑲᓐᓂᕈᑕᐅᓗᑎᓪᓗ ᑎᑎᖅᑐᒐᕐᒧᑦ, ᐱᕚᓕᕈᑕᐅᓗᑎᒃ, ᑕᐃᒪᐃᒻᒪᑦ ᐃᓚᕙᓪᓕᐊᓲᒃᑲ,” ᐅᖅᑲᖅᑐᖅ. “ᑕᐅᑐᙳᐊᖅᑕᖃ ᐱᕙᓪᓕᐊᒻᒪᑦ .... ᑎᑎᖅᑐᒐᖅ ᐃᓚᕙᓪᓕᐊᑦᓯᒍ ᑕᒡᒐᓕ ᑕᐅᑐᓕᖅᑯ ᐱᔭᕇᖅᑐᖅ; ᑕᐃᒪ.”[19]

ᕿᓐᓄᐊᔪᐊᑉ ᑎᑎᖅᑐᒐᕐᓂᖓ ᑲᔪᓯᓚᐃᓐᓇᖅᑕᖃᓗᐊᖅᑎᑦᑐᒍ, ᐊᒥᐊᓇᓂᐊᖅᑕᖏᓐᓂᒃ ᑎᑎᖅᑐᒐᖅᑕᖓᑕ ᓂᕈᐊᖅᐸᕇᔫᖅ. ᓄᑖᑦ ᑎᑎᖅᑐᒐᕈᑦᓴᐃᑦ ᐊᑐᐃᓐᓇᐅᕈᖅᐸᓪᓕᐊᒻᒪᑕ, ᑎᑎᖅᑑᑎᑐᐃᓐᓇᐃᑦ ᐊᑐᖅᐸᓚᐅᖅᓯᓂᒋᑦ ᐊᒥᐊᓕᓐᓂᒃ ᑎᑎᖅᑑᑎᓂᒃ ᐊᑐᖅᑲᑦᑕᓕᖅᓯᒪᔪᖅ ᐃᒪᓕᓐᓂᓪᓗ ᑎᑎᖅᑑᑎᓂᒃ. ᑎᑎᖅᑐᓕᐊᓚᐅᙱᓐᓂᕐᒥᓂ ᐊᒥᐊᕈᑎᓂᒃ ᐊᑐᕐᓂᐊᖅᑐᒥᓂᒃ ᓄᐊᓯᕙᕉᖅᓯᓂ ᐊᑐᕐᓂᐊᖅᑲᐅᔭᓂᓗ ᐊᓯᔾᔨᕐᓇᑦ ᑎᑎᖅᑐᒐᖓ ᐱᕙᓪᓕᐊᑎᑦᑐᒍ. “ᐊᒥᐊᕈᑏᑦ ᐊᑐᕐᓂᐊᖅᑕᒃᑲ ᐃᓕᐅᖅᑲᓲᒃᑲ ᐋᖅᑭᓱᖅᓯᒋᑦ; ᐃᑉᐱᒋᒋᐊᖅᓯᒋᑦ ᑕᖅᓴᖏᑦ... ᒪᕐᑮᓂᒃ ᓴᓂᓕᓈᑎᑦᓯᓗᖓ ᑲᑎᒪᒍᓇᖅᑑᑎᒋᔭᓐᓂᒃ,” ᑐᑭᓯᑎᑦᓯᒋᐊᖅᑐᖅ. ᓱᕐᓗ ᑕᐅᑦᑐᖅᑲᑦᓴᐅᑎᒋᓗᓂ ᑕᐅᑐᙳᐊᖅᑎᑦᑕᖃᓗᐊᖃ, ᓴᓇᒻᒪᖓ ᖅᑲᓄᐃᓕᐅᕐᓂᐊᕐᒪᖔᕐᒥ ᑕᐅᑐᙳᐊᖅᑕᖃᓗᐊᖃᐅᑉ.”[20]

ᕿᓐᓄᐊᔪᐊᖅ ᓂᕈᐊᖃᔪᖅᑲᑦᑕᖅᓯᒪᔪᖅ ᖅᑲᐅᒪᔪᓂᒃ, ᑲᑎᒪᒍᓇᖅᑑᑎᓂᒃ ᐊᒥᐊᖑᒐᔪᑦᑐᓂᒃ, ᐊᑐᖅᐸᑦᓯᒋᑦ ᑕᐃᒫᑦᓴᐃᓐᓇᖅ ᑕᑯᑦᓴᐅᑦᓯᐊᖅᓯᑎᒃ ᑲᓱᖅᓯᒪᓂᖏᓐᓈᖓᕗᑦ, ᖅᑲᑕᓈᑕᖅᓯᒪᕗᑦ, ᓱᕐᓗ ᐊᐅᓚᓂᑖᑦ ᑎᑎᖅᑐᒐᐃᑦ. ᐱᔭᓅᖅᓯᒪᔪᖅ ᑎᑎᖅᑐᒐᖅ ᑕᑯᒥᓇᖅᑐᐹᓘᑦᓯᓂ, ᐃᓗᑕᖅᑐᔫᑦᓯᓂ, ᐊᑦᓯᐃᑦᑐᒻᒪᓕᐅᑦᓯᓂ ᑕᐅᑦᑐᓕᔭᐅᔪᖅ ᑲᓱᖅᓯᒪᔪᖅ ᐃᓗᑕᑕᒫᖏᓐᓄᑦ ᓄᑦᑕᐅᓂᖅᓯᐅᕈᑕᐅᑕᖅᓯ ᑕᑯᑦᓴᒃᑯᑦ ᓴᐃᒪᓂᕐᒥᒃ.

ᕿᓐᓄᐊᔪᐊᕐᒧᑦ, ᑎᑎᖅᑐᒐᕈᓯᖓ ᒥᑦᓯᖅᑲᖅᑐᖅ ᐃᓯᐊᓄᓄᑦ—ᑕᑯᒥᓇᖅᑑᑏᑦ. ᐊᓯᖏᑦᑕ ᑎᑎᖅᑐᒐᖅᑎᐅᖅᑲᑎᖏᑦ ᐅᓂᒃᑳᖅᑐᐊᖅᑎᐅᒐᓗᖅᑎᑦᓗᒥ ᐅᓂᒃᑳᖅᑐᐊᖅᑎᑎᐅᓯᒪᙱᒻᒪᑦ ᐅᓂᒃᑳᖅᑎᐅᓯᒪᒐᓂᓗ. ᐱᔪᒪᔭᑦᑐᐊᑕᓕᓯᒪᔭᖓᑕ ᐃᓯᒫᓘᑎᑐᐊᓕᑦᓯᒍᓗ ᑎᑎᖅᑐᒐᕐᓂᖅ. ᐃᓯᒪᒋᔭᐅᓯᒪᔪᖅ ᑎᒻᒥᐊᓂᒃ ᑎᑎᖅᑐᒐᖅᑎᐅᒋᐊᖓ ᑭᙵᕐᓂ—ᐃᓘᓐᓇᑦᓯᐊᑎᒃ ᐋᒡᒐᑐᐊᒃ ᒪᕐᕿᒃ ᑭᙵᕐᓂ ᐊᖅᕿᒍᑕᒫᑦ

ᑕᑯᑦᓴᐅᑎᑦᓯᔪᑦ ᑎᑎᖅᑐᓕᐊᖑᓯᒪᔪᓂᒃ ᐱᕐᑲᓯᐅᔾᔨᔪᑦ ᕿᓐᓄᐊᔭᐊᑉ ᑎᒻᒥᐊᙳᐊᓕᐊᓇᓯᒪᔭᖕᒋᓐᓂᒃ, ᐅᑉᐲᑦ, ᑐᑐᒐᐃᓪᓗ ᐱᓗᐊᖅᑐᒥᒃ. ᑭᓯᐊᓂ ᑳᑯᐊᖑᒐᓗᐊᖅᑎᓪᓗᒋᒃ ᑎᑎᖅᑐᓇᐊᖕᒋᒃ ᖁᕕᐊᕆᓂᖅᐹᖕᒋᒃ, ᐃᖏᑐᐃᓐᓇᖅᑐᓂ ᐃᓛᓃᖅᑐᓂ ᑎᑎᖅᑐᖅᑲᑦᑕᖅᓯᒪᖖᒋᑦᑕᖕᒋᑦ. ᐊᐱᓇᔭᐅᒐᒥ ᑲᑎᒪᔨᒧᑦ ᑲᓇᑕᒥ ᐃᓄᐃᑦ ᓴᓇᐅᒐᖕᒋᓐᓄᑦ ᑲᑎᒪᔨᓂ, ᐱᓪᓚᕆᐅᕆᔭᖅᑲᖅᒪᖕᖢᖅ ᐅᒃᐱᒃᔪᐊᕐᓂᒃ, ᕿᓐᓄᐊᔭᐊᖅ ᑭᐅᓯᒪᔪᖅ ᐅᒃᐱᒃᔪᐊᕐᓂᒃ ᐊᓚᒃᒐᐃᔨᐊᖅᑲᖖᒋᓐᓂᖃᖅᓱᓂ, ᑭᓯᐊᓂ ᑎᑎᖅᑐᓯᓂᑕᒫᑦ, ᐅᒃᐱᒃᔪᐊᖅ ᑎᑭᓐᓂᐅᓴᑐᐃᓐᓇᖅᑑᔭᖅᑐᖅ.[21] ᑕᑯᑦᓴᐅᑎᑦᓯᓪᓚᕆᖅᑲᑦᑕᖅᓯᒪᖖᒋᒃᑲᓗᐊᖅᓱᓂ ᐃᓄᐃᑦ ᐅᓂᒃᑳᖅᑐᐊᖕᒋᓐᓂᒃ ᑐᕋᐃᓐᓇᖅᑐᑎᒃ ᑎᑎᖅᑐᖕᒋᓐᓂ, ᑐᑭᓯᓯᒪᑦᓯᐊᖅᑐᑦ ᑲᔫᒪᖅᑲᑎᑮᓐᓂᖕᒋᓐᓂᒃ ᐃᓅᓯᐅᑉ ᐆᒪᔪᓕᒫᑦᓯᐊᓪᓗ ᑳᑯᐊᓗ ᑐᙵᕕᐅᑦᓯᑎᒃ ᐃᓄᐃᑦ ᐅᓂᒃᑳᖅᑐᐊᖕᒋᓐᓄᑦ ᓯᓚᕐᔪᐊᕐᒨᖓᔪᕗᑦᓗ. ᐅᖃᐅᓯᖕᒋᓂᖕᒋᑦ ᖃᐅᒪᓂᐅᑉ ᑖᖅᑑᑦᓗ ᑭᒡᓚᖅᑐᖅᑕᐅᔪᑦ ᓯᕿᓂᕐᒧᑦ ᑕᖅᑭᕐᒧᑦᓗ, ᐅᒃᐱᒃᔪᐊᕐᒧᑦ ᑐᓗᕐᒧᑦᓗ, ᑎᑎᖅᑐᖕᒋᑦᓗ ᐱᕙᓪᓕᐊᑐᐃᓐᓇᕐᒪᑕ, ᐊᑦᓯᐃᑦᑑᑉ ᐊᕐᓇᐅᑉ ᖀᓇᖕᒐ ᕿᑎᖕᒐᓃᑦᓯᓂ.

ᑎᑎᖅᑐᒐᐃᑦ ᑎᑎᖅᑐᓕᐊᖑᔪᑦ

ᕿᓐᓄᐊᔭᐊᖅ ᖃᐅᔨᒪᔭᐅᑦᓯᐊᖅᑐᖅ ᑎᑎᖅᑐᓕᐊᖑᓯᒪᔪᓄᑦ, ᑭᓯᐊᓂᓕ ᓇᓪᓕᓂᖅ, ᑎᑎᖅᑐᓕᐅᖅᑎᐅᖕᒋᑦᑐᖅ. ᑕᐃᑦᓱᒪᓂᒋᐊᖅ ᑎᑎᖅᑐᓕᐅᖅᑐᖅᑲᖅᑲᑦᑕᐸᓪᓕᐊᓕᖅᑎᓪᓗᒍ, ᐊᖑᑏᑦ ᐃᓕᓐᓂᐊᖅᑎᑕᐅᖅᑲᑦᑕᖅᓯᒪᔪᑦ ᑎᑎᖅᑐᓕᐅᖅᑎᐅᓂᕐᒥᒃ, ᐃᓅᓇᓴᓚᕆᓐᓂᒃ, ᑎᑎᖅᑐᓕᐅᖅᑲᑦᑕᖅᓯᒪᔪᑦ ᐊᓯᒥ ᑎᑎᖅᑐᖕᒋᓐᓂ. ᑕᒪᓐᓇ ᐊᐅᓚᓂᐅᔪᖅ ᐋᖅᑭᑦᑕᐅᓚᐅᖅᓯᒪᔪᖅ ᐊᑕᐅᓯᕐᒥᑦᑐᒥᒃ ᐱᔾᔪᑎᖃᖅᓱᑎᒃ, ᑕᐃᑦᓱᒪᓂᓗ, ᐃᓅᓇᓴᓚᑎᒃ ᐃᓄᐃᑦ ᓱᓕ ᓄᓇᖅᑲᔪᓪᒪᑕ ᑭᖕᒐᐃᑦ ᓯᓚᑖᓂ ᑎᑭᑉᐸᑦᓯᑎᒃ ᑭᖕᒐᕐᓄᑦ ᖃᑦᑐᓐᓂᐊᓕᕋᐃᒐᒥᒃ ᕿᔫᓇᐊᖅᑐᖅᓯᑎᑦᓗ/ᐊᒦᑦ. ᑕᐃᒃᑯᐊᓗ ᑎᑎᖅᑐᒐᕈᒪᔪᑦ, ᐊᖑᑏᑦ ᐊᕐᓇᐃᑦᓗ ᑕᒪᕐᒥᒃ—ᑎᑎᖅᑐᕐᕕᑦᓴᖅᑖᖅᑎᑕᐅᕙᑦᓯᑎᒃ ᑎᑎᖅᑑᑎᓂᑦᓗ ᓄᓇᒥᓅᕈᑎᒐᑦᓴᖕᒋᓐᓂᒃ ᐅᑎᖅᑎᓖᖅᓯᑎᒃ ᑎᑎᖅᑐᖅᓯᒪᓕᕐᓗᑎᒃ ᓂᐅᕕᐊᕆᔭᐅᓗᑎᑦᓗ. ᐊᕐᓇᐃᑦ ᐱᕕᕐᑲᕐᓂᖅᓴᐅᔾᔮᖅᑲᑦᑕᖅᓯᒪᔪᑦ ᑎᑎᖅᑐᕐᓂᖅᓴᐅᑦᓯᑎᓪᓗ ᐊᓯᖕᒋᓂᒃ ᑲᒪᒋᒋᐊᓕᒻᒥᓂᒃ ᑲᒪᓯᓈᖅᓯᑎᒃ, ᐊᖑᑎᖕᒋᓪᓗ ᓅᓯᒪᔪᑦ ᐊᓯᕚᖅᓯᒪᔪᑦ, ᐃᓚᖓᓂ ᐅᑦᓱᖅᓴᐃᑦ. ᑎᑎᖅᑐᓕᐅᖅᑏᑦ, ᐃᑦᓱᐊᓂ, ᓄᓇᓕᓐᓃᑐᒐᓇᖅᓯᒪᔪᑦ ᖃᓂᑭᔅᓂᑑᓐᓂᑦ ᓄᓇᓖᑦ ᐃᑲᕐᖃᖃᓴᓐᓂᒃ ᐃᖅᑲᓇᐃᔭᓯᕙᑦᓯᑎᒃ ᑎᑎᖅᑐᓕᐅᕐᕕᒻᒥ. ᑕᒪᓐᓇ ᐃᖅᑲᓇᐃᔮᑦ ᐊᕙᑦᑐᖅᓯᒪᓂᖓᑦ ᐱᕙᖅᑲᕈᑕᐅᓯᒪᔪᖅ ᑎᑎᖅᑐᖅᑎᓄᑦ ᐃᓯᒪᖅᓱᖅᓯᑎᒃ ᐊᖏᕐᕋᒥᓂ ᓴᓇᒍᓐᓇᖅᓯᑎᒃ ᐊᕐᕕᑕᖅᓯᓐᓈᑦ, ᑎᑎᖅᑐᓕᐅᖅᑎᓄᑦᓗ ᐃᓱᒪᖅᓲᑕᐅᒍᓐᓇᖅᓯᒪᑦᓱᑎᒃ ᑎᑎᖅᑐᒐᕐᒨᖓᔪᖅ. ᑎᑎᖅᑐᓕᐅᖅᑏᑦ ᐱᓯᑎᐹᓗᕈᓚᐅᖅᓯᒪᔪᑦ ᖃᓄᖅᑑᕈᑎᖅᑲᕈᓐᓇᓕᖅᓯᑎᒃ ᓴᓇᐅᒐᓐᓅᖕᒐᔪᓂᒃ. ᐊᓚᒃᒐᐃᓐᓂᖕᒐᑦ ᑲᒪᒋᔭᖕᒐᑦᑕ ᐃᓕᑕᕆᔭᐅᓯᒪᔪᖅ ᑎᑎᖅᑐᓕᐅᕐᕕᐅᑉ ᓇᕐᑭᑦᑕᒐᖕᒐᑎᒍᑦ, ᓇᕐᑭᓯᒪᔪᖅ ᐃᓅᓇᑦᓯᐊᖕᒋᓇᓂ ᓴᒃᑯᑕᐅᓯᒪᔪᓂ ᑎᑎᖅᑐᕐᕕᒻᒥᒃ ᑕᐃᒪᖕᒐᓂᑦ 1960–ᒥᓂᑦ.

ᕿᓐᓄᐊᔭᐊᖅ ᑐᑭᓯᓯᒪᓚᐅᖅᓯᒪᔫᒐᓗᐊᖅ ᑎᑎᖅᑐᓕᐅᕐᓂᐅᑉ ᐊᐅᓚᓂᖕᒋᓐᓂᒃ, ᑭᓯᐊᓂ ᓇᔫᑎᒐᔭᐃᑦᑑᓯᒪᔪᖅ ᑎᑎᖅᑐᒐᖅᓯᒪᔭᖕᒋᑦ ᑎᑎᖅᑐᓕᐊᖑᑎᑦᑐᒋᑦ. ᐊᑎᓕᐅᖅᐸᒃᑲᓗᐊᖅᓱᓂ ᑎᑎᖅᑐᓕᐊᒥᓂᕐᓂᒃ ᐱᔮᕆᖅᑕᐅᕙᓪᓕᐊᑎᓪᓗᒋᑦ ᓂᓪᓕᕈᑎᒋᓗᐊᖅᑲᑦᑕᖅᓯᒪᓇᒋᓪᓗ. ᑲᓐᓄᔭᒦᑦᑐᑦ, ᐆᑦᑐᖅᑕᐅᕆᐊᖕᒐᓚᐅᖅᓯᒪᔪᑦ 1962–ᒥ, ᑲᒪᒋᓚᐅᖅᓯᒪᔭᕋᑐᐊᖕᒋᑦ. ᐊᒥᓱᐊᓗᓐᓂᒃ ᑲᓐᓄᔭᒦᑦᑐᓂᒃ ᓴᓇᓯᒪᔪᖅ ᐊᔪᕈᓐᓃᖅᓯᒪᓗᒍ ᑲᒪᒋᒋᐊᖕᒐ, ᑭᓯᐊᓂ ᖁᕕᐊᕆᓚᐅᖅᓯᒪᖖᒋᑦᑕᖕᒐ. ᐊᓪᓚᐅᑎᖕᒐᓄᑦᓗ ᐊᓪᓚᖕᒐᓄᑦᓗ ᐊᑲᐅᒐᓂ, ᑭᓪᓕᑲᓪᓕᔭᙳᖕᒋᓇᖅᓯᓂᓗ.[22] ᑕᐃᒫᒃ ᐃᓱᒪᓚᑑᓯᒪᖕᒋᑦᑐᖅ ᖃᓐᓄᔭᓚᓇᓂᐅᑉ ᒥᑦᓵᓄᑦ; ᐊᒥᓱᑦᑕᐅᖅ ᑎᑎᖅᑐᖅᑏᑦ ᐆᑦᑐᖅᑲᑦᑕᖅᓯᒪᔪᑦ ᐱᔭᓇᐊᑐᓗᐊᖅᓴᖅᓯᒪᔪᑦ, ᑕᐃᒪᐃᓐᓂᖕᒐᓄᑦ ᑲᓐᓄᔭᓚᓇᓂᖅ ᐊᑯᓃᖅᓯᒪᖕᒋᓚᖅ.

ᕿᓐᓄᐊᔭᐊᑉ ᑎᑎᖅᑐᑦᓚᓇᓚᒫᖕᒋᑦ ᒫᓐᓇ ᓄᖑᑕᐅᓯᒪᑦᓯᐊᓕᖅᑐᖅ ᓂᐅᕕᐊᖑᓯᒪᑦᓯᑎᒃ. ᐊᑭᑦᑐᖅᓴᐅᑎᔪᖅᑲᖅᑎᑦᓗ ᓴᖅᑭᔮᑦ ᐊᑭᖕᒋᑦᓗ ᖁᕝᕙᐸᑦᓚᐊᖕᒋᓇᖅᓯᑎᒃ. 1960–ᒥ ᐅᔭᖅᑲᓂᒃ ᑎᑎᖅᑐᓕᐊᒥᓂᖅ ᐅᒃᐱᒃᔪᐊᖅ ᓂᐅᕕᐊᖑᔪᔪᖅ 2018–ᒥ ᐊᑭᖃᖅᓱᓂ $216,000—ᓯᑯᒥᑦᓯᑦᓱᓂ ᐊᑭᑐᓂᖅᐸᐅᓯᒪᔪᓂᒃ ᑎᑎᖅᑐᖅᑕᐅᓯᒪᔪᓂᒃ ᑲᓇᑕᒥ ᑎᑎᖅᑐᖅᑎᒧᑦ.

ᖃᐅᔨᒪᔭᕆᐊᖃᓕᖅᐸᓪᓕᐊᓂᖅ

ᓄᓇᕐᔪᐊᕐᒥᒃ ᑕᑯᒋᐊᖕᒐᓚᐅᖅᓯᒪᔪᖅ ᕿᓐᓄᐊᔭᐊᖅ ᐊᖅᑯᑕᐅᑦᓗᓂ 1963 ᑲᓇᑕᒥ ᑕᕐᓇᔭᓕᐅᖅᑎᒃᑯᑦ ᑕᕐᓇᔭᓇᔭᓕᐊᖕᒐᓄᑦ ᐃᓄᒃ ᑎᑎᖅᑐᖅ – ᕿᓐᓄᐊᔭᐊᖅ. ᓄᓇᕐᔪᐊᖕᒐ—ᑲᓇᑕᒥ ᐅᑭᐅᖅᑕᖅᑐᖅ—ᑕᐃᑦᓱᒪᓂ ᐅᖕᒐᓯᐊᑦᑐᐊᓘᓚᐅᖅᓯᒪᔪᖅ, ᑐᑭᓯᐅᒪᓇᖕᒋᑦᓯᐊᖅᓱᓂ ᓄᓇ, ᐊᓯᐊᒍᑦ ᐃᓱᒪᒋᔭᐅᓗᐊᓚᐅᖅᓯᒪᖕᒋᑦᑐᖅ ᓄᓇᓕᕐᔪᐊᓄᑦ ᑭᓯᐊᓂ ᐆᒪᓇᓯᐊᕐᕕᑦᓴᐅᖕᒋᕆᐊᖕᒐ ᓯᓚᖕᒐ ᐊᒻᒪᓗ ᐃᓄᖅᑲᓇᐊᖕᒐ “ᐃᐊᓯᑭᒨᓂᒃ” ᐃᓄᓐᓂᒃ, ᖃᓄᐊᓗᑭᐊᖅ ᐊᓐᓇᑦᑑᓚᓗᐊᑦ ᑕᐃᑲᓂ. ᑳᑯᐊ ᑕᐸᐃᖃᑦᓯᐊᖅᑐᑦ ᑕᕐᓇᔭᐃᑦ ᒪᑐᐃᕈᑕᐅᓚᐅᖅᓯᒪᔪᑦ ᐊᒥᓱᓄᑦ ᐃᓴᓄᑦ ᓯᓚᑖᓂᑦᑐᓄᑦ ᐊᑦᓯᐃᑦᑐᒻᒪᓇᒻᒥᒃ ᐃᓅᓯᖅᑲᓇᐊᖕᒐ ᑕᑯᒥᓇᖅᑐᓂᑦᓗ ᓴᓇᐅᒐᖅᑲᓇᐊᖕᒐ

ᑖᓐᓇ ᐃᓐᓇᕈᖅᐸᓪᓛᐊᔪᖅ ᐊᕐᓇᖅ, ᐊᑑᑏᓐᓇᕐᓂᐊᓕᖅᑕᖕᒐᓗ ᐃᖕᒋᕐᖁᓯᓪᓗᓂ. ᐊᕐᕿᑐᑕᓖᑦ ᑎᑎᖅᑐᒐᐃᑦ ᑕᑯᔅᓴᐅᑎᑕᐅᓕᖁᐃᒻᒪᑕ ᑭᙵᕐᓂᒃ "ᖃᓪᓗᓈᑦ ᓄᓇᖕᒐᓐᓂ," ᐊᑎᖓ ᕿᓐᓄᐊᔪᐊᑉ ᑐᓴᕐᓴᑦᓵᖅᑲᑕᐅᓯᑦᑕᖅᑯᖅ, ᑐᑭᓯᐅᒪᓇᙱᑦᓯᐊᖅᑐᓄᑦ ᐊᒥᒐᙱᑦᑐᓄᑦ ᑲᔾᔮᓇᕐᓂᖕᒐᓄᓪᓗ ᑲᓇᑕᐅᑉ ᐅᖕᒐᓯᑦᑐᒥ ᐅᑭᐅᖅᑕᖅᑐᖕᒐᓂ.

ᓄᓇᕐᔪᐊᕐᒥ ᑐᓴᐅᒪᔭᐅᑦᓯᐊᓕᓚᐅᖅᓯᒪᒍᖅ ᕿᓐᓄᐊᔪᐊᖅ ᐊᕐᕿᑐᐃᑦ ᓯᑕᒪᑦ ᐊᓂᒍᕐᒪᑕ, ᓅᕙᐃᕝᕙ 1967−ᖑᑎᓪᓗᒍ, ᔩᓂᕝᕗᒃᑯᒃ ᐋᑐᕚᓕᐊᖅᓯᑎᒃ, ᑕᐃᑲᓂ ᐃᓕᑕᕆᔭᐅᓂᖅᑲᓚᐅᖅᓯᒪᓪᒪᑦ ᐃᕐᔨᒻᒥᓕᖅᑕᐅᑦᓱᓂ ᐃᓕᑕᕆᔭᐅᔾᔪᑎᓪᒪᕆᐊᓗᒻᒥᒃ ᖁᑦᓯᓂᖅᐹᒥᒃ ᑲᓇᑕᒥ ᒐᕙᓇ ᔭᓄᕈ ᕉᓚᓐ ᒪᐃᑲᓇᓗᑦ. ᑖᓐᓇ ᓄᑖᕐᒧᑦ ᓯᕗᓕᖅᐸᐅᓚᐅᖅᓯᒪᔪᖅ ᑲᓇᑕᒥ ᐃᓕᑕᕆᔭᐅᔾᔪᑎᒧᑦ, ᐱᕙᓪᓕᐊᔪᓂᒃ ᐅᖃᐅᓯᐅᑦᓱᓂ, ᕿᓄᐊᔪᐊᖅ ᐅᖃᐅᓯᐅᓚᖅᓯᒪᔪᖅ "ᐱᐅᔪᒻᒪᕆᐊᓗᒃ."[23] ᕿᓐᓄᐊᔪᐊᒃᑯᒃ ᔩᓂᕝᕗᒃᑯᒃ ᐅᑎᓕᓚᐅᖅᓯᒪᓪᒥᔫᒃ ᐋᑐᕚᒧᑦ ᐊᕐᕌᒎᒃ ᒪᕐᕉᒃ ᐊᓂᒍᕐᒪᑎᒃ ᑕᖅᑮᓐᓂᒃ ᒪᕐᕉᓐᓂᒃ ᑕᐅᓇᓃᒋᐊᖅᑐᖅᓯᑎᒃ ᑲᑐᔾᔭᖅᑎᕆᔪᑎᖅᓯᑎᒃ ᑎᑎᖅᑐᒐᕐᒥᒃ ᑐᕋᕐᖓᔪᒥᒃ ᑲᓇᑕᒥ ᓄᓇᕐᔪᐊᕐᒥ ᓇᓪᓕᐅᓂᖅᓯᐅᕐᓂᕐᒧᑦ ᐊᑉᓴ 70, ᓯᐃᑕ, ᐅᓵᑲ, ᔭᐹᓐᒥ. ᑐᓴᕐᓴᓕᓂᐹᓪᓕ ᑐᓵᒐᓂᓚᐅᖅᑕᖕᒐᑦ ᑖᒃᑯᐊ ᑎᑎᖅᑐᒐᖅᑎᒃ ᐊᐃᑉᐸᓃᒃ ᑲᑐᔾᔭᖅᑎᕆᔪᑎᖕᒐᑦ, ᐃᓚᖕᒐᑦ ᐅᖃᐅᓯᐅᔪᖅ ᐃᒪᐃᓕᖕᒐᑦᓱᓂ, "ᐅᑯᐊ ᑎᑎᖅᑐᒐᖅᑏᑦ ᑕᕝᕙᓂᙶᓐᓇᖅ ᓯᓂᑉᐸᑦᑑᒃ ᐃᓕᖅᒥ ᐊᑐᖅᑎᕆᑉᐸᑦᓯᑎᓪᓗ ᑖᑦᓯᒪᙵᖓᓐᓇᖅ ᑎᑎᖅᑐᒐᖃᕐᕕᒻᒥᒃ."[24] ᒪᕐᕉᒃ ᐊᕐᕿᑑᒃ ᐊᓂᒍᕐᒪᑎᒃ, ᐅᑎᓚᐅᖅᓯᒪᓪᒥᔫᒃ ᖃᓪᓗᓈᑦ ᓄᓇᖕᒐᓄᑦ, ᕼᐊᓕᕚᒃᓯᒧᑦ, ᒪᑐᐃᖅᑕᐅᒪᓂᓐᓂᖅᑲᖅᑎᓪᓗᒍ ᓄᑖᖅ ᓴᐃᓐᑦ ᒥᐅᓇ ᓯᓚᑦᑐᓴᕐᕕᔾᔪᐊᕐᒥ ᑕᑯᔭᒐᖅᑲᕝᕙᖕᒐᑦ. ᓱᓇᐅᕙᓕ, ᑖᓐᓇ, ᑭᖑᓪᓕᖅᐸᐅᓕᖅᑐᒥᓂᖅ ᐊᐅᓪᓚᖅᓯᑎᒃ ᓇᓪᓕᐅᓂᖅᓯᐅᖅᑕᐅᖅᑎᕆᑦᓯᑎᓪᓗ. ᔮᓐᓂᕗ ᐃᓅᒍᓐᓃᓚᐅᖅᓯᒪᔪᖅ 1972−ᒥ ᕿᐱᙳᒥᐅᑦᓯᖅᓱᓂ. ᖃᖕᒐᑕᔫᒥᒃ ᑎᑭᑎᑦᓯᔪᖅᑲᖁᓯᐊᓚᐅᖅᓯᒪᔫᒐᓗᐊᖅ ᐃᖅᑲᓪᓕᐊᕈᔾᔨᐊᔪᑦᓴᒥᒃ ᐱᓚᑦᑕᐅᓂᐊᕐᒪᑦ, ᑭᓯᐊᓂᓕ ᖃᖕᒐᑕᔫᖅ ᒥᒍᓐᓇᖅᓯᒪᙱᑦᑐᖅ ᓯᓚ ᐱᔾᔪᑕᐅᓪᓗᓂ. ᑕᒪᓐᓇ ᐅᖁᒪᐃᑦᑐᐊᓘᓚᐅᖅᓯᒪᔪᖅ ᐃᓅᒍᓐᓃᕐᓂᖓ ᕿᓐᓄᐊᔪᐊᕐᒧᑦ.

ᓇᒧᑐᐃᓐᓇᑦᓯᐊᖅ ᕿᓐᓄᐊᔪᐊᖅ ᐊᐅᓪᓚᖅᑦᑕᓕᓚᐅᖅᓯᒪᔪᖅ ᑎᑎᖅᑐᒐᖕᒋᑦ ᐱᕙᓪᓕᐊᑐᐃᓐᓇᑎᓪᓗᒋᑦ, ᑕᓇᐅᑉ ᐊᑭᐊᓅᖅᓱᓂ, ᒥᐊᓕᒐᐃᑦ ᓄᓇᖕᒐᓄᑦ ᓇᒧᑐᐃᓐᓇᕐᓗ ᑲᓇᑕᒥ. ᐱᖅᑯᓯᕐᒥ ᑭᒡᒐᖅᑐᐃᔾᔨᑎᑦ ᐱᔭᐅᓯᒪᖅᑕᖅᓯᒪᔪᖅ ᐃᔾᔭᖅᓴᐅᓂᕐᒧᑦᓗ ᐊᕐᓇᓄᑦ. ᕿᓐᓄᐊᔪᐊᖅ ᐊᖅᑯᓯᐅᕆᓯᒪᔪᖅ ᐊᓯᒥᒃ ᐊᓇᓂᒃ ᐃᓄᓐᓂᒃ ᓴᓇᐅᒐᖅᑎᓂᒃ, ᑕᐃᒪᐃᒃᑯᐊᒥᓂᒃ ᐊᒻᒪᓗ ᑭᖑᕚᕆᔭᐅᔪᓂᒃ. ᐃᓐᓇᕈᖅᐸᓪᓕᐊᓕᖁᒥ, ᐅᖃᓕᒫᒍᑎᖅᓴᐅᓕᓚᐅᖅᓯᒪᔪᖅ ᑎᑎᖅᑐᒐᖅᑎᐅᓂᕐᒥ ᒥᑦᓵᓄᑦ, ᒪᑭᒪᑦᓯᑦᓯᓂᓗ ᐃᓚᒥᓂᒃ ᑮᓇᐅᔭᓕᐊᕆᕙᑦᑕᒥᒍᑦ. ᑭᐅᓴᐅᖅᑐᖅᑲᑦᑕᖅᓯᒪᔪᖅ ᐊᐱᖅᑯᑎᓂᒃ ᖃᖓ ᑎᑎᖅᑐᒐᕈᓐᓃᑦᓚᕆᖕᒑᖅ: "ᐃᓄᐃᑦ ᐃᓯᒪᖅᑲᖁᔾᔪᒪᑕ ᑎᑎᖅᑐᒐᖅᑎᐅᓂᕐᒥᒃ ᐊᔾᔨᐅᖏᑦᑑᒋᐊᖓ ᐊᓯᖏᓐᓂᒃ ᐃᖅᑲᓇᐃᔮᓂᒃ ᐊᐱᖅᓯᓕᖅᓯᑎᒃ, ᓯᓪᒪᑦ ᑎᑎᖅᑐᒐᐃᓐᓇᕈᒪᑦᑕᖅᑭᑦ? ᑕᒪᓐᓇᓕ ᐃᖅᑲᓇᐃᔮᖁ ᖁᕝᕙᐊᕆᑦᓯᒍᓗ. ᑕᐅᑦᑐᙳᐊᕈᓐᓇᙱᑦᑕᖁ ᐃᓅᓯᖁ ᑎᑎᖅᑐᒐᖅᑎᐅᖏᓪᓗᖓ."[25]

ᕿᓐᓄᐊᔪᐊᖅ ᖁᕝᕙᐊᕆᔭᐅᑦᓯᐊᓕᓚᐅᖅᓯᒪᓪᒥᔪᖅ ᐃᓕᑕᕆᔭᐅᑦᓯᐊᖅᓱᓂ ᓄᓇᒥᓂ, 1999−ᖑᑎᓪᓗᒍ ᐃᖅᑲᐅᒪᕆᔭᐅᑎᓪᓗᒍ ᓴᖅᑭᖅᑕᐅᓂᖓ ᐃᓄᐃᑦ ᓄᓇᖓᑦ, ᓄᓇᕗᒻᒥ, ᑕᐸᐃᕐᓇᓂᖅᐸᐅᖅᑲᑎᒧᑦ ᑎᑎᖅᑐᒐᖕᒐᓄᑦ—ᓯᓚᕗᑦ, ᓄᓇᕗᑦ. 2003−ᖑᑎᓪᓗᒍ, ᐃᓇᑕᐅᓚᐅᖅᓯᒪᓪᒥᔪᖅ ᐊᑦᕆᓐᓯ ᑲᓇᑖᒃᑯᓐᓄᑦ ᐳᓖᖅᑎᕆᔭᐅᒍᒪᑦᓯᓂ ᐃᖕᒋᖅᑲᓂᐊᖅᓯᑎᒃ ᐅᑭᐅᖅᑕᖅᑐᒃᑯᑦ. 76−ᖑᑦᓯᓂ, ᐊᕆᐊᒐᓚᐅᖅᓯᒪᔪᖅ ᑖᓂᓯᖅᓱᓂᓗ ᐃᑳᖅᐸᓪᓚᐊᓯᓐᓈᑦ ᑕᓯᐅᔭᕐᔪᐊᕐᒥᒃ. ᐅᒥᐊᕐᔪᐊᖅ ᑎᑭᒻᒪᑦ ᑭᙵᕐᓄᑦ, ᐅᓂᒃᑳᓕᐅᖅᑏᑦ ᐃᓚᖕᒐᑦ ᑎᑎᖁᖅᓯᒪᔪᖅ, "ᓲᕐᓗ ᑯᐃᓐ ᑎᑭᑦᑐᖅ.... ᐃᓚᖏᑦ, ᑐᙵᓱᑦᑎᑦᓯᐋᖏᑦ, ᐃᖅᑲᓪᓕᐊᖅᑏᓪᓗ ᓯᓅᓅᖅᓯᑎᒃ. ᑎᑎᖅᑐᒐᖅᑏᓪᓗ ᓴᓇᐅᒐᖅᑏᑦ ᑎᒎᑎᖁᓕᓪᓯᑎᒃ ᕿᓐᓄᐊᔪᐊᕐᒥᒃ."[26] 2009−ᖑᑎᓪᓗᒍ, ᓯᕗᓪᓕᖅᐹᒥ ᓇᔫᑎᓚᐅᖅᓯᒪᔪᖅ ᓴᓇᐅᒐᑐᐊᖏᑦ ᑕᑯᔅᓴᐅᑎᑕᐅᑎᓪᓗᒋ ᓄᓇᕗᒻᒥ ᓄᓇᑦᑕ ᓯᓇᒃᑯᑖᖏᑦ ᑕᑯᔭᒐᖅᑲᕝᕕᒻᒥ ᐃᖅᑲᓗᓐᓂ, ᐊᒻᒪᓗ 2012−ᒥ, ᐃᓕᑕᕆᔭᐅᓂᖅᑲᓚᐅᖅᓯᒪᔪᖅ ᐃᓕᑕᕆᔭᐅᔾᔪᑎᒻᒪᕆᒻᒧᑦ ᓄᓇᕗᒻᒥ, ᖁᑦᓯᓂᖅᐹᖅ ᐃᓕᑕᕆᔭᐅᔾᔪᑎᓂ ᓄᓇᕗᒻᒥ.

ᕿᒪᐃᔾᔪᑎᖏᑦ

ᕿᓐᓄᐊᔪᐊᖅ ᐱᖅᑯᓯᓕᕆᓂᖅ ᒪᑐᐃᖅᑕᐅᒪᓂᓐᓂᖅᑲᓚᐅᖅᓯᒪᔪᖅ ᑭᙵᕐᓂ ᓯᑦᑕᐱᕆ 2018−ᖑᑎᓪᓗᒍ. ᐊᑯᓂᐊᓗᒃ ᐸᕐᓇᑕᐅᓯᒪᔪᖅ. ᐸᕐᓇᑕᐅᓂᖓ ᐱᖅᑯᓯᓕᕆᓂᕐᑉ ᑭᙵᕐᓂ ᐸᕐᓇᑕᐅᕙᓪᓕᐊᓯᒪᔪᖅ ᐊᕐᕿᑐᐃᑦ 20 ᐅᖓᑖᓄᑦ, ᑭᓯᐊᓂ ᐊᐳᖅᑕᕝᕚᑦ ᐊᐅᓚᓂᖕᒋᓐᓅᖓᔪᑦ ᒐᕙᒪᐃᑦ ᐊᒻᒪᓗ ᑮᓇᐅᔭᓂᒃ ᐱᕈᖅᓴᐃᓂᕐᒨᖓᔪᑦ ᐊᑑᑎᔫᒪᑕ ᑕᐃᑦᓱᒨᓇ, ᐊᐅᓚᓂᑦᓴᐅᔪᖅ ᑭᖑᕚᕆᐊᖅᑕᐅᓪᓚᕆᓕᖅᓱᓂ. ᑭᓯᐊᓂ ᐳᐃᒍᖅᑕᐅᓯᒪᒐᓂ. ᑭᙵᐃᑦ ᓴᓇᐅᒐᖅᑎᐅᓂᖅᐸᐅᖅᑕᐅᔪ ᑐᓴᐅᒪᔭᐅᑦᓯᐊᖅᓯᑎᒃ ᓄᓈᓪ ᓄᓇᕗᒻᒥ, ᐱᔪᑎᑦᓴᐃᓪᓗ ᓴᓇᓂᕐᒧᑦ ᐱᖅᑯᓯᓕᕆᓂᕐᒥᒃ ᑕᒪᔾᔭᐅᑦᓯᑎᒃ—ᓇᓪᓕᐅᓂᖅᓯᐅᕈᑕᐅᓗᓂ ᓴᓇᐅᒐᓅᖕᒐᔪᑦ ᕿᒪᐃᔾᔪᑕᐅᔪᑦ—ᐊᓯᔾᔨᓚᐅᖅᓯᒪᙱᑦᑐᑦ ᐊᒻᒪᓗ, ᓴᙱᔪᕈᖅᐸᓪᓕᐊᑐᐃᓐᓇᖅᓯᒪᔪᑦ ᑭᖑᕚᕆᔭᐅᔪᑦ ᑲᔪᓯᑎᑦᓯᓂᖏᑦᑎᒍᑦ ᓴᓇᕙᑦᓯᑎᒃ ᐅᑭᐅᖅᑕᖅᑐᒥ ᐱᐅᓂᖅᐹᓂᒃ ᓴᓇᐅᒐᓂᒃ.

ᐊᑯᓂ ᐅᑕᖅᑭᔭᐅᓯᒪᔪᖅ ᓇᓪᓕᐅᓂᖅᓯᐅᕐᓂᐅᔪᖅ—ᓇᔫᑎᔭᐅᑦᓱᓂ ᑎᑭᓯᒪᔪᓄᑦ, ᑮᓇᐅᔭᖅᑲᖅᑎᑦᓯᔩᓄᑦ ᐊᒻᒪᓗ ᐅᖓᑖᓃᑦᑐᓄᑦ 600 ᐃᓄᐃᑦ ᓄᓇᓕᖕᓂᑦ—ᐃᑉᐱᓇᓪᓚᑦᓚᑦᓱᓂ ᓇᓪᓕᐅᓂᖅᓯᐅᕐᓂᐅᔪᔪᖅ. ᓇᑦᓯᕋᔭ ᐊᑦᓱᓈᖅ ᐃᑳᖅᑎᓯᒪᔪᖅ ᐹᖓᓂ ᑭᐱᔭᐅᑦᓱᓂ ᐊᑐᖅᓱᑎᒃ ᓴᕕᑦᓴᔭᑐᕐᑲᕐᒥᒃ ᐊᐳᓯᓚᔾᔪᑎᒥᒃ, ᐃᓄᐃᑦ ᐃᓗᐊᓄᑦ ᑑᖓᓱᑦᑎᑕᐅᓕᖅᓱᑎᒃ ᓄᑖᕚᔾᔪᐊᕋᓗᒻᒧᑦ ᐅᓪᓗᒥᓯᐅᑎᓅᖓᔪᓄᑦ ᑎᑎᖅᑐᓚᓕᐅᕐᕕᓐᓄᑦ, ᑎᑎᖅᑐᓚᕐᕕᒻᒧᓪᓗ ᑎᑎᖅᑐᓚᖅᑎᓄᑦ ᑎᑎᖅᑐᓚᕐᕕᐅᙳᓂᐊᖅᑐᓄᑦ, ᐃᓄᑐᕐᑲᕐᓄᑦ ᑲᑎᑦᑕᕐᕕᒃ ᐊᓯᖔᓄᓪᓗ ᓄᓇᓕᓐᓃᖕᖒᖅᑐᓄᑦ, ᑕᑯᑦᓴᐅᑎᑦᓯᕕᓪᓗ—ᓯᕗᓪᓕᖅᐹᑦᓯᐊᖅ ᓴᓇᔭᐅᓯᒪᔪᖅ ᑕᑯᑦᓴᐅᑎᑦᓯᕕᐅᒍᓐᓇᕐᑯᔭᐅᑦᓱᓂ ᓴᓇᐅᒐᖕᖏᓐᓂᒃ ᐸᐃᑉᐹᕆᑦᑐᓂᒃ ᓄᓇᕗᒻᒥ. ᐊᑭᓐᓇᕐᕿᑦᓱᑎᒃ 31 ᑎᑎᖅᑐᓚᐃᑦ ᐊᒻᒪᓗ ᐱᖓᓱᑦ ᑎᑎᖅᑐᓕᐊᖑᓯᒪᔪᑦ ᕿᓐᓄᐊᔪᐊᑉ ᑎᑎᖅᑐᖏᑦ, ᐱᖅᑯᓯᓕᓂᕗᓪᓗ ᐊᑦᓯᖅᑕᐅᓯᒪᑦᓱᓂ ᑖᑦᓱᒪᖓᑦ.

ᑎᑎᖅᑐᓚᐃᑦ ᒪᑐᖅᑕᐅᓂᖓᓂ ᑕᑯᑦᓴᐅᑎᑕᐅᔪᑦ ᐱᓯᒪᔪᑦ ᐃᑦᓴᕐᓂᑦᕐᑯᔾᔨᖏᓐᓂᒃ ᑯᐊᐸᒃᑯᑦ. ᑯᐊᐸᒃᑯᑦ ᓄᐊᓯᒪᔭᖏᑦ ᑎᑎᖅᑐᓚᔭᐅᔪᑦ ᐅᖓᑖᓃᑦᑐᓄᑦ 200 ᐃᓄᐃᑦ ᑭᙵᕐᒥᐅᑦ ᑎᑎᖅᑐᕋᓯᐊᖅᑲᑦᑕᖅᓯᒪᔪᑦ ᐊᕐᕌᒍᓂ ᐊᓂᒍᖅᑐᓂ. ᐃᓚᖏᑦ ᓴᐱᓕᖅᓯᒪᔪᑦ, ᐱᔪᓇᙱᓗᐊᒧᑦ ᑲᑦᓱᖓᒧᑦᔫᓐᓃᑦ ᑕᒪᒃᑮᑦᔫᓐᓃᑦ, ᐊᒥᓱᑦᓗ ᑲᔪᓯᓯᒪᑦᓱᑎᒃ, ᑐᙵᕕᓕᐅᓕᖅᓱᑎᒃ ᑎᑎᖅᑐᓚᐅᕐᓂᕐᒧᑦ ᓴᒃᑯᑕᐅᓂᖏᓐᓄᑦᑐ ᐊᕐᕋᒍᑕᒦᑦ ᑎᑎᖅᑐᓚᐊᖑᓯᒪᔪᑦ ᑭᙵᕐᓂᒃ. ᑭᓯᐊᓂ ᐊᒥᓱᐊᓗᐃᑦ ᑎᑎᖅᑐᓚᐃᑦ ᓂᐅᕕᐊᖑᓯᒪᔪᑦ ᑯᐊᐸᒃᑯᓐᓄᑦ ᐊᒥᓱᓕᐊᖑᓗᑎᒃ ᑎᑎᖅᑐᓚᐊᖑᓯᒪᙱᑦᑐᑦ, ᑕᒫᓂ ᒥᑦᓵᓕᕋᑦᑕᖅᓱᑎᒃ 100,000 ᑎᑎᖅᑐᓇᐊᙱᑦᑕᓅᑦ. ᑖᒃᑯᐊ ᐊᒥᓱᑦ ᐊᑯᓃᖅᑐᒧᑦ ᐊᑐᖅᑐᐊᖅᑕᐅᔪᑦ ᒪᒃᒪᐃᑯᑦ ᑲᓇᑕᒥ ᑕᑯᔭᒐᖅᑲᕐᕕᒻᒧᑦ ᑲᑕᐃᓐᓂᒋ ᐋᓐᑎᐅᕆᐅᒥ, ᐊᓯᖏᑦᑐ ᐸᐸᑕᐅᔪᑦ ᓴᓂᕐᕙᖅᑕᐅᓯᒪᔪᑦᑐ ᑯᐊᐸᒃᑯᓐᓄᑦ, ᑭᙵᕐᓂ, ᑐᐊᕐᓴᑦ ᕙᐃᓐ ᐋᕐᑦᓴ–ᑯᓐᓂ ᑐᕌᓐᑐᒥ.

ᒪᒥᐊᓇᕐᕈᑎᑦᓚᑦᓇᐊᑐᐊᓕ ᑭᙵᐃᑦ ᓴᓇᐅᒐᖅᑎᖏᑦᑐ ᖃᐅᔨᒪᔭᐅᑦᓯᐊᕋᑐᐊᖅᑎᑦᑐᕐᑦ ᓄᓇᕐᔪᐊᕐᒥ, ᓄᓇᓕᖕᓂᑦ ᑮᑕᐹᑐᒃ ᐊᑐᐃᓐᓇᖅᑲᖏᓯᐊᒻᒪᑎᖅᑕᖅᓯᒪᔪᑦᑑᓐᓃᑦ ᓇᒻᒥᓂᖅ ᓴᓇᐅᒐᕐᓂᕐᒧᑦ ᐱᐅᓯᑎᓯᒪᔭᒥᓂᒃ. ᑯᐊᐸᒃᑯᑦ ᐃᑦᓴᕐᓂᑕᐃᑦ ᑎᑎᖅᑐᕐᑯᑎᖏᑦ ᑎᑎᖅᑐᓚᐊᖑᓯᒪᔪᑦᑐ ᓅᑕᐅᓯᒪᔪᑦ ᐊᑦᓱᖏᖅᓯᒪᔫᑦᓯᐊᕐᑯᑦᑐᑎᑦ—ᐱᑐᐊᖅᑐᒥᒃ ᐃᑯᐊᑦᓚᑲᑦᓚᕐᑯᖖᒋᒧᑦ, ᓱᒃᑯᒍᑕᐅᓯᒪᔪᑦ ᓴᓇᐅᓪᓚᓇᐊᑐᓐᓄᑦ ᐸᓂᖅᑑᕐᒥ ᖃᒪᓂᑦᑐᐊᕐᒥᑐ. ᒫᓇᓕ, ᕿᓐᓄᐊᔪᐊᖅ ᐱᖅᑯᓯᓕᓂᕕᒃ ᒪᑐᐃᖕᒐᓕᖅᑐᖅ ᑖᖅᑲᐅᖕᒐ ᐃᓄᓐᓄᑦ, ᓇᑐᓇᐃᖅᑕᐅᓯᒪᑦᓱᓂᑐ ᑕᑯᑦᓴᐅᑎᑦᓯᕕᑦᓴᖅ, ᓄᓇᓕᖕᖏᑦ ᑕᑯᖅᑲᑦᑕᕈᓇᖅᑐᖅ ᓴᓇᐅᒐᖕᖏᓐᓂᒃ ᓯᕗᓕᖕᖏᑦᑕ ᐃᓕᖕᖏᑦᑕᑐ ᓯᕗᓪᓕᖅᐹᑦᓯᐊᒥ.

ᑕᑯᑦᓴᐅᑎᑦᓯᓂᖅ—ᕿᓐᓄᐊᔪᐊᖅ ᐋᓯᕚᒃ - ᐃᓅᓯᖓ ᖀᒪᐃᔾᔪᑎᖏᑦᑐ—ᓯᕗᓕᖅᐹᑦᓯᐊᖑᓯᒪᔪᖅ ᑲᓇᑕᐅᑉ ᐅᑭᐅᖅᑕᖅᑐᖓᓂ ᑭᖑᕐᖓᒍᑦ ᑲᓇᑕᒥ ᐳᓚᕋᑑᔾᔭᐅᒍᒫᖅᓱᑎᒃ. ᐋᖅᑭᑦᓱᐃᖅᑕᐅᓯᒪᑦᓱᓂ ᓗᐃᓴ ᐹ ᕿᓐᓄᐊᔪᐊᖅ ᐱᖅᑯᓯᓕᓂᕕᒻᒧᑦ ᐊᒻᒪᓗ ᐅᐃᓕᐊᒻ ᕼᐊᒡᒪᓐ ᑭᙵᐃᑦ ᑯᐊᐸᒃᑯᖏᓐᓄᑦ, ᑕᑯᑦᓴᐅᑎᑕᐅᔪᑦ ᐃᖅᑲᓯᐅᔾᔨᔪᑦ ᑕᑯᑦᓴᐅᓚᐅᖅᓯᒪᙳᑦᑐᓂᒃ ᑎᑎᖅᑐᕐᓂᒃ ᑲᑦᓱᖓᐃᓕᕈᑕᐅᓯᒪᔪᓂᒃ ᑎᑎᖅᑐᓚᐊᕐᓂᕐᒧᑦ ᐅᔭᖅᑲᒥ, ᑎᑎᖅᑐᓚᐊᕐᕕᖓᓂ ᑳᓄᔭᓂᑐ. ᑭᙵᕐᒥᐅᑦ ᐃᓇᑕᐅᓯᒪᓪᓕᔪᑦ ᑐᓂᓯᕐᑯᔭᐅᑦᓱᑎᒃ ᓇᒻᒥᓂᖅ ᐱᕐᑯᑎᒥᓂᒃ ᓱᓇᑐᐃᓐᓇᕐᓂᒃ ᐃᓚᒋᔭᐅᓂᐊᖅᑎᑦᑐᒋᑦ ᑎᑎᖅᑐᕐᓄᑦ, ᑕᑯᑦᓴᐅᑎᑦᓯᑲᓂᕈᑎᑦᓴᓂᒃ ᑲᒪᒋᖅᑲᑦᑕᖅᓯᒪᔭᖕᖏᓐᓂᒃ ᕿᓐᓄᐊᔪᐊᑉ ᐱᕙᓪᓕᐊᑎᑕᐅᑎᑦᑐᒍ ᑕᑯᔭᐅᑦᓚᑎᓕᖅᐸᓪᓕᐊᑎᑦᑐᒍᒧ ᐃᓄᐃᑦ ᓴᓇᐅᒐᖏᑦ ᐱᖅᑯᓯᖏᑦᑐ.

ᕿᓐᓄᐊᔪᐊᖅ ᐃᓅᒐᔭᕐᓂᕈᓂ ᓱᓕ ᑕᑯᒍᓇᖅᓯᒧᓂ ᑕᒪᑦᓱᒥᖓ ᑎᑭᐅᑎᓯᒪᔭᒥᓂᒃ ᐃᓕᑕᕆᔭᐅᔾᔪᑎᒥᓂᑦᑐ, ᖁᕕᐊᒃᑯᔾᔨᑦᓚᕆᑲᔭᖅᑐᖅ ᑖᒃᑯᐊ ᑭᖑᕚᖑᓂᐊᖅᑐᑦ ᒫᓇ ᐱᕕᑦᓴᖅᑕᕐᒪᑕ ᐃᓕᓐᓂᐊᕈᓇᖅᓯᑦᑐᑎᑦᑐ ᐊᑦᓱᕈᑎᕆᓚᐅᖅᑕᖕᖏᓐᓂᒃ ᐊᑖᑕᑦᓯᐊᒃᑯᖏᑦᑕ, ᓯᓚᐱᕈᒃᑯᖏᑦᑕ ᓇᒻᒥᓂᖅ ᐅᖅᑲᐅᓯᖅᑲᕈᓇᓕᕐᑐᑎᒃ ᓴᓇᐅᒐᕐᓂᕐᔫᖓᔪᓂᒃ. ᐃᓱᓖᑐᕆᔭᖅᑲᐃᓇᖅᑲᑦᑕᖏᓇᓰᖑᔪᓪᓚᑦ ᑭᖑᕚᑦᓱᓂᒃ, ᖁᑐᖕᒐᒥᓂᑦᑐ ᐃᓱᒪᖅᑲᖅᓯᓂ ᓯᕗᓂᑦᓵᖏᓐᓂᑦᑐ ᐱᕕᓕᒃᑯᑦᑐ ᐃᑲᔪᑦᓯᐊᕈᒪᑦᑐᓂᕆᑦ. ᖁᔭᕆᔭᖅᑲᑦᑕᖅᓯᒪᐃᓇᔪᓪᒥᔪᖅ ᑎᑎᖅᑐᖅᑎᓪᓚᓇᕈᕐᓂᓇᐊᑦᓴᖅ, ᓴᓇᖅᑲᑕᓇᐊᕐᑐ "ᐱᐅᔪᐊᐱᓐᓂᒃ." ᐃᓕᑕᓇᔭᐅᓚᐅᖅᓱᓂ ᑲᒻᐹᓂᐊᒧᑦ ᐃᓕᑕᓇᔭᐅᒍᑎᕐᔪᐊᕐᒧᑦ ᑲᓇᑕᒥ 1982–ᒥ, ᐊᐱᓇᔭᐅᓚᐅᖅᓯᒪᔪᖅ ᖃᓄᖅ ᐃᓱᒪᖅᑲᖓᓚᖖᒍᖅ ᐃᓕᑕᓇᔭᐅᓂᕐᒥᓂᒃ: "ᐃᒻᒥᓃᓐᓇᖅ ᐃᓱᒪᒋᔾᔫᖏᑦᑐᖓ, ᑭᓯᐊᓂᑦᑕᐅᖅ ᖄᑐᖕᖓᒃᑲ ᐃᓱᒪᒋᖅᑲᓯᐅᑎᓗᒋᑦ... ᐅᓪᓗᒥᑐᐃᓐᓇᕐᔫᖓᔪᓂᒃ ᐃᓱᒪᖅᔾᔫᖏᑦᑐᖓ, ᑭᓯᐊᓂ ᐃᕐᓃᒥᐅᑉ ᑐᑭᒋᓂᐊᖅᑕᖓᓂᒃ ᓯᕗᓂᑦᑎᓐᓂ, ᓱᓇᒥᓪᓗ ᐱᔾᔪᑎᖅᑲᖅᒪᖖᒍᖅ, ᔫᑎᐅᓪᓚ ᐊᖕᖓᑦ ᐃᓗᐊᓃᑉᐳᑦ. ᑕᐃᒫᓪᓚ ᑕᑯᓈᖅᑕᕋ."[27]

NOTES

1 ᐊᑎᖓ ᑐᑭᓕᒃ ᑭᐳᑎᓂᒃ ᑲᓱᕈᑕᐅᓛᑦᑐᓂᒃ ᕿᑭᖅᑕᒧᑦ ᕿᑭᖅᑖᓗᒻᒧᑦ ᑎᓃᖓᓕᕋᐃᒻᒪᑦ.

2 ᐸᑐᓇᓴ ᕋᐃᔭᓐ, "ᐃᒻᒥᓅᖓᔪᑦ ᐅᓂᒃᑳᖏᑦ ᕿᓐᓄᐊᔪᐊᑉ," ᐅᓗᓂ ᕿᓐᓄᐊᔪᐊᖅ, ᓃᓐ ᓘᑖᔅᓯᑦ (Toronto: Firefly Books, 1985), 7.

3 ᕋᐃᔭᓐ, "ᐃᒻᒧᓅᖓᔪᑦ ᐅᓂᒃᑳᖏᑦ ᕿᓐᓄᐊᔪᐊᑉ," ᐅᓗᓂ ᓘᑖᔅᓯᑦ, ᕿᓐᓄᐊᔪᐊᖅ, 8.

4 ᕋᐃᔭᓐ, 8.

5 ᕋᐃᔭᓐ, 10.

6 ᕋᐃᔭᓐ, 11.

7 ᕋᐃᔭᓐ, 12.

8 ᐲᑕ ᐱᑦᓯᐅᓛᖅ ᓯᕗᓕᖅᑎᐅᓚᐅᖅᓯᒪᔪᖅ ᓄᓇᓕᓐᓂ ᐊᒻᒪᓗ ᑭᙵᕐᓂ ᖃᐅᔨᒪᔭᐅᑦᓯᐊᖅᓯᓂ ᑎᑎᕋᖅᑎ ᐊᔾᔨᓕᐅᕆᔨᐅᑦᓯᓂᓗ. ᐃᓅᓯᕆᓂᒃ ᐅᓂᒃᑳᖏᑦ, ᐃᓄᐃᑦ ᐊᑭᑦᑎᓐᓂᙱᓚᖅᑐᑦ, ᑎᑎᕋᖅᑕᐅᓚᐅᖅᓯᒪᔪᑦ 1975–ᒥ (Edmonton: Hurtig Publishers).

9 ᐃᓄᐃᑦ ᐅᐱᓕᖅᐸᓪᓚᐊᓂᖏᑦ ᐊᑕᓂᕐᒧᑦ ᐱᒋᐊᖅᐸᓪᓚᐊᓕᖅᑎᓪᓗᒋᑦ 1900–ᖏᑦ, 1920–ᖑᓕᖅᑎᓪᓗᒍᓗ ᐃᓐᓇᐃᑦ ᐅᖅᑲᓕᒫᕈᓐᓇᖅᓂᖏᑦ ᑎᑭᐅᒪᑲᓴᑦᓯᐊᖅᑐᑦ 100%–ᒧᑦ.

10 ᕋᐃᔭᓐ, "ᐃᒻᒧᓅᖓᔪᑦ ᐅᓂᒃᑳᖏᑦ ᕿᓐᓄᐊᔪᐊᑉ," ᐅᓗᓂ ᓘᑖᔅᓯᑦ, ᕿᓐᓄᐊᔪᐊᖅ, 18.

11 ᐃᓄᐃᑦ ᑕᐱᕆᓐ ᑲᓇᑕᒥ, ᐃᓄᓐᓅᖓᔪᑦ *ᑭᓪᓕᓯᓂᐊᖅᑕᐅᓯᒪᔪᑦ 2018*, 2018, 11, https://www.itk.ca/wp-content/uploads/2018/08/Inuit-Statistical-Profile.pdf.

12 Hᐃᐅᕈᑦ ᓗᐃᓗ ᓄᑲᖓ, ᐅᐊᓪᑕ ᓗᐃᓗ, ᐃᓚᒋᔭᐅᓯᒪᔪᖅ ᔫᑦᑖᕐᔪᐊᕐᓄᑦ ᓇᔫᑎᔪᓄᑦ ᐊᓐᓂᐊᕙᓕᐊᖅᓯᒪᔪᓄᑦ ᐊᓐᓂᐊᕙᒻᒥ.

13 ᕋᐃᔭᓐ, "ᐃᒻᒧᓅᖓᔪᑦ ᐅᓂᒃᑳᖏᑦ ᕿᓐᓄᐊᔪᐊᑉ," ᐅᓗᓂ ᓘᑖᔅᓯᑦ, ᕿᓐᓄᐊᔪᐊᖅ, 20.

14 ᑭᙵᐃᑦ ᑯᐊᐸᒃᑯᖏᑦ, *ᑭᙵᐃᑦ 77: ᑭᙵᕐᓂ ᐊᕐᕖᒍᑕᒦᖅᓯᐅᑏᑦ ᑎᑎᖅᑐᓕᐊᖑᓯᒪᔪᑦ ᓄᐊᑕᐅᓯᒪᔪᑦ 1977* (Toronto: M.F. Feheley Publishers Limited, 1977), 48.

15 ᑭᙵᐃᑦ ᑯᐊᐸᒃᑯᖏᑦ, *ᑭᙵᐃᑦ 79: ᐊᓗᑎᒋᓕᖅᑕᖓᓂᒃ ᑭᙵᕐᓂ ᐊᕐᕖᒍᑕᒦᖅᓯᐅᑏᑦ ᑎᑎᖅᑐᓕᐊᖑᓯᒪᔪᑦ ᓄᐊᑕᐅᓯᒪᔪᑦ* (Toronto: M.F. Feheley Publishers Limited, 1979), 37.

16 ᕋᐃᔭᓐ, "ᐃᒻᒧᓅᖓᔪᑦ ᐅᓂᒃᑳᖏᑦ ᕿᓐᓄᐊᔪᐊᑉ," ᐅᓗᓂ ᓘᑖᔅᓯᑦ, ᕿᓐᓄᐊᔪᐊᖅ, 20.

17 ᓃᓐ ᓘᑖᔅᓯᑦ, "ᑎᑎᖅᑐᒐᖏᑦ ᕿᓐᓄᐊᔪᐊᑉ," ᐅᑯᓇᓂ ᕿᓐᓄᐊᔪᐊᖅ (Toronto: Firefly Books, 1985), 39.

18 ᓘᑖᔅᓯᑦ, "ᑎᑎᖅᑐᒐᖏᑦ ᕿᓐᓄᐊᔪᐊᑉ," ᐅᑯᓇᓂ ᕿᓐᓄᐊᔪᐊᖅ, 38.

19 ᓘᑖᔅᓯᑦ, 38.

20 ᓘᑖᔅᓯᑦ, 41.

21 ᓘᑖᔅᓯᑦ, 37.

22 ᓘᑖᔅᓯᑦ, 52.

23 ᓵᓗᔅ ᓕᓐᑦᓴ, "ᖃᐅᒪᓂᖅᐹᑦ ᖃᐅᒪᕗᑦ," ᐋᑐᕚᒥ ᐅᖃᓖᒪᒐᐃᑦ, ᓅᕙᐃᕝᕙ 25, 1967.

24 "ᐅᑯᐊ ᑎᑎᖅᑐᒐᖅᑏᑦ ᑕᕝᕙᓂᑦᓴᐃᓐᓇᖅ ᓯᓂᑉᐸᑦᑑᒃ ᐃᓕᕐᒥ ᐊᑐᖅᑲᑎᒌᑉᐸᑦᓯᑎᓪᓗ ᑖᑦᓯᒪᙵᓴᐃᓐᓇᖅ ᑎᑎᖅᑐᒐᕐᕕᒻᒥᒃ," ᓯᑖᕐ ᑐᓴᕋᑦᓴᐃᑦ ᐱᓇᓱᐊᕈᓯᑕᒫᑦ (Toronto), June 28, 1969.

25 ᒪᓃᓇ ᔭᒥᓇᔅ, "ᑎᑎᖅᑐᕐᓂᖅ ᐃᖅᑲᓇᐃᔮᓇᓚᒃᑯ ᖁᕕᐊᒋᑦᓯᒍᓗ," *Globe and Mail* (Toronto), ᐅᑦᑑᕙ 20, 2003.

26 ᔨᒪᓐᓯ, "ᑎᑎᖅᑐᕐᓂᖅ ᐃᖅᑲᓇᐃᔮᖅ."

27 "ᐃᓄᒃᑎᑐᑦ ᐊᐱᖅᓱᖅᑐᖅ ᕿᓐᓄᐊᔪᐊᕐᒥᒃ ᐃᓅᓯᖓᑕ ᒥᑦᓵᓄᑦ ᑎᑎᖅᑐᖅᑎᐅᑦᓯᓂ ᐊᓈᓇᐅᓯᓐᓈᑦ," ᐃᓄᒃᑎᑐᑦ ᐅᖃᓕᒫᒐᐃᑦ, ᔮᓐᓄᐊᕆ 1983, 13.

SELECTED EXHIBITIONS, COLLECTIONS, AND PUBLICATIONS

SOLO EXHIBITIONS

1967 *Kenojuak Prints*
National Library, Ottawa, Ontario

1971 *Kenojuak Drawings*
The Innuit Gallery of Eskimo Art, Toronto

1979 *Kenojuak Lithographs*
Waddington Galleries, Toronto

1982 *Kenojuak: The Renowned Dorset Artist*
Canadiana Galleries, Edmonton, Alberta

1983 *Kenojuak: Original Drawings and Mixed Media*
Waddington and Shiell Galleries, Toronto

1988 *Kenojuak: Premier Graphic Artist of the Arctic*
Arctic Artistry, Hartsdale, New York

1995 *Kenojuak: Original Drawings*
The Albers Gallery of Inuit Art, San Francisco

2000 *Kenojuak Ashevak: A Decade of Drawings*
Feheley Fine Arts, Toronto

2002 *Kenojuak Ashevak: To Make Something Beautiful*
National Gallery of Canada, Ottawa, Ontario

2005 *Kenojuak Ashevak: Form and Colour*
Art Gallery of Ontario, Toronto

2008 *Kenojuak Ashevak*
Inuit Gallery of Vancouver, British Columbia

Kenojuak: From Drawing to Print
McMichael Canadian Art Collection, Kleinburg, Ontario

2009 *Kenojuak*
Nunatta Sunakkutaangit Museum, Iqaluit, Nunavut

2013 *Fantastique Kenojuak Ashevak*
Centre Culturel Canadien, Paris

Kenojuak Ashevak: The Light of Happiness
Spirit Wrestler Gallery, Vancouver, British Columbia

2013–2014 *Kenojuak Ashevak: In Memoriam*
Art Gallery of Ontario, Toronto

2014 *Kenojuak Ashevak: A Retrospective*
Feheley Fine Arts, Toronto

GROUP EXHIBITIONS

1959–2013 Cape Dorset Graphics Annual Print Collection

1961 *Contemporary Canadian Eskimo Art*
Gimpel Fils, London

1963 *Art Eskimo*
Galerie de France, Paris

1967 *Inoonoot Eskima: Grafik och Skulptur från Cape Dorset och Povungnituk*
Konstfrämjandet, Stockholm

Cape Dorset – A Decade of Eskimo Prints and Recent Sculptures
National Gallery of Canada, in cooperation with the Canadian Eskimo Art Committee, Ottawa, Ontario

1970 *Graphic Art by Eskimos of Canada: Second Collection*
Cultural Affairs Division, Department of External Affairs, Canada, Ottawa, Ontario (touring exhibition)

1971 *Canadian Eskimo Sculpture*
Canadian Embassy, Washington, DC

1971–1973 *Sculpture/Inuit: Masterworks of the Canadian Arctic*
Canadian Eskimo Arts Council, Ottawa, Ontario

1974 *Prints, Drawings and Sculptures by Kenojuak and Johnniebo*
Nova Scotia Technical College, Halifax

Arts of the Eskimo: Prints
Musée des beaux-arts de Montréal, Quebec

1975–1976 *Cape Dorset Prints*
Winnipeg Art Gallery, Manitoba

GROUP EXHIBITIONS (continued)

1977–1982 *The Inuit Print / L'estampe Inuit*
Department of Indian Affairs and Northern Development and the National Museum of Man, Ottawa, Ontario (touring exhibition)

1978 *Polar Vision: Canadian Eskimo Graphics*
Jerusalem Artists' House Museum, Israel

1982 *Inuit Art from the Art Centre Collection*
MacDonald Stewart Art Centre, Guelph, Ontario

1983 *Inuit Masterworks: Selections from the Collection of Indian and Northern Affairs Canada*
McMichael Canadian Art Collection, Kleinburg, Ontario

1983–1985 *Grasp Tight the Old Ways: Selections from the Klamer Family Collection of Inuit Art*
Art Gallery of Ontario, Toronto

Contemporary Indian and Inuit Art of Canada
Department of Indian Affairs and Northern Development, Ottawa, presented at the General Assembly Building, United Nations, New York

1984 *Cape Dorset Prints: Twenty-Five Years*
National Gallery of Canada, Ottawa, Ontario

1984–1985 *Stones, Bones, Cloth and Paper: Inuit Art in Edmonton Collections*
Edmonton Art Gallery, Alberta

1987 *The Swinton Collection of Inuit Art*
Winnipeg Art Gallery, Manitoba

1988–1989 *Im Schatten der Sonne: Zeitgenössische Kunst der Indianer und Eskimos in Kanada / In the Shadow of the Sun: Contemporary Indian and Inuit Art in Canada*
Canadian Museum of Civilization, Hull, Quebec (touring exhibition)

1991 *Sojourns to Nunavut: Contemporary Inuit Art from Canada*
Bunkamura Art Gallery, Tokyo, presented by University of British Columbia Museum of Anthropology and the McMichael Canadian Art Collection

1992 *Art Inuit*
Galerie Montador, Dieppe, France, presented by L'Iglou Art Esquimau, Douai

1993 *Arts from the Arctic*
Anchorage Museum of History and Art, Alaska

1993–1994 *Contemporary Inuit Drawings*
Muscarelle Museum of Art, College of William and Mary, Williamsburg, Virginia

1994–1995 *Isumavut: The Arctic Expression of Nine Cape Dorset Women*
Canadian Museum of Civilization, Hull, Quebec

1995 *Keeping Our Stories Alive: An Exhibition of the Art and Crafts from Dene and Inuit of Canada*
Institute of American Indian Arts Museum, Santa Fe, New Mexico

2001 *Creatures of the World: The Priscilla Tyler and Maree Brooks Collection of Inuit Art*
Carleton University Art Gallery, Ottawa, Ontario

2003 *Asingit: Inuit Art from the MacDonald Stewart Art Centre Collection; University of Guelph*
Náprstek Museum, Prague (tour)

2004–2005 *Our Land: Contemporary Art from the Arctic*
Peabody Essex Museum, Salem, Massachusetts

2008 *Winners' Exhibition: Governor General's Award in Visual and Media Arts*
National Gallery of Canada, Ottawa, Ontario

2010 *Nipirasait: Many Voices; Inuit Prints from Cape Dorset*
Canadian Embassy Art Gallery, Washington, DC

2011 *Inuit Prints: Japanese Inspiration*
University of British Columbia Museum of Anthropology, Vancouver

2013 *In Memoriam: Inuit Artists Remembered*
Winnipeg Art Gallery, Manitoba

COLLECTIONS

Amon Carter Museum of American Art, Fort Worth, Texas

Anchorage Museum, Alaska

Art Gallery of Greater Victoria, British Columbia

Art Gallery of Ontario, Toronto

Art Gallery of Sudbury, Ontario

Beaverbrook Art Gallery, Fredericton, New Brunswick

Canada Council Art Bank, Ottawa, Ontario

Canadian Museum of History, Gatineau, Quebec

Dennos Museum Center, Northwestern Michigan College, Traverse City

Glenbow Museum, Calgary, Alberta

Haffenreffer Museum of Anthropology, Brown University, Rhode Island

McMaster Museum of Art, Hamilton, Ontario

McMichael Canadian Art Collection, Kleinburg, Ontario

Musée des beaux-arts de Montréal, Quebec

National Gallery of Canada, Ottawa, Ontario

Prince of Wales Northern Heritage Centre, Yellowknife, Northwest Territories

Royal Ontario Museum, Toronto, Ontario

SFU Gallery, Simon Fraser University, Burnaby, British Columbia

Tate Gallery, London

Toronto-Dominion Bank Collection, Toronto

University of Michigan Museum of Art, Ann Arbor

Vancouver Art Gallery, British Columbia

Victoria and Albert Museum, London

Winnipeg Art Gallery, Manitoba

World Wildlife Fund Collection, Switzerland

SELECTED PUBLICATIONS

1971 *Eskimo Prints*
James A. Houston, Longman Canada, Don Mills, Ontario

1971 *Sculpture/Inuit: Masterworks of the Canadian Arctic*
Canadian Eskimo Arts Council, University of Toronto Press

1972 *The Eskimo Art Collection of the Toronto-Dominion Bank*
The Toronto-Dominion Bank

1973 *Eskimo Art*
Cottie Burland, the Hamlyn Publishing Group, London

1974 *Arts of the Eskimo: Prints*
ed. Ernst Roch, Signum Press, Montreal

1985 *Kenojuak*
Jean Blodgett, Firefly Books, Toronto

1985 "Kenojuak Ashevak," *The Canadian Encyclopedia*
ed. James H. Marsh, Hurtig Publishers, Edmonton

1986 *From Drawing to Print: Perception and Process in Cape Dorset Art*
Dorothy LaBarge, Glenbow Museum, Calgary, Alberta

1987 *Contemporary Inuit Drawings*
Marion E. Jackson, MacDonald Stewart Art Centre, Guelph, Ontario

1991 *In Cape Dorset We Do it This Way: Three Decades of Inuit Printmaking*
Jean Blodgett, McMichael Canadian Art Collection, Kleinburg, Ontario

1995 *Inuit Women Artists: Voices from Cape Dorset*
eds. Odette Leroux, Marion E. Jackson, and Minnie Aoudla Freeman, Douglas & McIntyre, Vancouver

1995 "Kenojuak (1927–)," *North American Women Artists of the Twentieth Century: A Biographical Dictionary*
eds. Jules Heller and Nancy G. Heller, Garland, New York

2006 *Arctic Spirit: Inuit Art from the Albrecht Collection at the Heard Museum*
Ingo Hessel, Douglas & McIntyre, Vancouver

2007 *Cape Dorset Prints: A Retrospective; Fifty Years of Printmaking at the Kinngait Studios*
ed. Leslie Boyd Ryan, Pomegranate, San Francisco

HONORS

1967 Appointed Officer of the Order of Canada, at the inaugural investiture, Rideau Hall, Ottawa

1974 Elected a member of the Royal Academy of Arts

1982 Appointed Companion of the Order of Canada, Rideau Hall, Ottawa

1991 Awarded an honorary doctorate from Queen's University, Kingston, Ontario

1992 Awarded an honorary doctorate from University of Toronto, Ontario

1995 Received the Lifetime Achievement Award from the National Aboriginal Achievement Foundation

2001 Received a star on Canada's Walk of Fame, Toronto, Ontario

2008 Awarded the Governor General's Award in Visual and Media Arts, Ottawa, Ontario

2012 Appointed to the Order of Nunavut by the Legislative Assembly of Nunavut, Iqaluit

INDEX OF ARTWORKS

KENOJUAK ASHEVAK

Raven Silhouette III, 1998
Stonecut on kizuki kozo natural paper,
26.5 x 38 cm
Edition of 50
Printer: Arnaqu Ashevak
Page 29

Ravens Return, 2000
Stonecut and stencil on kizuki kozo usunezumi paper, 63.2 x 72.9 cm
Edition of 50
Printer: Qavavau Manumie
Page 35

Red Fox, 2012
Stonecut on kizuki kozo natural paper,
52.7 x 68.8 cm
Edition of 50
Printer: Cee Pootoogook
Page 73

Sealskin bag, c. 1950s
17.8 x 26.7 x 7.6 cm
Collection of John and Joyce Price
Page 12

Serpentine Wolf, 2013
Lithograph on BFK Rives white paper,
57 x 76.5 cm
Edition of 50
Printer: Niveaksie Quvianaqtuliaq
Page 77

Siilavut, Nunavut (Our Environment, Our Land), 1999
Lithograph, diptych on Somerset paper,
113 x 76 cm
Edition of 99
Printer: Pitseolak Niviaqsi
Page 17

Six-Part Harmony, 2011
Stonecut and stencil on kizuki kozo white paper,
62 x 99.5 cm
Edition of 50
Printer: Qavavau Manumie
Page 69

Spectacular Ravens, 2003
Stonecut and stencil on Kozuke paper, 64 x 81.5 cm
Edition of 50
Printer: Qiatsuq Niviaqsi
Page 51

Starlit Ravens, 2001
Lithograph on Arches cover white paper,
57 x 71.3 cm
Edition of 50
Printer: Niveaksie Quvianaqtuliaq
Page 39

Summer Courtship, 2000
Stonecut and stencil on kizuki kozo natural paper,
58.5 x 68.8 cm
Edition of 50
Printer: Qavavau Manumie
Page 33

Swans at Sunset, 2002
Lithograph on Arches cover white paper,
57.2 x 76.8 cm
Edition of 50
Printer: Pitseolak Niviaqsi
Page 41

Tapestry of Owls, 2002
Lithograph on BFK Rives white paper,
66.3 x 51.4 cm
Edition of 50
Printer: Niveaksie Quvianaqtuliaq
Page 47

Untitled, 1959–1965
Graphite on paper, 42.3 x 53.3 cm
Collection of the West Baffin Eskimo Co-operative Ltd., on loan to the McMichael Canadian Art Collection, CD.40.112
Reproduced with the permission of Dorset Fine Arts
Page 14

Untitled (Between Friends), 2010
Ink and colored pencil on paper, 57 x 76.7 cm
Page 64

Untitled (Dancing Ravens), 2003
Ink and colored pencil on paper, 50.8 x 66 cm
Page 52

Untitled (Decorative Char), 2004
Ink and colored pencil on paper, 51 x 66 cm
Page 54

Untitled (Eternal Spirit), 2011
Ink and colored pencil on paper, 51.6 x 66 cm
Page 66

Untitled (Filigreed Raven), 1998
Ink and colored pencil on paper, 26 x 32.7 cm
Page 22

Untitled (Great Big Fish), 2011
Ink and colored pencil on paper, 57 x 76.1 cm
Page 78

Untitled (Inquisitive Bird), 2001
Ink on paper, 50.7 x 66 cm
Page 80

Untitled (Intruding Raven), 2001
Ink and colored pencil on paper, 50.7 x 66 cm
Page 36

Untitled (Iqalutsiavak [Beautiful Fish]), 2005
Ink and colored pencil on paper, 51 x 66 cm
Page 60

Untitled (Long Necked Goose), 2013
Ink and colored pencil on paper, 51 x 66 cm
Page 74

Untitled (Loons Protect the Owl), 2002
Ink and colored pencil on paper, 50.8 x 66.3 cm
Page 48

Untitled (Oracle), 1999
Ink and colored pencil on paper, 25.9 x 32.8 cm
Page 30

Untitled (Owl's Consort), 2012
Ink and colored pencil on paper, 77.7 x 122 cm
Page 70

ACKNOWLEDGMENTS

This publication was truly a team effort, with many individuals and organizations participating in its development. A heartfelt thank you to the West Baffin Eskimo Co-operative team, particularly President Pauloosie Kowmageak and General Manager Jason Paul for their support and leadership. The co-operative's Toronto team, comprising Richard Bonderenko, David Hannan, William Huffman, Donna McKie, Paige Connell, Marisha Pula, and John Westren, was vital in the realization of this project. The initiative also had the assistance of Research Residents Sara Paladino (Ryerson University), Emily Smith (McGill University), and Naia Wang (Humber College). The inclusion of French and Inuktitut translations was the contribution of Duncan McDonald and Nina Toonoo, respectively. Many thanks to the publication's intrepid editor and chief contributor, Leslie Boyd. Pomegranate Communications, especially Thomas Burke, Zoe Katherine Burke, and Cory Mimms, provided invaluable publication and distribution infrastructure. The Government of Nunavut's generous financial contribution, through its Department of Culture and Heritage, is greatly appreciated. Lastly, the lead supporter on this publication and its associated national touring exhibition is the Government of Canada through the Department of Canadian Heritage. And simply put, without the department's Senior Cultural and Heritage Consultant, Bruce Borysiuk, *Kenojuak Ashevak: Life and Legacy* wouldn't have been possible. Thank you, Bruce!

ABOUT THE AUTHOR

Leslie Boyd was employed by the West Baffin Eskimo Co-operative for thirty-two years, living in Cape Dorset, Nunavut, and in Toronto, where she was director of the co-op's marketing division, Dorset Fine Arts. As an independent writer and curator, Boyd has published essays in exhibition catalogues for private galleries and public institutions. She is editor of *Cape Dorset Prints: A Retrospective* (Pomegranate, 2007), a comprehensive illustrated history of the Kinngait Studios in Cape Dorset. She is also author of *Tim Pitsiulak: Drawings and Prints from Cape Dorset* (Pomegranate, 2018) and *Ningiukulu Teevee: Drawings and Prints from Cape Dorset* (Pomegranate, 2019). Boyd holds a master's degree in Environmental Studies from York University in Toronto, where she studied the history of the Inuit co-operative movement in northern Canada.